Fables of Modernity

Emmanuel Frémiet, *gorille enlevant une négresse (Gorilla Carrying Off a Negro Woman)* (1859). Musée des Beaux-Arts, Dijon, France. © Musée des Beaux-Arts, Dijon

FABLES OF MODERNITY

Literature and Culture in the English Eighteenth Century

LAURA BROWN

Cornell University Press
Ithaca and London

First published 2001 by Cornell University Press

Printed in the United States of America

Library of Congress Cataloging-in-Publication Data

Brown, Laura, 1949–
    Fables of modernity : literature and culture in the English eighteenth century / Laura Brown.
        p. cm.
    Includes bibliographical references and index.
    ISBN 0-8014-3756-3 (cloth : alk. paper)
    1. English literature—18th century—History and criticism. 2. Literature and society—Great Britain—History—18th century. 3. Literature and history—Great Britain—History—18th century. 4. Great Britain—Civilization—18th century. 5. Fables, English—History and criticism. 6. Imperialism in literature. 7. Animals in literature. 8. Women in literature.   I. Title.
    PR448.S64 B764 2001
    820.9'355—dc21

                                                                    2001001670

Cornell University Press strives to use environmentally responsible suppliers and materials to the fullest extent possible in the publishing of its books. Such materials include vegetable-based, low-VOC inks and acid-free papers that are recycled, totally chlorine-free, or partly composed of nonwood fibers. Books that bear the logo of the FSC (Forest Stewardship Council) use paper taken from forests that have been inspected and certified as meeting the highest standards for environmental and social responsibility. For further information, visit our website at www.cornellpress.cornell.edu.

1 3 5 7 9   Cloth printing   10 8 6 4 2

For the graduate students at Cornell who have joined me over the last twenty years in exploring the literature and culture of the English eighteenth century

Contents

Illustrations

Preface

THIS book originated in a discussion of Jonathan Swift's poem *A Description of a City Shower* in a graduate seminar on "Literary Anti-Feminism" at Cornell University in the spring of 1997. My contribution to that discussion was a failure; I was unable to persuade the group and even to explain to myself my conviction that the poem contained an extended reflection both on the nature of modern experience and on the female body. I discovered during that class that the compressed story that I saw in the *City Shower* required a different sort of explication and a different frame of reference than my students and I were able to define. The result was the idea of the cultural fable, which Swift's poem generated and which developed a momentum of its own, gathering strength as it moved in my imagination through the print culture of the period. I am grateful to my students for providing me with this occasion, and innumerable others, to think again about the literary culture of the eighteenth century.

I have received particular advice and help from friends, colleagues, and assistants. I would like to thank Srinivas Aravamudan, Martin Bernal, Fredric Bogel, Kellie Dawson, Michelle Elleray, Jody Greene, Anne Lyden, Sarah McKibben, Felicity Nussbaum, Adela Pinch, Hunter Rawlings, Shirley Samuels, Harry Shaw, Chi-ming Yang, and the Fellows of the Society for the Humanities at Cornell 1999/2000, especially Eric Cheyfitz, Frederick Neuhouser, and Priscilla Wald, for their involvement with various parts of this book. I am especially grateful to my research assistants, Zahid Chaudhary, Sarah Heidt, and Jennifer Hill, for their initiative in pursuing my needs; to Joe Pappa for calling my attention to the sculpture by Emmanuel Frémiet that appears as the frontispiece; to Katherine Reagan, Curator of Rare Books, Cornell University Library, for assisting me with the illustrations; and to Bernhard Kendler, Executive Editor of Cornell University Press, for his early support. I am also grateful to the Society for the Humanities at Cornell for a fellowship that supported the preparation of this book in its final stages.

And as always I am most deeply indebted to my first, last, and best critic, Walter Cohen.

Fables of Modernity

Introduction:
The Cultural Fable, the Experience of
Modernity, and the Paradigm of Difference

THE objects of this study—the cultural "fables of a new world"—are the phantoms of the eighteenth-century literary canon. Nowhere and everywhere, these are stories without a text, imaginative events without an author, and yet they are built from the concrete materials of modern European experience, and they pervade and surpass the various movements, forms, genres, and modes of eighteenth-century English print culture. This book attempts to establish the "cultural fable" as a critical category, and to use that category as a means of exploring the constitution of modernity in the English eighteenth century.

The phrase "cultural fable" might look at first like an oxymoron. By joining these terms, I mean to yoke the material and historical with the aesthetic, "culture" with "fable," in a way that enables a simultaneous reading both of literature and of history. As I deploy it here, the cultural fable is a formal construct in the sense that it is characterized by a set of related figures that have a distinctive structure or are in a dynamic relationship. These recurrent figures adhere to their own specific texts and develop from their own rhetorical traditions. But beyond that local function, and taken together, they intersect with and elaborate one another so as to project a set of meanings, affects, or even ironies that constitute a common imaginative project.

My approach has an affinity with the methods of rhetorical analysis that formalist criticism absorbed during the 1980s from the critical strategies of poststructuralism under the initial influence of Paul de Man, as well as with the critique of ideology developed during that same period from marxist literary theory, following the lead of Fredric Jameson. The readings that follow are informed also by the shifts in the understanding of ideology that have arisen in the marxist tradition from Antonio Gramsci to Ernesto Laclau and Chantal Mouffe, through which the determining status of the economic and the priority of class are replaced by a sense of the indeterminacy of the social and by a broadened and complicated definition of the cultural. Like a marxist notion of ideology, then, a cultural fable transcends particular writers and texts: it is generated collectively in many texts over a period of time. But unlike ideology, a cultural fable has a specific formal structure that can be defined and read as closely as a novel or a poem, and an aesthetic distinctiveness that enables it to develop a temporary life of its own, to attain the relative autonomy of a literary tradition, to be connected generically with other parallel cultural fables, or even to gain canonical status. But although it has a coherent form, a cultural fable is not necessarily coterminous with a single text. It may make up a small portion or a specific dimension of a text, and a particular text may contain more than one cultural fable. My treatment of texts focuses on specific images, sustained tropes, and recurrent rhetorical structures, and it highlights the contradictions, disjunctions, or tensions generated by those structures. But it moves through various modes of discourse—from canonical and noncanonical literary texts to periodical essays, medical treatises, philosophical works, and popular ballads, and it places these close rhetorical and intertextual readings in relation to other aspects of contemporary material history. In this regard, of course, my idea of the cultural fable reflects the influence of the culturalist and historicist approaches that have dominated critical work in the humanities in the 1990s, most directly that shaped by Michel Foucault in France, Raymond Williams and Stuart Hall in Britain, and Stephen Greenblatt in the United States.

In employing the idea of a fable, I have sought to emphasize the collectivity of this imaginative phenomenon, its cultural potency, and its formal dynamism. In general, we understand a fable to be more extended than a single text, and more momentous in its cultural import and influence than a story. A fable also has a narrative trajectory that moves beyond the local or static effect of a trope or a figure. Thus, while I do not mean to allude to the narrowly didactic connotation often popularly attached to the idea of the fable, I do mean to evoke the sense of the fable as a distillation of meaning and significance—in this case the significance of a historical moment. And while I do not intend in my use of the fable to include the idea of a transcendent aesthetic category, as in Northrop Frye's notion of myth, I do see the fable as marshaling a formidable aesthetic power.

Though it is formed from images, tropes, and sometimes even specific resonant words, the cultural fable as I understand it here is a complex imaginative work, which entails a process, an unfolding problem, or an evolving fate. Thus, a cultural fable can be said to tell a story whose protagonist is an emanation of contemporary experience and whose action reflects an imaginative negotiation with that experience. In this respect, my notion of the cultural fable has affinities with a structuralist or a neo-Aristotelian understanding of the shape or architecture of an imaginative construct, and shares some of the critical premises of Roland Barthes or R. S. Crane. My concern, however, is not to prescribe a series of paradigms to contain these imaginative events, but to use the idea of the cultural fable as a flexible model through which the various and diverse images and figures that collect around particular aspects of eighteenth-century material history can be understood in themselves and in relation to one another. The concept of the cultural fable is designed to generate a mode of analysis, rather than to impose a system of classification. As such, the notion of the cultural fable entails a proposition on my part about the nature of literary culture: that it is a collective enterprise which, through its collectivity, engages with the most vital, problematic, or prominent aspects of contemporary experience. This engagement links literary culture with the major forces of historical change. In other words, the cultural fable provides a way of reading not only literary texts, but the relation between literature and history.

A cultural fable is fundamentally tied to a specific aspect of material culture, imaginatively shaping, registering, or reflecting upon the experience of historical change condensed in that material phenomenon. Each of the chapters that follow thus begins with an account of the particular material ground which their respective cultural fable takes up: urban sanitation, shipping, the stock market, printing, "native" visitors to the metropolis, and relations with animals. The fables that are constructed around these material experiences are the collective expressions of a metropolitan European culture, but within that perspective, they belong to no single group. They are not necessarily the stories of a particular class, gender, or coterie, but the fables of a cultural experience, and in that sense they encounter their historical moment with a distinctive engagement. Through this engagement, the cultural fable can tell a story that seems to grasp the processes of history with a peculiar discernment, or to represent the contradictions of such processes with a striking clarity.

The cultural fable, then, can be a tool of demystification. But the grasp of history that we will observe in these cultural fables is less predictable than the systematic demystificatory function proposed by marxist ideology critique, just as the work of the cultural fable is more varied and indistinct than that of ideology. Because the cultural fable arises from a

polymorphous material contingency, in which specific contemporary social, economic, cultural, political, or even aesthetic pressures variously intersect, its conclusions are in turn variously prescient, pragmatic, anxious,
or speculative. Thus, a cultural fable might perform the demystifying tasks
of revealing the underlying contradiction of its historical moment or un-
covering the mystified social relations behind its formation, but it might
also augment a particular structure of judgment, consolidate a specific
contemporary prejudice, expose the problematic constituents of an accepted belief, or open an imaginative route to a new mode of knowing or
being.

My notion of the cultural fable is, finally, also meant to serve as an intervention in the ongoing project of cultural studies. In the field of literary criticism, cultural studies has had the effect of breaking down the boundaries
of traditional disciplines, and of opening up rich sources of material for research and analysis. But a conceptualization of the premises or the methods
driving this critical work has been elusive, despite its ties to the theoretically
self-conscious positions of critics like Raymond Williams or Michel Foucault. In its general practice in the 1990s, cultural studies has been diffuse,
multiform, and pragmatic. As a result, its practice has sometimes been uneven, its construction of models for critical thought often ineffective. At the
least, the cultural fable might serve as a helpful means of structuring the
critical encounter with print culture; and it might also provide a systematic
way of applying the insights of cultural studies to the reading of literary
texts. The former effort is the aim of this book as a whole; I demonstrate the
latter project at length in chapter 4, where I seek to build a sustained reading of a major canonical text—Alexander Pope's *Dunciad*—from an account of the relationships among several intersecting cultural fables.

I

The fables that I define in this study express some of the experiences centrally associated with modernity. Taken together, they suggest that in significant ways modernity is constituted, imaginatively and discursively, in
the eighteenth century, and that its constitution is circumscribed by alterity—by an imaginative negotiation with the figure of the woman or of the
non-European. In this sense, my reading of these cultural fables explores
the experience of modernity in ways that aim to illuminate both their period and modernity itself as it extends beyond the English eighteenth century into our own time.

I am engaged in a close reading of the experience of modernity, but
not in an extended negotiation with that concept. Of the rich, complex,

multidisciplinary twentieth-century debate on modernity, I have extracted one concrete area, focused on the collective effects of print culture. My treatment of these materials depends upon a widely accepted social, cultural, and economic understanding of modernity, which I do not challenge.[1] Thus I am not able to explore some of the recent positions that would modify or dispute the very idea of modernity, especially those dealing with the economic phenomena of modernization. Global or comparative economic and social historians who seek to account for major events—industrialization, revolution, or the rise of capitalism, money, markets, commodities, or modern finance—across divergent sites from Europe to Asia, may implicitly or explicitly undermine a notion of modernity that is tied closely to Western European history, though such internationalist accounts can often be seen to reconstitute a new comparative definition of modernity through the structural parallels that they draw across the globe.[2] My study, located as it is entirely within English history and culture, is not situated to contribute to this discussion.

Even more obviously, I am not prepared to intervene in the philosophical debates about the status and the moral and epistemological implications of modernity that have been engaged—alongside debates about enlightenment, humanism, science, discourse, and relativism—since the seventeenth century,[3] except to the extent that my readings of print culture might provide a perspective on ideological structures of modernity

[1] For a sample of some approaches to modernity compatible with mine, see Marshall Berman, *All That Is Solid Melts into Air: The Experience of Modernity* (New York: Penguin Books, 1982); Rita Felski, *The Gender of Modernity* (Cambridge: Harvard University Press, 1995); David Frisby, *Fragments of Modernity: Theories of Modernity in the Work of Simmel, Kracauer and Benjamin* (Cambridge: MIT Press, 1986); Jürgen Habermas, *The Philosophical Discourse of Modernity: Twelve Lectures*, trans. Fredrick Lawrence (Cambridge: MIT Press, 1987); Charles Taylor, *Sources of the Self: The Making of the Modern Identity* (Cambridge: Harvard University Press, 1989).

[2] For example, Andre Gunder Frank, *Reorient: Global Economy in the Asian Age* (Berkeley: University of California Press, 1998); Jack A. Goldstone, *Revolution and Rebellion in the Early Modern World* (Berkeley: University of California Press, 1991); Frank Perlin, *The Invisible City: Monetary, Administrative, and Popular Infrastructure in Asia and Europe, 1500–1900* (Aldershot, Hampshire: Variorum, 1993) and *Unbroken Landscape: Commodity, Category, Sign and Identity: Their Production as Myth and Knowledge from 1500* (Aldershot, Hampshire: Variorum, 1994); and Immanuel Wallerstein, *The Modern World-System* (New York: Academic Press, 1974).

[3] Some examples of the many recent redactions of such debates include Theodor Adorno and Max Horkheimer, *Dialectic of Enlightenment*, trans. John Cumming (New York: Seabury, 1972); Michel Foucault, "What is Enlightenment?" in *The Foucault Reader*, ed. Paul Rabinow (New York: Pantheon Books, 1984), 32–50; Habermas, "Modernity—an Incomplete Project," in *The Anti-Aesthetic: Essays on Postmodern Culture*, ed. Hal Foster (Port Townsend, Wash.: Bay Press, 1983), 3–15, and *The Philosophical Discourse of Modernity*, trans. Frederick Lawrence (Cambridge: MIT Press, 1987); Bruno Latour, *We Have Never Been Modern*,

relevant to issues like the status of the nonhuman in a humanist episte-
mology, or the connections between metaphysics and imperialist apologia. I must also necessarily neglect the question of the role of aesthetic
modernism in the constitution of modernity, since my materials precede
that movement. And finally, I am deliberately avoiding the problem of
postmodernism. My representation of modernity does not take on the
relation between the modern and the postmodern, except implicitly. By
claiming that the cultural forms defined through these eighteenth-
century materials are constitutive of a modern experience that retains a
currency in the present day, this book does subscribe to the view that locates the postmodern as an exfoliation of the modern, rather than as a
clearly demarcated epoch with a distinct nature.[4] In all these ways, my use
of modernity is limited. But on the other hand, I assume that my explication of these cultural materials—as a concrete sample of the nature of the
modern life experience—will have a place in the larger development of
the idea of modernity beyond this book and this period of English history.
And within its particular historical and material parameters, this study is
specifically aimed to take up another major challenge to accepted notions
of modernity: the suggestion that our understanding of Western European modernity should attend to the effects of gender and race. This particular complication in the idea of modernity is my central theme.

For the purposes of *Fables of Modernity*, then, my notion of modernity is
derived from the marxist and cultural materialist traditions. I understand
modernity not in the prescriptive sense of a liberal metanarrative in which
rationality and Enlightenment would be the prominent concerns, but in
the sense of the lived consequences of a complex of social and economic
formations that characterize a significant moment of historical transformation. Thus, I accept the broad definition of modernity that loosely
adopts a marxist economic frame while largely eliding the distinction of
base and superstructure, and that joins with it an engagement with material culture, a concern with the nature of bourgeois thought and the development of the private sphere, and an interest in the evolving phenomenon of nationalism. Centered in the triumph of capitalism in England in
the seventeenth and eighteenth centuries, modernity refers to the histor-

---

trans. Catherine Porter (Cambridge: Harvard University Press, 1993); and Barbara Maria
Stafford, "The Eighteenth Century at the End of Modernity: Towards the Re-Enlightenment,"
in *The Past as Prologue: Essays to Celebrate the Twenty-Fifth Anniversary of ASECS*, ed. Carla H. Hay
and Syndy M. Conger (New York: AMS Press, 1995), 403–416.

[4] In this respect, for instance, Frisby's conclusion—"to speak of postmodernity . . . would
therefore be premature"(272)—is compatible with my assumption, as is Fredric Jameson's
extended definition of postmodernism in *Postmodernism, or, The Cultural Logic of Late Capitalism* (Durham: Duke University Press, 1991).

ical transformations connected with that event: to changes in the nature of the economy and production, in the structures of social and political organization, in the orientation and significance of culture, and in the conceptualization of history itself. In the economy, modernity involves commercialization, commodification, the expansion of markets, and the priority of profit. In social and political terms, it manifests itself in the development of bureaucracy, urbanization, and the rise of the nation state, and in demographic shifts and upheavals that transform urban environments and that transport masses of people across the globe. In philosophical thought, modernity is represented in the definition of the social contract, the concept of private property, and theories of democracy. And in historiography, modernity is distinguished by an act of historical differentiation, an attention to the novelty of the present and its distance from the past, which makes possible ideas of progress, improvement, and change.

Michel Foucault describes this distinctive "attitude of modernity" as a "reflection on 'today' as difference in history" (38). The experience of these changes is symptomatically complex. Marshall Berman provides a compact summary:

> To be modern is to find ourselves in an environment that promises us adventure, power, joy, growth, transformation of ourselves and the world—and, at the same time, that threatens to destroy everything we have, everything we know, everything we are. . . . modernity . . . pours us all into a maelstrom of perpetual disintegration and renewal, of struggle and contradiction, of ambiguity and anguish. (15)

These dimensions of the experience of modernity are deepened and pointed by the rise of industrialization and technology in the nineteenth century, but many of the core elements of modernity are available in the English eighteenth century before the consolidation of the industrial revolution.

Indeed, the eighteenth century is now well-documented as an age of "revolutions": the triumph of mercantile capitalism and the privileging of property and profit; the acquisition of England's first non-European empire along with the institutionalization of slavery and a socially pervasive racism; the creation of the modern, post-dynastic nation state and of a discourse and political practice of national identity; the financial revolution and the rise of banking, credit, stock trading, and national debt; innovations in agriculture and the transformation of the countryside; the explosion of consumption and the rise of the retail market; the development of a self-perpetuating and self-disciplining bourgeois public sphere along with the consolidation of a culturally coherent middle class; the invention of advertising, middle-class fashion, and obsolescence; and fundamental changes in the structures of the family entailing companionate relationships among nuclear family members. Some of these "revolutions," of course, had their beginnings as early as the sixteenth century or earlier: enclosure has a three-hundred-year history; the rise of the middle class family took perhaps two hundred years; and Fernand Braudel has located "nascent capitalism" in the fifteenth century, in "forms of economic life . . . that are already modern," long before we find a coherent modern economy.[5] The industrial revolution of the late eighteenth century produced further visible and tangible transformations—of the economy, the countryside, and the nature and conditions of labor. But historians find that the period after 1660 marks a new epoch, in which a wide range of major shifts comes together.[6]

---

[5] Fernand Braudel, *Capitalism and Material Life 1400–1800* (New York: Harper and Row, 1967), xiii.

[6] These changes are described in many recent historical studies of the period. I cannot in the context of this introduction supply an exhaustive survey, but the following works will provide a selective access to this material: On capitalism, Braudel, *Capitalism and Material Life*; Albert O. Hirschman, *The Passions and the Interests: Political Arguments for Capitalism Before Its Triumph* (Princeton: Princeton University Press, 1977). On empire, John Brewer, *Sinews of Power: War, Money and the English State, 1688–1783* (New York: Alfred A. Knopf, 1989); *The Eighteenth Century*, ed. P. J. Marshall, vol. 2 of *The Oxford History of the British Empire* (Oxford: Oxford University Press, 1998). On slavery, Robin Blackburn, *The Making of New World Slavery: From the Baroque to the Modern, 1492–1800* (London: Verso, 1997); David Brion Davis, *The Problem of Slavery in the Age of Revolution* (Ithaca: Cornell University Press, 1975); *Slavery and the Rise of the Atlantic System*, ed. Barbara L. Solow (Cambridge: Cambridge University Press, 1991). On national identity, Benedict Anderson, *Imagined Communities: Reflections on the Origin and Spread of Nationalism*, rev. ed. (London: Verso, 1991); Linda Colley, *Britons: Forging the Nation 1707–1837* (New Haven: Yale University Press, 1992); Kathleen Wilson, *The Sense of the People: Politics, Culture, and Imperialism in England, 1715–1785* (Cambridge: Cambridge University Press, 1995). On the financial revolution, P. G. M. Dickson, *The Financial Revolution in England: A Study in the Development of Public Credit 1688–1756* (New York: St. Martin's Press, 1967); Larry Neal, *The Rise of Financial Capitalism: International Capital Markets in the Age of Reason* (Cambridge: Cambridge University Press, 1990). On the industrial revolution, Maxine Berg, *The Age of Manufactures: Industry, Innovation, and Work in Britain, 1700–1820* (New York: Oxford University Press, 1985); Pat Hudson, *The Industrial Revolution* (London: E. Arnold, 1992). On the public sphere, Habermas, *The Structural Transformation of the Public Sphere: An Inquiry into a Category of Bourgeois Society*, trans. Thomas Burger (Cambridge: MIT Press, 1989). On the middle class, Peter Earle, *The Making of the English Middle Class: Business, Society, and Family Life in London, 1660–1730* (Berkeley: University of California Press, 1989); Paul Langford, *A Polite and Commercial People: England, 1727–1783* (Oxford: Oxford University Press, 1992); E. P. Thompson, *The Making of the English Working Class* (New York: Pantheon Books, 1963). On consumption, advertising, and fashion: *Consumption and the World of Goods*, ed. John Brewer and Roy Porter (London: Routledge, 1993); Neil McKendrick, John Brewer, and J. H. Plumb, *The Birth of a Consumer Society: The Commercialization of Eighteenth-Century England* (Bloomington: Indiana University Press,

My claim, then, assumes a different perspective on this era of cultural history from that indicated in the prominent recent system of classification that includes the eighteenth century in an "early modern period" that extends from the sixteenth. Such a grouping usefully resituates the age previously known as the Renaissance in relation to the eighteenth century rather than the medieval period. But it highlights resemblances and continuities between the eighteenth century and the sixteenth and seventeenth where my argument, by contrast, would emphasize distinctions and innovations. And the idea of the "early modern period," by drawing a line between that and the "modern," implicitly separates the eighteenth century from the deep implication in the constitution of modernity that this study seeks to advance.

The economic, social, and cultural developments that emerged, strikingly, threateningly, sometimes suddenly and without precedent in the eighteenth century, captured the collective imagination of the age and shaped a print culture that directly registers their energies with a distinctive sense of novelty and immediacy. Fredric Jameson describes this "modern feeling" as "the conviction that we ourselves are somehow new, that a new age is beginning, that everything is possible and nothing can ever be the same again" (310). This novelty has consistently figured implicitly in the critical understanding of the eighteenth century, and it has come to special prominence in recent years. J. H. Plumb, in his essay on "The Acceptance of Modernity," suggests that in this period "quite humble men and women, innocent of philosophical theory, began to be fascinated not only by nature but also by the manipulation of nature; . . . their hobbies or their pets . . . led them to accept, perhaps unconsciously, the modernity of their world, and to relish change and novelty and to look with more expectancy towards the future."[7] Nancy Armstrong and Leonard Tennenhouse have taken this period, and the status of Milton within it, as the site of irreversible, "startling and profound," "changes in intellectual and artistic practice," indicating a "relationship between the origins of personal life and the onset of modernity."[8] Howard Erskine-Hill, in a recent summary reflection on Pope scholarship, eloquently describes this new world by evoking Pope's place within it: "His imagination . . . produced . . . a vision of time, ideas of the processes of the world, notions of

---

1982); Hoh-Cheung Mui and Lorna Mui, *Shops and Shopkeeping in Eighteenth-Century England* (Montreal: McGill-Queens University Press, 1989). On the family, Lawrence Stone, *The Family, Sex and Marriage in England 1500–1800* (New York: Harper and Row, 1977).

[7] Plumb, "The Acceptance of Modernity" in *The Birth of a Consumer Society*, 316–317.

[8] Nancy Armstrong and Leonard Tennenhouse, *The Imaginary Puritan: Literature, Intellectual Labor, and the Origins of Personal Life* (Berkeley: University of California Press, 1992), 7, 23.

the patterns of history, of the cycles of civilizations, within which hopes of progress, fears of decline and fall, could be urged, averted, at least understood"; in this way, Pope's vision represents the possibility for "modern minds to assess their world in the light of the past."[9] This is the vision that reflects the experience of modernity that I locate in the English eighteenth century, and that I attribute, not to the particular works of Pope's corpus, but to the collective cultural fables in which his works participate.

In the argument that follows, modernity is consistently involved with a problematic figure of difference. Women and non-Europeans provide a template, a catalyst, a reference point, a precedent, a strategy, or a conclusion for the imaginative exercises that these cultural fables undertake. Though modernity has often been understood as an exclusively masculine province, tied to the public sphere and associated with the political and the economic, as well as with rationalism and the enlightenment, recent perspectives open the possibility of the role of other, non-male, non-European influences upon the ways in which modernity was registered and lived. For instance, Rita Felski in *The Gender of Modernity* argues, in reference to a parallel moment in French culture, that the female figure "play[s] a central role in prevailing anxieties, fears, and hopeful imaginings about the distinctive features of the 'modern age,'" that she "crystallize[s] the ambivalent responses to capitalism and technology," and that she embodies some of the ideas most closely associated with the modern world—commodification, contamination, anonymity, the breakdown of social hierarchy, and the revulsion from and fascination with technology.[10] In *The Making of New World Slavery*, Robin Blackburn argues for a new understanding of the nature of slavery, which he sees as a development of modernity, rather than an antique, reactionary, or premodern system:

> [Slavery's] development was associated with several of those processes which have been held to define modernity: the growth of instrumental rationality, the rise of national sentiment and the nation-state, racialized perceptions of identity, the spread of market relations and wage labour, the development of administrative bureaucracies and modern tax systems, the growing sophistication of commerce and communication, the birth of consumer societies, the publication of newspapers and the beginnings of press advertising, 'action at a distance' and an individualist sensibility. . . . The

[9] Howard Erskine-Hill, introduction to *Alexander Pope: World and Word*, ed. Erskine-Hill (Oxford: Oxford University Press, 1998), 1.

[10] Felski, chap. 1.

dynamic of the Atlantic economy was sustained by new webs of social trust, and gave birth to new social identities. It required business planning and methods for discounting risk; it was associated with distinctive modern traditions of reflexive self-consciousness.[11]

In *The Black Atlantic: Modernity and Double Consciousness*, Paul Gilroy develops a definition of a transnational, compound, "black Atlantic" culture from this notion of the modernity of plantation slavery. Modernity in Gilroy's account is thus deeply involved with "ideas of . . . ethnicity, authenticity, and cultural integrity," and registers the "impact of issues like 'race' and gender on the formation and reproduction of modern selves." From Gilroy's perspective "the modern subject [is] located in historically specific and unavoidably complex configurations of individualization and embodiment—black and white, male and female, lord and bondsman."[12]

The readings that follow will variously substantiate and develop these newly conceived conjunctions of race or gender and modernity. I do not claim that alterity determines our experience or understanding of the modern, though my exploration of these particular fables of modernity might lead in that direction. Rather, I mean to highlight a repeated connection between modernity and the encounter with difference, a connection that accords a distinctive, persistent, and powerful significance to the woman and the non-European.

II

The three parts of this study—"Expansion," "Exchange," and "Alterity"— are not strictly equivalent. Each reflects a broad dimension of modern experience, but though alterity is the stated theme of part 3 alone, difference is a common thread throughout. In the fables of expansion and exchange of parts 1 and 2, the female figure is the imaginative touchstone of the encounter with the material transformations of the modern world, framing, explaining, or reigning over those stories of heterogeneity, hysteria, and apocalypse. Difference, in the fables that form the subject of these first two parts, is a pervasive subtext. But in part 3, where difference is confronted in the form of the cultural divide between the European and the non-European, alterity enters directly into the action of the fable,

---

[11] Robin Blackburn, *The Making of New World Slavery: From the Baroque to the Modern, 1492–1800* (London: Verso, 1997), 4.

[12] Paul Gilroy, *The Black Atlantic: Modernity and Double Consciousness* (Cambridge: Harvard University Press, 1993), 2, 46.

as the protagonist of a strenuous engagement. These fables address difference as an immediate imaginative crisis rather than a mode of explanation or an underlying cause. The discrepancy here—between the first two parts of this study and the third—reflects the very substantial social, historical, and material dissimilarities between the woman and the non-European, which the loose notion of alterity obscures. But though my large claim about the status of difference in the constitution of modernity places the representation of the woman and that of the non-European together in that same loose category, my particular explorations of these cultural fables in the chapters that follow provide distinctive readings of these separate figures.

Part 1, "Expansion," explores two closely related images prominent in the canonical poetry of the period: the sewer and the torrent. Chapter 1, "The Metropolis: The Fable of the City Sewer" uses Swift's poem, *A Description of a City Shower*, as a springboard for the argument that the problem of urban sanitation in the rapidly growing modern metropolis exerts a material pressure on the contemporary imagination and generates a collective story that represents a complex engagement with the experience of modernity. This chapter takes up various contemporary images of the sewer in the misogynist poetry of Rochester and Swift, and in urban poetry by Swift, Pope, and Gay. I argue that together these works participate in a cultural fable that understands modern urban experience as a vortex of heterogeneity—fluid, dispersed, and transformative—and that makes meaning from that experience by seeing it as female. The fable of the city sewer uses the female body to explain the vitality, the indiscriminacy, and the transforming powers of modernity.

The feminized floods of the urban sewer system are projected beyond the metropolis into the expansionist fable of torrents and oceans that forms the topic of the next chapter. Chapter 2, "Imperial Fate: The Fable of Torrents and Oceans," pursues the fluid energy of the urban sewer into the poetry of national identity and imperial expansion, where images of oceans, floods, and torrents reflect a similar vital and threatening power. The material context for this essay is the burgeoning shipping industry, and the powerful and pervasive impact of ships and maritime trade on the contemporary imagination. I argue that the growth of shipping and the visibility of maritime expansion generates a cultural fable whose currency shapes both the literature of imperialist apologia and that of metaphysical speculation. This chapter takes Samuel Johnson's *Vanity of Human Wishes* as a touchstone, placing that poem in the context of imperialist poetry by Dryden, Denham, Pope, and others. The figure of torrents and oceans that these works share plays the role of the protagonist in a story that depicts the headlong, tumultuous, and paradoxical process of modern history, a story of an apocalyptic fate directed by a fluid, inexorable, expansive and dangerous force, which poses glory against destruction, hope against fear.

The second part of the book, "Exchange," locates a fable of feminized volatility in the rise of public credit and stock speculation, and links that fable with the apocalyptic "new world" of unfettered capitalism generated by another female protagonist, the Mighty Mother, Dulness, of Pope's *Dunciad*. Chapter 3, "Finance: The Fable of Lady Credit," describes the financial revolution of the early eighteenth century, its innovations in financial instruments and the nature of exchange, and its provocative relation to mystery, imagination, and the female body. This chapter reads closely the figure of "Lady Credit" from Defoe's *Review* essays and one of Addison's *Spectator* papers, defining the cultural characteristics of that female figure, especially her tendency to hysteria and her evocation of commodification. The fable of Lady Credit represents a way of grasping the historical phenomenon of a credit-based economy in terms of the female body. But reciprocally, this fable also shapes a feminized and sexual changeability out of an experience of financial volatility, drawing from the world of finance a female character directly linked to the sentimental protagonist of the cult of sensibility. I argue that finance might make sensibility possible; Clarissa might be the long lost daughter of Lady Credit.

The second chapter of this part, "Capitalism: Fables of a New World," is designed to demonstrate the generic connections among a group of cultural fables—fables of finance, urban expansion, imperialism, and commodification—by describing their integration within a single literary text, Alexander Pope's *Dunciad*. The *Dunciad* constructs its alignment of these fables out of the material context of the capitalization of the printing industry and uses their mutual affiliations to generate a multidimensional imaginative vision of capitalism and its power to transform not only the world, but the experience of the world: reality itself. This vision is variously and consistently feminized, through an interweaving of images and effects derived from these cultural fables' engagements with the figure of the woman. Dulness, the poem's female protagonist, absorbs the insubstantiality of Lady Credit; but that effect is joined with the leveling energies of the feminized city sewer, the indiscriminacy generated by the commodification of the body of the woman, and the female mystery associated with the transformation of capitalist exchange. Thus, I argue that the scope and complexity of the poem is the result of its engagement with so many rich and resonant fables of modernity, and that its famous canonization of the figure of the woman is a formal effect of that engagement: the female figure informs all the affiliations among the *Dunciad*'s fables of a new world. In exploring the generic alignment of these cultural fables within a single work, this chapter demonstrates a sustained application of the idea of the cultural fable to the explication of a particular literary text.

Chapter 4 serves as a summary and conclusion to the first two parts of the book, which take up the relationship between difference and modernity through the representation of woman. My reading of the *Dunciad* provides a perspective on the connections among the fables of Lady Credit, torrents and oceans, the city sewer, and commodification, a perspective that demonstrates their generic mutuality as fables of the "new world" of modernity. The third and final part of this study, "Alterity," moves from the subtext of the female body to the open cultural encounter with difference in two related figures prominent in eighteenth-century representations of Africans, Amerindians, and Polynesians—the "native prince" and the nonhuman being. In the first of these chapters, chapter 5, entitled "Spectacles of Cultural Contact: The Fable of the Native Prince," I describe, in both historical and fictional accounts of royal "native" visitors to London, the typical rhetorical structures through which these non-European heroes are often imagined. By that means I develop a reading of the larger cultural fable underlying these local figures of sentimental identification. I claim that this fable transforms the ways in which the heroic is imagined as a source of identification in the development of the cult of sensibility: in this way the non-European becomes an influential model for the European man of feeling.

The second chapter in this part and the final chapter of the book, chapter 6, "The Orangutang, the Lap Dog, and the Parrot: The Fable of the Nonhuman Being," explores modern constructions of difference by defining the rhetoric of eighteenth-century representations of the nonhuman. This is the age of the invention of the pet, the discovery of the great apes, and the development of the modern system of biological classification, when animals took on a new role in relation to humankind. Here I examine the imaginative status of a cohort of nonhuman beings—apes, parrots or talking birds, and lap dogs—to develop a reading of a specific, repeated representation of a "leap of affinity" that supercedes the distance between the human and the nonhuman. This experience is directly linked to the encounter with cultural difference in the form of the African—native and slave—who shadows the fable of the nonhuman being in many of its manifestations. The strange arrangement here—in which the nonhuman being negotiates an approach to the non-European human being—is a central irony of the modern encounter with alterity.

These two final chapters are meant to serve as paired explications of a formative experience of this major era of European global expansion, the experience of cultural difference. They describe the construction of alternative fables, imaginative counterparts which taken together express an irony characteristic of the implication of modernity with alterity. We might hope that "native" visitors to London would provide an occasion for a contemplation of the question of cultural difference, enabling the English metropolitan population to see the multiform diversity of the peoples of the world. And we might assume that orangutangs, parrots, and lap dogs would appear to be so different from human beings as to fall outside the modern contemplation of alterity altogether. But it is the fable of the "native prince" that ignores the question of cultural difference by assuming a sentimental identification between the native and the European. And it is the fable of the nonhuman being, in imagining an affinity between radically alien species, that opens up the possibility of a new way of being that has the potential to rise above difference. This reversal of interpretive expectations—in the counterposition of two contemporary imaginative approaches to the question of alterity—represents an irony that appears as one of the common themes in the chapters that follow, an irony that characterizes this study's understanding of modernity itself—its yoking of exploitation and liberation, brutality and progress, fears and hopes. Each of the following fables gives a distinctive form to that paradox.

PART I : EXPANSION

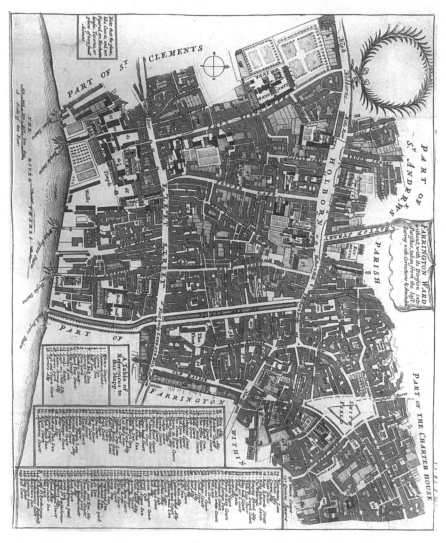

Map of Farrington Ward (1720). Showing Smithfield, St. Sepulchre's Church, Holborn Bridge, and Fleet Ditch—here designated as the New Canal. By permission of the Division of Rare and Manuscript Collections, Cornell University Library.

CHAPTER 1

The Metropolis:
The Fable of the City Sewer

A FEW days after the publication of his *Description of a City Shower* in *The Tatler* for October 7, 1710, Jonathan Swift recorded his friends Nicholas Rowe's and Matthew Prior's praise of the poem in his *Journal to Stella*: "both fell commending my *Shower* beyond any thing that has been written of the kind: there never was such a Shower since Danaë's."[1] Rowe's and Prior's juxtaposition of the *City Shower* with the classical myth, is, of course, a mock-heroic one. In this sense, it reproduces the mock classical formulae that appear within this poem and its companion piece, Swift's *Description of the Morning*.[2] In these examples of urban "Local Poetry," classified and promoted as such by Richard Steele in his *Tatler* essays on the subject,[3] the description of a sordid city scene is structured in terms of neoclassical allusion. The *Description of the Morning*, for example, represents the approach of the Virgilian "Ruddy Morn" in London in terms of the sexual indiscretions of the chambermaid Betty as she slips from the bed of her master, and the various street cries, moppings, and sweepings of the urban laboring classes.[4] And in the *City Shower*

---

[1] Jonathan Swift, *Journal to Stella* (27 October 1710), ed. Harold Williams (Oxford: Clarendon Press, 1948), 1:74.

[2] *A Description of the Morning* was first printed a year and a half before the *City Shower* in *The Tatler*, no. 9 (30 April 1709).

[3] Richard Steele, *The Tatler*, no. 238 (17 October 1710), ed. Donald F. Bond (Oxford: Clarendon Press, 1987), 2:225.

[4] *A Description of the Morning*, in *Swift: Poetical Works*, ed. Herbert Davis (London: Oxford University Press, 1967), line 2. Subsequent references to Swift's poems, except for *The Progress of Beauty*, are to this edition; line numbers are given within the text. The "ruddy Morn" is a familiar trope in the *Aeneid*; see, for instance, in Dryden's translation: "The rosy morn was risen from the main" (4.182), in *The Poetical Works of Dryden*, ed. George R. Noyes,

Swift compares the sound of the downpour on the roof of a sedan chair
with that of Laocoon's spear on the side of the Trojan horse:

> So when *Troy* Chair-men bore the Wooden Steed,
> Pregnant with *Greeks,* impatient to be freed,
>
> . . . .
>
> *Laoco'n* struck the Outside with his Spear,
> And each imprison'd Hero quak'd for Fear.

(ll. 47–52)

These Virgilian comparisons have the same general deflationary effect
that Rowe and Prior must have been suggesting in evoking the myth of
Danaë as the precedent for Swift's *Shower.* Danaë was imprisoned in an underground house of bronze (in Horace, a tower) by her father, King Acrisius of Argos, who had learned from the Delphic priestess that Danaë's son
would be his murderer. The bronze house was Acrisius's necessarily futile
attempt to control Danaë's sexuality. But predictably Danaë was not con-
strained by her father's devices. Zeus, in the form of a golden shower dropping through the open roof of the house, impregnated her, and she conceived Perseus, slayer of Medusa and, accidentally, of his own grandfather.
Acrisius's death was inevitable from the outset, of course. This is a myth of
the inaccessibility of female sexuality to male control or supervision.

The comparison with Danaë demonstrates the contemporary association of the *City Shower* with the female body at the same time that it dram-
atizes the distance between classical mythology and contemporary life,
and specifically between the divine distillation of irrepressible procreativity and the profane concretization of modern urban experience. The distance evoked here calls attention to the sordidness of the modern world,
but the effect of the comparison is not simply dismissive of the local and
the mundane. Like much Augustan mock-heroic writing, this juxtaposition gives the unflattering evocation of contemporary experience an at-
tractive immediacy and an enigmatic energy. The tangible scents and
scenes of the London street have a certain intensity, which makes them
different from but not necessarily inferior to the classical precedent. It is
this compensatory vitality that enables a critic like Irvin Ehrenpreis to observe that "only an admirer could have gathered together the sharp observations" that fill the *City Shower.*[5] But this is a vitality whose source and

---

rev. ed. (Boston: Houghton Mifflin, 1937). Subsequent references to Dryden's poetry are to
this edition; line numbers are given within the text.

[5] Irvin Ehrenpreis, *Swift: The Man, His Works, and the Age,* vol. 2 of *Dr. Swift* (Cambridge:
Harvard University Press, 1967), 2:384. This affirmative reading represents one pole of the

nature are notoriously difficult to pin down, here and elsewhere in Augustan mock-heroic verse. What is it about Swift's London or, for that matter, Pope's Dulness, that could be said to attract "admiration"?[6] Where, in the cultural imagination of this period, is this peculiar intensity generated? And why is it figured as female?

The contrast between Danaë's shower and Swift's is typical of the formal structure of the Augustan mock-heroic. But if, instead of holding apart these two showers as if their relationship should be understood solely by their deflationary contrast, we bring them together, the vivid precedent of Danaë can provide a purchase on the significance of the urban deluge, and a means of locating the source of the enigmatic vitality of contemporary urban experience for the writers of this period. Rowe's and Prior's female figure evokes a powerful cultural fable, of which the *City Shower* is a prominent expression, a modern fable of irrepressible procreativity whose images of vitality preoccupy the literary culture of the early eighteenth century. This fable is engaged with the representation of an ungovernable and omnivorous female sexual energy, located in the female body, associated with female desire, and through that association evocative of a force that seeks to transform, reorder, or overwhelm established systems of coherence, genealogy, or hierarchy. It is a story of the crisis of modern urban sanitation: a fable of the city sewer. It has its own particular shape and theme, but it belongs to a larger contemporary genre of cultural fables that includes a closely related story, also premised upon a fluid and transforming force, the fable of the torrents and oceans of nationalist and imperialist apologia.

---

interpretation of the poem. For instance, Peter Schakel also describes the *Shower* as "a celebration rather than a condemnation of city life"; see *The Poetry of Jonathan Swift: Allusion and the Development of a Poetic Style* (Madison: University of Wisconsin Press, 1978), 59. The affirmative reading is countered by a reading that sees the *Shower* as an unambiguous attack on the contemporary. For example, Patricia Meyer Spacks argues that the last lines of the poem "provide a more forceful indictment of the disorder and filth of the city than could be achieved by ten times their bulk in moral or sociological commentary. The horror, the obscenity that Swift felt inherent in chaos are here directly evoked"; see introduction to *Eighteenth Century Poetry*, ed. Spacks (Englewood Cliffs, N.J.: Prentice Hall, 1964), xxxiii–xxxiv. On the relation between these two positions, and the interpretive "paradox" of the poem, see John I. Fischer, "Apparent Contraries: A Reading of Swift's *A Description of a City Shower*," *Tennessee Studies in Literature*, ed. Richard M. Kelly (Knoxville: University of Tennessee Press, 1974), 21–34.

[6] *The Rape of the Lock* also depends on a classical juxtaposition whose contemporary pole is enigmatically affirmative, resulting in an interpretive paradox much like that of the *Shower*. For a representative statement along these lines, see Murray Krieger, "The 'Frail China Jar' and the Rude Hand of Chaos," in *Essential Articles for the Study of Alexander Pope*, ed. Maynard Mack, rev. ed. (Hamden, Conn.: Archon Books, 1968), 301–319.

I

Danaë's shower, in its diffuse permeation of the enclosed space of Danaë's bronze prison, is an apt emblem of the ineluctability of female sexuality; no constraints could be effective against Danaë's receptivity to that golden deluge. Though the shower is male, it is represented in Swift's paraphrase of Rowe's and Prior's praise as a female force: Danaë's shower. Zeus's liquid form is in this sense the perfect instantiation of the woman's desire. In Swift's case, however, the choice of the shower is less immediately explicable. What makes the shower the visceral epitome of eighteenth-century urban experience, for Swift and his appreciative friends?

We might guess that the vitality of this image arises from its connection with the tangible and local. The shower elicits sights and smells that can only belong to London: the "pensive Cat" sensing the coming storm, the "double Stink" of the city sewer (ll. 3, 6). Or perhaps the shower expresses the essence of the city because it brings together the full spectrum of the London populace in their flight from the deluge: the "daggled Females" crowding into shops, the "Templer spruce" pretending to call a coach, the "tuck'd-up Sempstress" hastening down the street, the "triumphant Tories" mingling with "desponding Whigs," and the impatient "Beau" "Box'd in a Chair" and trembling at the thunderous beating of the rain on its sides (ll. 33–43). The shower might act as a geographical summary of London as well, encompassing in its deluge the whole town, and giving the poet an occasion to trace some of the main districts and landmarks of the city, from "*Smithfield* or St. '*Pulchre's* . . . to *Holborn-Bridge*," and from there down the "Flood" of Fleet Ditch to the Thames (ll. 58–63). Furthermore, the shower is a venerable classical motif; a famous rain storm staged by Juno precedes Dido's ill-fated union with Aeneas in the cave at Carthage,[7] and the first book of the *Georgics* contains a sustained storm scene which structures Swift's poem from "Prognosticks" to preliminaries to the deluge itself,[8] and provides the model—"And cakes of rustling ice come rolling down the flood"—for Swift's final line, "Dead Cats and Turnip-Tops come tumbling down the Flood."[9] In this context, the shower gives Swift and his audience that link that the Augustans treasured between the Roman and the British empire, centered, in this case, on the burgeoning metropolitan scene of the city of London. The shower is a

---

[7] See Dryden's *Aeneid*, 4.161–246.

[8] See Ehrenpreis, 384.

[9] The storm occupies the last two hundred lines of *Georgics* 1, in Dryden's translation. Ehrenpreis notes the resemblance between Swift's concluding line and that of Dryden's Virgil (385 n. 1).

polymorphous figure in the urban local poetry that Swift is defining here. But it has an underground history that governs all these effects.

The shower, like Virgil's "imber" for his own audience, was no simple meteorological term to an eighteenth-century English ear.[10] As the *Oxford English Dictionary* documents, in the second half of the seventeenth century "shower," "shore," and "sewer" were the dominant but not unique spellings of three nouns designating, respectively: rainfall or an observer; a strip of land bordering on a body of water, a menace, a prop, or a sewer; and a conduit for waste disposal or a steward. In the seventeenth century, "shower" was also spelled "shewre," "shewer," and "shore"; "sewer" was also spelled "sure" and "shewer"; and "shore" was also spelled "showre" and "shower." Behind this conflation was a phonological change that tended to equate the pronunciation of "shower" and "sewer." In the late seventeenth century an "s" (phonetic [s]) followed by, roughly, the modern consonantal sound "y" (phonetic [j]) becomes "sh" (phonetic [ʃ]). This is in some cases a temporary change; the "sh" ([ʃ]) reverts to "s" ([s]) usually in the eighteenth century. The modern "sure," however, is an example of a case in which the change is retained. Relatedly, the vowel sound originally following the "s," pronounced roughly like"you" (phonetic [ju:]), with the change to "sh" drops the consonantal "y" sound ([j]) and comes close to the vowel sound following the "s" in modern "sewer" (phonetic [u:]). In short, it seems likely that "shower," "shore," and "sewer" were for a time in the late seventeenth and early eighteenth century pronounced alike; all sounded like the modern word, "sure."[11]

Semantically, the *Oxford English Dictionary* tells us that "shore," in the sense of a piece of land bordering on a body of water, was regularly used as a variant of "sewer," meaning a conduit for waste disposal. The editors of the *Oxford English Dictionary* suggest that the use of "shore" as "sewer" was probably derived not from a common linguistic source, which they indicate was the traditional view, but from the contemporary use of the phrase "common shore," which denoted a piece of land bordering on a body of water that was used for refuse disposal. A "common shore" was a sort of natural "sewer," whose use preceded the rise of urban planning and the various civil regulations that gradually transformed the "common

[10] For Virgil such storms could be indicative of the anger of the gods and predictive not only of natural destruction but of a disorder in the state that paralleled that of the natural world. In Dryden's *Georgics*, for instance, the storm to which Swift's *Shower* alludes foretells "fierce tumults, hidden treasons, open wars" (1.627). For Swift's relation to Virgil, see Brendan O Hehir, "Meaning of Swift's *Description of a City Shower*," *ELH* 27 (1960): 194–207.

[11] On phonetics, see E. J. Dobson, *English Pronunciation 1500–1700* (Oxford: Clarendon Press, 1957), 2:706–707, 711–712, 789–799, 799–803, 957, 958–967.

shore" into the underground sewer systems of the twentieth century. Thus the contemporary phrase "common sewer" seems to have been derived from that semantic connection with the "common shore." Semantically as well as phonetically, then, in the period of Swift's poem, one person's "sewer" was another person's "shore," a word that sounded like and was sometimes spelled as "shower."

Indeed, the notion of a "sewer" as we understand it, as a separate, planned, covered waterway for the disposal of urban or suburban refuse and waste water, is a very recent one. There were few sewers that were not "common shores" in London until the mid nineteenth century. In fact, until the major project to enclose London sewers was initiated in 1858 after the crisis of the Great Stink in which the windows of the Houses of Parliament had to be draped with lime-soaked curtains so that the Members could meet, the notion of the "common shore" was the most accurate description of the means of discharging refuse and waste water in the city. In *The Lost Rivers of London* N. J. Barton has documented the expansion of the city across the original alluvial flood plain. Like most other substantial English and European cities, London grew up around a major waterway, the Thames. With the demographic explosion of the metropolis in the seventeenth and eighteenth centuries, the Thames's tributary rivers—the Fleet, the Walbrook, the Tyburn, and many other local streams—were gradually incorporated into a network of open sewers into which all urban waste was deposited. Even today urban geographers can match the underground sewer system of the city with the ancient waterways of the pre-urban alluvial flood plain, like a palimpsest in which the overlay defines the modern city as its sewer system.[12] An anonymous writer, perhaps Defoe, describes these "common shores" in the decade after the publication of Swift's *Shower*:

> These filthy places receive all the sinks [local sewers] . . . and drains from dye houses, wash houses, fell [hide] mongers, slaughter houses and all kinds of offensive trades; they are continually full of carrion and the most odious of all offensive stench proceeds from them; also the other part of the said ditches westward as far as Lambeth, many of which lye a great depth in mud. . . . The like of these are to be seen below Bridge from Horseleydown to Battle Bridge and all along the back of Rotherhithe . . . and are justly the terror even of the inhabitants themselves. . . . Such notorious fountains of

[12] N. J. Barton, *The Lost Rivers of London. A study of their effects upon London and Londoners, and the effects of London and Londoners upon them* (London: Leicester University Press, 1962).

stench, [are] enough to corrupt the very air and make the people sick and faint as they pass by.[13]

Urban sanitation had become a massively complex and highly visible matter whose impact was evident to every city dweller and whose prevalence extended from the most minute and local detail of the smallest household cesspit and streetside ditch to the large scale pollution of the Thames itself. In this period latrines were located directly over urban waterways. Waste water and refuse from dwellings and businesses, including slaughter houses, hog yards, butchers, coal yards, brick works, and dye works, were either discharged into cesspits, from which they were periodically removed to the sewage "ditches" flowing through local neighborhoods, made to flow directly into local "sinks," "drains," or "sluices," the smaller channels that ran behind or between buildings, or carried out to the "kennels" that ran down the center of many urban thoroughfares. The sheer number of and names for the city sewer in this period, in itself, indicates its prominence in everyday life. Residents were subjected not only to the smells and sights of the open sewers all around them, they were forced to ford the sewers almost every time they crossed a street and to see their own contributions deposited directly from the latrines or through the discharge of chamber pots and household refuse containers into those open ditches before their doors and beneath their windows. Contemporary residents and modern urban historians alike have recognized this network of open sewers as a kind of thoroughfare in itself, a system of communication—much more effective than the crowded streets and alleys—that served to connect and to define the modern city. In Pat Rogers's description: "Open sewers . . . were among the few direct communicating links from one part of London to another, in some areas of the town where the streets were little better than a maze."[14]

The first major attempt to reform urban sanitation was the Sewage and Paving Act of 1671, which initiated a change in the location of the kennel, removing it from the center of the street to an open side drain, set off by a raised pavement.[15] The concern here, however, seems to have been mainly the safety of the main thoroughfares of the city, which by this legislation were also to be cambered—built up in the middle for drainage—and paved. As a result, some streets were improved, though central kennels remained common well into the eighteenth century. The notion of

[13] *Due Preservation from the Plague as well for Soul as Body* (1722). Cited in M. Dorothy George, *London Life in the XVIIIth Century* (London: Kegan Paul, 1925), 349 n. 66.

[14] Pat Rogers, *Grub Street: Studies in a Subculture* (London: Methuen, 1972), 144.

[15] Roy Porter, *London: A Social History* (Cambridge: Harvard University Press, 1994), 89.

covering over the sinks, drains, ditches, and tributary rivers of the city's burgeoning sewage system did not arise until two decades after Swift's *Shower*. Fleet Ditch, the contemporary name for the Fleet River, the largest of the Thames's tributaries, was the most notorious site of urban filth and pollution, not only in Swift's poem, but in almost every other account of the material degradation of city life for two centuries running.[16] This "nauceious and abominable sink of nastiness"[17] was the main focus of a series of largely futile efforts to improve urban sanitation. In the late seventeenth century the lower section of the river was dredged and flanked with wharves to form a canal, but this structure had deteriorated to such an extent by the time of Swift's poem that in 1733 the short-lived Fleet Canal was covered over from Fleet Bridge to Holborn Bridge (Barton, 76–78, 105–106).[18] The Fleet was thus a physical, social, and cultural emblem of urban life; in Rogers's words: "The Fleet . . . was a conduit which linked virtually all the most wretched corners of the city" (149).

As Swift's poem shows us, London's system of waterways also came under strain during rainstorms; the city affords no porous soil to absorb a sudden shower. Floods in these open urban waterways after heavy rains were notorious for carrying dead animals and property down the sewers to the Thames. In a storm in 1679, according to a contemporary observer, not only cattle, but,

> property and goods of all sorts and descriptions, including barrels of ale and spirits from the wrecked houses on its route, were carried down to Hockley-in-the-Hole, to become Flotsam for a greedy and excited rabble.[19]

Even today the underground sewers of London are dangerously swollen by a downpour. A twentieth-century sewerman describes the effects of a deluge:

> A heavy shower can quickly flood the main sewer as water pours in from 2,500 miles of small local lines. Within minutes of a downpour a man could be swept away. First comes a noisy gust of wind,

---

[16] See Barton for a detailed historical account of the degradation of the Fleet River "from a river to a brook, from a brook to a ditch, and from a ditch to a drain" (29). For an account of the status of Fleet Ditch in contemporary culture, see Rogers's essay on the "Artery of Dulness" in *Grub Street*.

[17] Cited in George, 85.

[18] For a history of the desultory and unsuccessful attempts to improve the Fleet, see Rogers, 146–149.

[19] Cited in Barton, 104.

echoing down the tunnels; then the deluge, and the water rushes over the weirs into the dry storm-relief sewers. (Barton, 116)

His language matches Swift's in a way that shows the continuity in the modern experience of the city sewer.

II

The titular image of Swift's poem, then, is a graphic, unacknowledged pun that calls attention to one of the defining dimensions of modern urban experience. Many of Swift's contemporaries, notably Addison, did not countenance open punning. Swift, however, enjoyed and exploited puns, especially in his *Journal to Stella*.[20] In this case the sewer seems so deeply inseparable, semantically and phonetically, from the shower as to almost eliminate the effect of surprise for a contemporary reader. The poem matches the sewer and the shower with a perfect reciprocity. Certainly the vigorous image of the torrent of Fleet Ditch, which concludes and summarizes the progress of the poem, comes as no surprise, but rather as an apt culmination of the account of the shower. This well-known triplet describes the "swelling Kennels" flowing through the city from Smithfield market and St. Sepulchre's Church on Snow Hill to be collected in Fleet Ditch at Holborn Bridge:

Sweepings from Butchers Stalls, Dung, Guts and Blood,
Drown'd Puppies, stinking Sprats, all drench'd in Mud,
Dead Cats and Turnip-Tops come tumbling down the Flood.
(ll. 61–63)

Even without the phonetic connection between "sewer" and "shower," the shower of Swift's poem leads in an inexorable rush—characteristic of the vitality of this figure—to the urban sewer.

The sewer seems to share and even underpin the shower's cultural force in evoking the immediacy and significance of urban life, the energy that tempts us to claim that Swift must be, paradoxically, its admirer. We might speculate that the sewer is the figure of choice because it represents a sign of the demographic explosion of the urban population: sewers indicate the need for urban planning and sanitation, and thus serve as a focal point for the tensions around urban growth. Sewers epitomize the

---

[20] Ann Cline Kelly, *Swift and the English Language* (Philadelphia: University of Pennsylvania Press, 1988), 18. On Swift's puns and contemporary science and economics, see David Nokes, "'Hack at Tom Poley's': Swift's Use of Puns," in *The Art of Jonathan Swift*, ed. Clive Probyn (New York: Barnes and Noble, 1978), 43–56.

sordid nature of the city, exhibiting the most pungent smells and the most graphic sights that would strike the senses of an eighteenth-century urban dweller. And sewers are omnipresent in the urban scene. In fact, the sewer is a phenomenon that structures urban geography, tying the distant and socially disparate parts of the city to one network with the common necessary purpose of waste disposal, to the same effect as the shower's assembling of disparate urban regions and social classes. All these roles make the sewer a sordid counterpart to the shower—the classical figure's contemporary urban alter ego.

The impact of urban geography on late seventeenth and early eighteenth-century English culture has been explored in detail by Cynthia Wall, in a way that bears directly on our understanding of the rhetorical and literary materials of the period. Wall shows that the rebuilding of London following the great fire of 1666 is a crucial stage in the constitution of the modern city. She finds in these decades "various topographically obsessed forms of literature"—like the urban local poetry of Swift and others—which reflect a "new cultural awareness," a "sense of spatial motion," a "jumbling and jostling," and a rhetorical and social indiscriminacy "that captures and exploits or seeks to sort and contain the topographical and social intercrowding of the modern metropolis."[21] Wall both connects this new urban culture with earlier discursive traditions and distinguishes it from them:

> Some of the power of the new narratives of urban landscapes
> derives from a much older literary tradition of inscribing London's
> streets with social, commercial, and traditional topographical
> meaning . . . that . . . emerged from and negotiated a different but
> also specifically *urban* crisis. . . . the new literature and new spatial
> representations swallowed whole or in part the rhetorical patterns
> of the past. The rupturing of spatial stability brought on by the Fire
> and the rebuilding . . . ignited a widespread cultural effort within
> the City to remap itself imaginatively, to resignify its spaces, to
> rename itself. . . . In particular, the constant litany of street names
> in the sermons and journalized accounts, the indexing and itemiza-
> tion of streets in the topographies, the grammatical and imagina-
> tive change from a relative sense of spatial fixity to a relative sense
> of spatial motion, and the cleanswept two-dimensionality of the sur-
> veys and groundplans replacing the three-dimensional birds-eye-
> views, all found themselves in the employ of poetry, drama, [and]
> prose fiction. (116)

[21] Cynthia Wall, *The Literary Spaces of Restoration London* (Cambridge: Cambridge University Press, 1998), chap. 4; this quote, 116–117.

The fable of the city sewer is a condensation of the distinctive modern urban environment that Wall defines, its social and geographical tropes reflecting the particular experiences of physical crowding, social indiscriminacy, and especially spatial mobility characteristic of the modern metropolis. The defining features of modernity have long been located in the social space of the metropolis. In the marxist tradition especially, the critique of modernity has been inspired by the streets, crowds, and architectural structures of the major European cities—of Paris, London, or Berlin.[22] The cultural experience of the eighteenth-century sewer represents an original moment in that modern encounter with urban space, a moment that condenses various dimensions of its historical significance, and that finds expression in a coherent, collective fable.

The confluence of sewer and shower, a defining feature of this fable, sets it off from prior literary sewerscapes, confirming both its connection with and its distinctions from the earlier period. A century before the *City Shower*, for instance, Ben Jonson's extended sewer poem, "The Voyage it selfe" (1616), sets many precedents for the later accounts of the London sewers in the urban local poetry of the eighteenth century. But Jonson's work lacks that rush of vitality and impetuous energy that marks the eighteenth-century sewer/shower. The Jacobean poem is framed as a mock-heroic voyage to hell, as its protagonists, after an evening of merriment at the "Mermaid" in Bread-street, "Propos'd to goe to *Hol'borne* in a wherry,"[23] that is, to travel up the Fleet River from Bridewell to Holborn bridge in a row boat. At the outset of the voyage, the reader is enjoined to "stop thy nose" (l. 60), the boat's oars stir up a hot stench from the mud, and the travelers make their way "through [the] wombe" of the Fleet (l. 66) and between her "two walls," from which privies and sinks pour their contents down on them. Forced close to the wall by a passing liter, they draw even nearer to the overhead latrines, with the predictable result:

> Alas, they will beshite vs.
> No matter, stinkards, row. What croaking sound
> Is this we heare? of frogs? No, guts wind-bound,
> Ouer your heads: Well, row.

> (ll. 90–93)

---

22 See David Frisby, *Fragments of Modernity: Theories of Modernity in the Work of Simmel, Kracauer and Benjamin* (Cambridge: MIT Press, 1986), for a summary of the role of the city in the marxist tradition.

23 Ben Jonson, "The Voyage it selfe" in *Epigrammes* (1616), in *Ben Jonson*, vol. 3 of *The Poems, The Prose Works*, ed. C. H. Herford Percy and Evelyn Simpson (Oxford: Clarendon Press, 1947), line 38. Subsequent references to Jonson's poem are to this edition; line numbers are given within the text.

Farts descend from above, or rise like ghosts from the stream, shit is "stucke upon the wall," "precipitated downe the jakes," swimming in the pool "in ample flakes," or "heap'd" up in a mass on all sides (ll. 136–139). Refuse from the cooks on Fleet lane adds to this accumulation:

> The sinkes ran grease, and haire of meazled [diseased] hogs,
> The heads, houghs [hocks], entrailes, and the hides of dogs:
> . . . .
> Cats there lay diuers [which] had beene flead, and rosted,
> And, after mouldie growne, againe were tosted,
> . . . .
> . . . here they were throwne in wi'the melted pewter,
> Yet drown'd they not. They had fiue liues in future.
>
> (ll. 144–154)

And finally the travelers encounter a being who, after he has "thrise diu'd" into the stream, addresses them:

> .   How dare
> Your daintie nostrils . . .
> . . . .
> Tempt such a passage? when each priuies seate
> Is fill'd with buttock? And the walls doe sweate
> Vrine, and plaisters? when the noise doth beate
> Vpon your ears, of discords so vn-sweet?
>
> (ll. 164–171)

Defying him, the voyagers finish the trip, and then, making bystanders witnesses of their success, they return the way they came.

As we shall see, the constituents of this urban local poem—the heaps of excrement, the stopped-up nose, the diving into the mud, the denizen of the deep, the jakes and privies, the drowned dogs and cats, the potency of Fleet Ditch—become the familiar constituents of the eighteenth-century fable of the city sewer. But the earlier poem tells an upstream story; it represents a steady, methodical, slow rowing through a viscous medium, in a dark, claustrophobic womb of mud. Although Swift's *City Shower* in its last couplet occupies the same locale as Jonson's poem, Holborn Bridge, its geographical trajectory and its formal dynamic is downstream from the bridge to the Thames, with the rapid rush of the urban deluge. This vital deluge is the signature item of the eighteenth-century fable of the city sewer.

A sustained account of a city shower—clearly indebted to Swift's poem—forms the centerpiece of the first book of John Gay's urban pastoral, *Trivia: Or, The Art of Walking the Streets of London* (1716). This poem's account of the sewer begins with the inclusive "you" that characterizes this metropolitan experience:

> When Sleep is first disturb'd by Morning Cries;
> From sure Prognosticks learn to know the Skies,
> Lest you of Rheums and Coughs at Night complain;
> Surpriz'd in dreary Fogs, or driving Rain.[24]

And it quickly moves to the vital trope of urban torrents:

> But when the swinging Signs your Ears offend
> With creaking Noise, then rainy Floods impend;
> Soon shall the Kennels swell with rapid Streams,
> And rush in muddy Torrents to the *Thames.*
>
> (1.157–160)

The "rushing" impetus of these descriptions of the sewers is the rhetorical counterpart to the energy of the rainstorm, with its winds, spouts, and torrents:

> . . . you'll hear the Sounds
> Of whistling Winds, e'er Kennels break their Bounds;
> Ungrateful Odours Common-shores diffuse,
> And dropping Vaults distil unwholesom Dews,
> E'er the Tiles rattle with the smoking Show'r,
> And Spouts on heedless Men their Torrents pour.
>
> (1. 169–174)

A representation of flowing motion characterizes Gay's metropolis. The pedestrian is urged to "swiftly shoot along" (3.51) the crowded streets and warned that "the Tide / Tumultuous" might bear his companion from his side (3.91–92). Flowing crowds mingle with the floods and torrents of shower and sewer, as the pedestrian struggles to keep his place beside the protective wall of housing and far from the street-side mud:

> When from high Spouts the dashing Torrents fall,
> Ever be watchful to maintain the Wall;
> For should'st thou quit thy Ground, the rushing Throng
> Will with impetuous Fury drive along;

---

[24] John Gay, *Trivia: Or, The Art of Walking the Streets of London* (London: Daniel O'Connor, 1922), 1.121–124. Subsequent references to Gay's poem are to this edition; book and line numbers are given within the text.

All press to gain those Honours thou has lost,
And rudely shove thee far without the Post.
Then to retrieve the Shed you strive in vain,
Draggled all o'er, and soak'd in Floods of Rain.
Yet rather bear the Show'r, and Toils of Mud,
Than in the doubtful Quarrel risque thy Blood.

                                        (3.205–214)

For Gay, these swelling energies are a source of potential disruption, physical and social, soaking the wig of the unprepared pedestrian (1.202) and threatening the shoes of the ladies, who are saved, in a mock-heroic excursus, only by Vulcan's invention of the elevated patten (1.271–276). Wrecked coaches often accompany the poem's accounts of the urban deluge. At night the sewer's "gulph" catches a passing carriage:

Where a dim Gleam the paly Lanthorn throws
O'er the mid' Pavement; heapy Rubbish grows,
Or arched Vaults their gaping Jaws extend,
Or the dark Caves to Common-Shores descend.
. . . .
E'er Night has half roll'd round her Ebon Throne;
In the wide Gulph the shatter'd Coach o'erthrown,
Sinks with the snorting Steeds; the Reins are broke,
And from the cracking Axle flies the Spoke.

                                        (3.335–345)

In book 2, the shower produces a physical enactment of social leveling, when the Beau is overturned into the sewer by the storm, chariot and all:

I've seen a Beau, in some ill-fated Hour,
When o'er the Stones choak'd Kennels swell the Show'r,
In gilded Chariot loll; he with Disdain,
Views spatter'd Passengers, all drench'd in Rain;
With Mud fill'd high, the rumbling Cart draws near,
Now rule thy prancing Steeds, lac'd Charioteer!
The *Dustman* lashes on with spiteful Rage,
His pond'rous Spokes thy painted Wheel engage,
Crush'd is thy Pride, down falls the shrieking Beau,
The slabby Pavement crystal Fragments strow,
Black Floods of Mire th' embroider'd Coat disgrace,
And Mud enwraps the Honours of his Face.

                                        (2.401–411)

Here again, the epic simile sets up that familiar mock-heroic paradox of deflation and vitality that we have seen in Swift's *Shower* and in Rowe's and Prior's Danaë. Like Ehrenpreis on Swift's shower, Pat Rogers registers the unexpected admiration generated by Gay's unflattering evocation of urban experience:

> Gay makes something almost pretty out of the showers of mud that bespatter citizens; the dirt can perhaps be identified with the lower segments of society—it has certainly become part of the moving stream of the city, a kind of urban hormone which sets the activity of the whole town in motion. (164)

A motion that can have disruptive, even threatening, implications. In Gay's poem the images of the torrential shower/sewer become the rhetorical basis for an account of urban conflagration that evokes the Great Fire that devastated the city and cleared the way for the building of modern London:

> At first a glowing Red enwraps the Skies,
> And born by Winds the scatt'ring Sparks arise;
> From Beam to Beam, the fierce Contagion spreads;
> The spiry Flames now lift aloft their Heads,
> Through the burst Sash a blazing Deluge pours,
> And splitting Tiles descend in rattling Show'rs.
>
> (3.355–360)

These lines suggest the cataclysmic implications of the urban deluge—sewer and shower—for the contemporary imagination.[25] The sewer, however, has a specific contemporary history of its own, which rivals the classical genealogy of the shower.

In fact, sewers in literary culture are not unique to Swift's or Gay's urban local poetry.[26] John Wilmot, the Earl of Rochester, suggests the currency of the figure in *On Mrs. Willis* (1681), a poem attacking a notorious London prostitute. This essay in graphic misogyny ends with a sewer image that parallels Swift's in its climactic positioning and its summary effect:

[25] Wall sees Gay's poem as more confident and optimistic than Pope's and Swift's: "his imagery remains 'cleaner' than Swift's, softer than Pope's. . . . Gay's poem is closer to the agendas and tones of the textual topographies . . . than to his fellow Scriblerians' outwardly similar verse satire" (133). My impression of the poem's evocation of a cataclysmic energy, on the other hand, derives from my focus on the common representation of the sewer in these works.

[26] On the geographical presence and the cultural prominence of the sewer in the period, see Rogers, 145–166.

> Bawdy in thoughts, precise in words,
> Ill-natured though a whore,
> Her belly is a bag of turds,
> And her cunt a common shore.[27]

Here is the common shore/sewer that we have seen underlying the *City Shower*'s pun, but in this case the sewer is a figure for the female genitalia. The effect of this metaphor is both to express the filthiness of Willis's body and to evoke a sense of the sordid indiscriminacy of female sexuality. The common shore/sewer is a location of heterogeneous mingling where all sorts of waste may be deposited or where all sorts may deposit their waste. This image gives the female body a specific figurative function within the fable of the city sewer: that of homogenizing relationships of difference or leveling systems of hierarchy.

The leveling function defined here, with its implication in the image of urban waste disposal, is a consistent dimension of the representation of the female body in the poetry of the late seventeenth century. In another poem attacking women, *A Ramble in St. James's Park* (ca. 1680), Rochester describes his rejection by his mistress Corinna in favor of "three confounded asses" who carry her off in a hackney coach (l. 81). Corinna's preference for these other men is described through a metaphor of indiscriminacy similar to Willis's "common shore," this time in the form of a chamber pot:

> But to turn damned abandoned jade
> When neither head nor tail persuade;
> To be a whore in understanding,
> A passive pot for fools to spend in!
>
> (ll. 99–102)

Here the feminized site for the collection of waste is meant to indicate a kind of intellectual leveling where the three "fools," whom the poem characterizes at some length, are made to mingle with the poet, who sees himself in a very different category from them: "Gods! that a thing admired by me / Should fall to so much infamy" (ll. 89–90). The description of the setting of this poem also serves to emphasize this function of leveling or of categorical promiscuity. St. James's Park is defined at the opening of the poem as a locus of social indiscriminacy:

> Unto this all-sin-sheltering grove
> Whores of the bulk [shop-front] and the alcove,

[27] *On Mrs. Willis*, in *The Complete Poems of John Wilmot, Earl of Rochester*, ed. David M. Vieth (New Haven: Yale University Press, 1968), lines 17–20. Subsequent references to Rochester's poems are to this edition; line numbers are given within the text.

Great ladies, chambermaids, and drudges,
The ragpicker, and heiress trudges.
Carmen, divines, great lords, and tailors,
Prentices, poets, pimps, and jailers,
Footmen, fine fops do here arrive,
And here promiscuously they swive.

(ll. 26–32)

And Corinna, we learn, has practiced exactly this sort of promiscuity before:

When your lewd cunt came spewing home
Drenched with the seed of half the town,
My dram of sperm was supped up after
For the digestive surfeit water.
Full gorgèd at another time
With a vast meal of nasty slime
Which your devouring cunt had drawn
From porters' backs and footmen's brawn,
I was content to serve you up
My ballock-full for your grace cup.

(ll. 114–123)

Here female sexual insatiability is identified with categorical indiscriminacy—fools mix with wits and social classes mingle in the omnivorous female body. This dismantling of hierarchical and categorical order is a pervasive and determining dimension of the representation of women in this period and a central theme of the fable of the city sewer that, as we shall see, is shaped by these images of the female body.[28]

Robert Gould's poem, *Love given o're: or, A Satyr against the Pride, Lust, and Inconstancy, &c. of Woman* (1682), another contemplation of female sexuality from the decades before the *City Shower*, gives us yet another feminized sewer, this time a "sluce" that is made to characterize female inconstancy. The speaker advises men to avoid any intercourse with women, but when celibacy is impossible, the best object is a sexually insatiable fe-

---

[28] Feminist critics have provided various perspectives on this poetry's treatment of the female figure, against which my reading of the role of the sewer could be viewed. For instance, Valerie Rumbold situates the poems in relation to the historical women to whom they refer in *Women's Place in Pope's World* (Cambridge: Cambridge University Press, 1989). Felicity A. Nussbaum surveys their misogynist themes and effects in *The Brink of All We Hate: English Satires on Women 1660–1750* (Lexington: University Press of Kentucky, 1984). And Ellen Pollak explicates the relation between this poetry and cultural myths about gender in *The Poetics of Sexual Myth: Gender and Ideology in the Verse of Swift and Pope* (Chicago: University of Chicago Press, 1985).

male body, which can absorb the "deluge" of male lust in a sewer that, in this image, has no "shore":

> But if the Tyde of Nature [male desire] boist'rous grow,
> And would Rebelliously its Banks o'reflow,
> Then chuse a Wench, who (full of lewd desires)
> Can meet your flouds of Love with equal fires;
> And will, when e're you let the Deluge flie,
> Through an extended Sluce straight drain it dry;
> That Whirl-pool Sluce which never knows a Shore,
> Ne're can be fill'd so full as to run ore,
> For still it gapes, and still cries—room for more![29]

In Gould's poem and more generally in the figurative culture of the period, the deluge, like Danaë's shower, is only nominally male; it implies the force of female insatiability and desire, and, symptomatically, it is used both to describe male "flouds" and female sexuality. Elsewhere in Gould's poem the "deluge" represents an explicitly female power:

> Forgive me Modesty, if I have been
> In any thing I've mention'd here, Obscene;
> Since my Design is to detect their [women's] Crimes,
> Which (like a Deluge) overflow the Times.
>
>   (6)

Connected to this complex of images around the urban sewer and the deluge that feeds it is the related venerable rhyming conjunction of womb and tomb.[30] In the poetry of this period, the feminized tomb is a redaction of the feminized sewer. For Gould it "gapes" like the "extended Sluce":

> [she] drain'd 'em dry; exhausted all their store;
> Yet all could not content th' insatiate Whore,
> Her C—— like the dull Grave, still gap't for more.
>
>   (4)

[29] Robert Gould, *Love given o're: or, A Satyr against the Pride, Lust, and Inconstancy, &c. of Woman,* in *Satires on Women* (Los Angeles: William Andrews Clark Memorial Library, 1976), 3. Subsequent references to Gould's poem are to this edition; page numbers are given within the text.

[30] For such connections, see Hugh Kenner, "Pope's Reasonable Rhymes," *ELH* 41 (1974): 74–88.

Gould's female figure is insatiable to the same effect as Rochester's: her body's omnivorous appetite gathers indiscriminate things—like the items washed down to Hockley-in-the-Hole by the London rainstorm:

> . . . the Womb
> [is] as greedy as the gaping tomb:
> Take Men, Dogs, Lions, Bears, all sorts of Stuff,
> Yet it will never cry——there is enough.
>
> (5)

This is Gould's most compact account of the leveling function of the female body. Here the womb is the locus which mingles not just different sorts and classes of people, but people with animals, and animate with inanimate "Stuff."

Gould's "insatiate Whore" is Messalina, wife of the Emperor Claudius of Rome and famous for her sexual exploits. Messalina is a common figure for female lust in this period, regularly connected also with the leveling of class distinction. Dryden in his translation of Juvenal's Sixth Satire (1692) also gives her a prominent place, describing her return from the "brothel-house" (l. 173) after servicing all comers:

> Old Cæsar's bed the modest matron seeks;
> The steam of lamps still hanging on her cheeks
> In ropy smut; thus foul, and thus bedight,
> She brings him back the product of the night.
>
> (ll. 186–189)

Dryden's translation emphasizes the transgression of class and even racial boundaries: women will have sex with dancing masters (l. 89), fencers (l. 117), slaves (l. 449), watermen (l. 450), and "Ethiops" (l. 777). Indiscriminacy is the constitutive function of the female body, the city sewer its most eloquent contemporary emblem.

Swift himself, in his misogynist poetry, evokes this intimacy between the sewer and the female body. In *A Beautiful Young Nymph Going to Bed* (1734) the prostitute who undresses by removing not only clothes but body parts, hair, eyes, and teeth, dreams of her origins on the shore of Fleet Ditch. In fact, Corinna seems to have emerged from that king of all London sewers:

> . . . near *Fleet-Ditch*'s oozy Brinks,
> Surrounded with a Hundred Stinks,

Belated, [Corinna] seems on watch to lye,
And snap some Cully passing by.

(ll. 47–50)

Indeed, Corinna appears like some denizen of the sewer, or some sewer
goddess, surrounded with the same "Stinks" as the *City Shower*, and connected, through the indiscriminate numerousness of these surroundings,
with the same leveling function as Gould's greedy womb. By the end of this
poem, Corinna's body has itself dispersed to indiscriminacy, as the pieces
of her limbs and face are scattered throughout her "Bow'r." In the last
line of the poem, Corinna becomes an embodied epitome of the urban
sewer: "Who[ever] sees [her], will spew; who smells, be poison'd" (l. 74).
But it would be hard to argue that Swift was "an admirer" of this feminized
redaction of the urban scene, even though it belongs to the same cultural
fable as the *City Shower*. Whatever "admiration" we might be tempted to locate in this fable must be strangely and powerfully qualified.

Corinna's personal dispersal is comparable to the fate of Celia in
Swift's *Progress of Beauty* (1718), a poem written only eight years after the
City Shower. Celia flows away, a female embodiment of the sewer. At first
the "Complexions" of her "artificiall Face" run together overnight:

Three Colours, Black, and Red, and White,
So gracefull in their proper Place,
Remove them to a diff'rent Light
They form a frightfull hideous Face,

For instance; when the Lilly slipps
Into the Precincts of the Rose,
And takes Possession of the Lips,
Leaving the Purple to the Nose.[31]

But later on in the poem this mingling appears to be a result of the "rot-
ting" (l. 103) of syphilis or of mercury poisoning, as (in the analogy of the
moon) "Each Night a Bit drops off her Face" (l. 87). As Celia's features indiscriminately stream together, she turns into a "mingled Mass" (l. 20)
with the same liquid qualities as the flowing urban waste at the end of the
City Shower, when the streams from all the "swelling Kennels" come together, "And in huge Confluent join'd at *Snow-Hill* Ridge, / Fall from the

---

[31] *The Progress of Beauty*, in *The Poems of Jonathan Swift*, ed. Harold Williams (Oxford:
Clarendon Press, 1958), lines 30, 7, 21–28. Subsequent references to this poem are to this
edition; line numbers are given within the text.

Conduit prone to *Holborn-Bridge*" (ll. 57–60). In Celia's case, the same streams convert a coherent visage into a geography of flowing effluent:

> The Paint by Perspiration cracks,
> And falls in Rivulets of Sweat,
> On either Side you see the Tracks,
> While at her Chin the Conflu'ents met.
>
> A Skillfull Houswife thus her Thumb
> With Spittle while she spins, anoints,
> And thus the brown Meanders come
> In trickling Streams betwixt her Joynts.

(ll. 37–44)

Here the sewer and the female body come together in a complex and sustained figure that joins a variety of effects that we have seen elsewhere: a geographical image that evokes the assembling of the features of a complex landscape, and the representation of a fluidity that mixes, merges, or disperses a coherent body or system of order into a surprising, revolting, or sordid image of incoherence or indiscriminacy.

III

Less than two decades after Swift's publication of the *City Shower*, Alexander Pope, the preeminent eighteenth-century poet of the city sewer, published the first version of this period's most ambitious urban local poem, *The Dunciad* (in three books, 1728; in four books, 1743).[32] This poem as a whole will form the centerpiece of my description of the conjunction of the fables of sewers, floods, finance, and commodification in chapter 3. But book 2 of the *Dunciad* contains one of the period's major representations of the fable of the city sewer, in its evocation of urban waste and of the convergence of urban sanitation with the female body. This book describes the "high heroic Games" staged by Dulness "to glad her sons" (ll. 17–18) and celebrate the accession of the king of the dunces. First comes the booksellers' race for the phantom of a poet; second is the pissing contest, whose reward is a woman writer; third is the tickling contest, for the favors of the patron; fourth the noise contest, which seems its own

[32] The *Dunciad* was published first in three books in 1728, then in the Variorum edition in 1729. In 1742 Pope published the fourth book, and in 1743 all four books, revised, with Cibber replacing Theobald as king of the dunces. *The Dunciad, in Four Books* is my text in this chapter. References are to *The Dunciad,* in *The Poems of Alexander Pope,* vol. 5, ed. James Sutherland (London: Methuen, 1943); book and line numbers are given within the text.

reward; fifth the famous diving contest, whose venue is Fleet Ditch; and finally the dunces are challenged with the sleeping contest, which ends the book.

The movement within and through these games sketches an urban geography that includes the Strand, the Temple, Tottenham Fields, Chancery Lane, Westminster Hall, Hungerford Market, Bridewell, Fleet Ditch, St. Paul's Cathedral, Aldgate, Ludgate, and Fleet Street.[33] Pope traces the urban perambulations of the dunces in a note connected with the opening lines of the diving contest: "the games begin in the Strand, thence along Fleet-street (places inhabited by Booksellers), then they proceed by Bridewell toward Fleet-ditch, and lastly thro' Ludgate to the City and the Temple of the Goddess" (n. to l. 269ff). Individual games name numerous additional locations, producing an impression of inclusiveness that seems to embrace all of London; indeed, Pope has Curl announce this geographical scope with pride: "what street, what lane but knows, / Our purgings, pumpings, blankettings, and blows?" (ll. 153–154). But this evocation of a network of locales returns persistently to the connected waterways of the Thames and Fleet Ditch, which in their fluid ubiquitousness collect and epitomize the diffuseness of the urban landscape.

The famous sewer of Fleet Ditch, or the vast natural sewer of the Thames to which it leads, is the geographical center of book 2. In fact, this book is obsessed by and premised upon the figure of urban waste. At the climax of the games, the dunces dive into Fleet Ditch in a contest that viscerally connects them and their products with the sewer:

This labour past, by Bridewell all descend,
(As morning pray'r, and flagellation end)
To where Fleet-ditch with disemboguing streams
Rolls the large tribute of dead dogs to Thames,
The King of dykes! than whom no sluice of mud

[33] The Strand is the site of the first game; it is located on the border between the City of London and the City of Westminster (line 28). The Temple is the dwelling place of the sewer goddess Cloacina upon whom Curl calls in the course of the first game (l. 98); Pope refers specifically here to the "black grottos" or coal wharves at the Thames in this London district. Tottenham Fields, Chancery Lane, Westminster Hall, and Hungerford Market are the areas where the spreading noise of the dunces in the fourth contest are heard. The dunces proceed past Bridewell to Fleet Ditch, the location of the fifth contest (ll. 269–271). The "branch of Styx" that Smedley discovers in his visit to the underworld affects the inhabitants of the Temple, St. Paul's Cathedral, and Aldgate (ll. 345–36). The dunces pass through Ludgate and along Fleet Street to the site of the sixth contest (l. 359). The Thames appears, explicitly and as a backdrop to the locales named, in the following passages: ll. 98, 265, and 272. Fleet Ditch is in the foreground and background at ll. 271, 359 (as Fleet Street), and l. 427.

With deeper sable blots the silver flood.
"Here strip, my children! here at once leap in,
"Here prove who best can dash thro' thick and thin,
"And who the most in love of dirt excel,
"Or dark dexterity of groping well."

(ll. 269–278)

In this exploration of the sewer, Smedley, in a mock journey to the underworld, meets the "Mud-nymphs" who vie for his love (ll. 332–335) and discovers a "branch of Styx" that rises out of the sewer and from there,

Pours into Thames, and hence the mingled wave
Intoxicates the pert, and lulls the grave:
Here brisker vapours o'er the Temple creep,
There, all from Paul's to Aldgate drink and sleep.

(ll. 338–346)

The powers emanating from the "mingled" effluent disperse over the city in a movement that reverses the conventional one of waste removal, and that suggests that the sewer confers its peculiar qualities upon the urban setting that it pervades.

This effluent is visible in the opening game as well. In the race of the booksellers for the phantom of a poet, Curll slips in a puddle of excrement left by Corinna and loses the lead to Lintot:

Full in the middle way there stood a lake,
Which Curl's Corinna chanc'd that morn to make:
(Such was her wont, at early dawn to drop
Her evening cates before his neighbors shop).

(ll. 70–73)

The practice of locating ditches for waste disposal in the "middle way," at the center of urban streets, remained common practice through the first half of the eighteenth century. This passage evokes the perilous centrality of urban "ordure" (l. 103). But it defines such filth as a female product even before it connects it to the sordid, profit-making pursuits of the printing industry. Curll is attacked for his contact with "Corinna," from whom he obtained some of Pope's private letters. His fall into the sewer defines his "wickedness" as the absorption of a female quality: "Obscene with filth, the miscreant lies bewray'd, / Fal'n in the plash his wickedness has made" (ll. 75–76). In the event, this filth, once absorbed, confers special powers, enabling Curll to win the race:

> Renew'd by ordure's sympathetic force,
> As oil'd with magic juices for the course,
> Vig'rous he rises; from th' effluvia strong
> Imbibes new life, and scours and stinks along;
> Re-passes Lintot, vindicates the race,
> Nor heeds the brown dishonours of his face.
>
> (ll. 103–108)

This happy outcome is secured through the intervention of another female figure, "fair Cloacina" (l. 93), the "Roman Goddess of the common-sewers," according to Pope's gloss (l. 93n.). From her home beside the Thames coal wharves, she has listened on previous occasions to Curll's prayers, and at this crisis in the contest she intervenes with Jove, to whom Curll as he falls in Corinna's "plash" sends a petition for help. Jove receives these prayers seated over a "spacious vent" in "A place . . . betwixt earth, air, and seas, / Where, from Ambrosia, [he] retires for ease" (ll. 83–85), a private latrine well supplied for the purpose with "reams" of "vain petitions," which he returns "Sign'd with that Ichor which from Gods distils" (ll. 87, 92). Cloacina can readily exert her influence in this private place, since "In office here fair Cloacina stands, / And ministers to Jove with purest hands" (ll. 93–94).

This scene recalls the privies that line the Fleet in Jonson's "Voyage," and echoes a central passage in Dryden's urban local poem, *Mac Flecknoe*, to which Pope's *Dunciad* is indebted. At his coronation as poet laureate, Dryden's hero Shadwell appears "High on a throne of his own labors," attended by the works of "neglected authors": "Martyrs of pies, and relics of the bum."[34] The representation of urban waste disposal moves from the latrine to the street, where it almost impedes the coronation procession, when "loads of Sh— almost chok'd the way" (l. 102). In the case of Pope's Cloacina, the Goddess serves not only to further feminize the energies "imbibed" by Curll, but to evoke the familiar connection of both sewer and woman with the function of leveling: Cloacina listens indiscriminately to "link-boys and watermen" (l. 100) in the same way that in his translation of Juvenal Dryden's women demand "slaves, / and watermen, a race of strong-back'd knaves" (ll. 449–50), or Rochester mingles "Carmen, divines, great lords, and tailors, / Prentices, poets, pimps, and jailers, /

---

[34] John Dryden, *Mac Flecknoe*, in *John Dryden: Selected Works*, ed. William Frost (1953; reprint, New York: Holt, Rinehart and Winston, 1971), lines 107, 101.

Footmen, [and] fine fops" in Saint James's Park (*St. James's Park*, ll. 29–31).

The next game in the *Dunciad's* perverse Olympics, the pissing contest, confirms this sense of the potency conferred upon Curll by his connection with Corinna, Cloacina, the chamber pot, the latrine, and the sewer. In a scene of notable self-display, Curll wins the prize, the woman writer Eliza Haywood, through his "vigour and superior size" (l. 171):

> . . . impetuous spread
> The stream, and smoking flourish'd o'er his head.
> So (fam'd like thee for turbulence and horns)
> Eridanus his humble fountain scorns;
> Thro' half the heav'ns he pours th' exalted urn;
> His rapid waters in their passage burn.
>
> (ll. 179–184)

Curll's "vigour," like Zeus's in the myth of Danaë, is effected through female potency, and it has a familiar fluidity to it, a fluidity that lies at the core of this urban fable and generates both its attack on hierarchy as well as its enigmatic energy.

Images of fluidity—rivers, waterways, and seas—carry a distinctive discursive charge in the poetry of this period. This is a trope with a broad and rich cultural significance, extending from the fable of the sewer and the female body to another, corollary contemporary fable: the fable of torrents and oceans, a collective story of imperial expansion represented through images of the ocean and the Thames. As we shall see, these are overlapping and mutually resonant fables, which represent, in their various redactions, a fluid force of power, vitality, and transformation. Their congruence is most evident in Pope's *Windsor Forest* (1713), a poem that highlights this image in its long concluding account of the Thames. Indeed, this local poem should be seen as the rural counterpart to the *Dunciad*, a sort of encomium to the global force of the city sewer. *Windsor Forest*, too, is organized around the figure of a waterway that carries in its potent fluidity the significance of contemporary experience. The Thames and its tributaries occupy the backdrop of the rural scene of the poem in much the same way that those streams flow behind and beneath the London scene of the *Dunciad*. And *Windsor*'s Thames, too, is feminized by its identification with its tributary, the Loddon, which Pope explains through the myth of Lodona, the "injur'd Maid" who is transformed into a stream to escape from Pan's pursuit. This female waterway then "foaming pour[s] along, and rush[es] into the *Thames*" with an energy that is an expression of the force of the imperialist project, which, as we shall see in chapter 2, will produce an "unbounded Thames" that will "flow for all Mankind."[35] The same system of tributary rivers that makes up the sewers of the urban poetry, then, becomes the source of the *pax britannica*, the historical force of modern imperial expansion. And *Windsor* too finally characterizes that force in terms of a rushing, rolling, rapid flood, deluge, or torrent, in the same way and with the same rhetorical effect as Swift's *Shower.*

> Filths of all Hues and Odours seem to tell
> What Streets they sail'd from, by the Sight and Smell.
> They, as each Torrent drives, with rapid Force
> From *Smithfield* or St. *'Pulchre*'s shape their Course,
> And in huge Confluent join'd at *Snow-Hill* Ridge,
> Fall from the *Conduit* prone to *Holborn-Bridge.*
> Sweepings from Butchers Stalls, Dung, Guts, and Blood,
> Drown'd Puppies, stinking Sprats, all drench'd in Mud,
> Dead Cats and Turnip-Tops come tumbling down the Flood.
>   (ll. 55–63)

The "Flood" in both of these poems names the irresistible energy at the core of contemporary experience, a potency which in the urban local poetry is ascribed to the city sewer through its shower's irresistible downstream momentum, and which in the expansionist literature of national identity, as we shall see in the following chapter, is attributed to the waterways of global commerce.[36]

The sewer also ends book 2 of the *Dunciad.* At the close of the final contest, when everyone has been put to sleep by the reading of Dulness's favorite authors, the dunces disperse—in their inspired dreams—throughout the city to jails, brothels, and the banks of the sewers:

> Why should I sing what bards the nightly Muse
> Did slumb'ring visit, and convey to stews;
> Who prouder march'd, with magistrates in state,
> To some fam'd round-house, ever open gate!

---

[35] Alexander Pope, *Windsor Forest,* in *The Poems of Alexander Pope,* vol. 1, ed. E. Audra and Aubrey Williams (London: Methuen, 1961), lines 218, 398. Subsequent references to this poem are to this edition; line numbers are given within the text.

[36] My reading of Swift and Pope here diverges from Wall's; she sees these poems as working "to *immobilize* the swift shifting modernity, to stop it in its tracks . . . to dissolve the differences in a 'tumbling down the Flood'" (129). Her account, at this point, grasps the critique of modernity evident in the *Dunciad* and the *City Shower,* rather than their exuberant representation of the experience, which she elsewhere acknowledges, for instance when she sees Swift and Pope as "the loudest, sharpest, strongest voices articulating modernity and overfilling space" (130).

How Henley lay inspir'd beside a sink [a sewer],
And to mere mortals seem'd a Priest in drink:
While others, timely, to the neighb'ring Fleet
(Haunt of the Muses) made their safe retreat.

(ll. 421–428)

Pope's gloss at the last couplet locates that final "retreat" as "A prison for insolvent Debtors on the bank of the Ditch." The movement toward the sewer at the close of the poem is part of a reciprocity that we have already observed in the structure of this fable. The dunces have never left the sewer, though they are shown to return to it; and it is never clear whether they derive their powers from or confer their powers upon it, in the same way that the powers of the sewer both emanate from the tributary of the Styx and are brought there by the agency of Dulness.

The effect of the final sleeping contest is metaphorized through yet another sewer image, a figure that shapes the climactic moments of the *Dunciad* in this book and at the poem's conclusion at the end of book 4. When Dulness takes over the world, she does so through a metaphor from urban sanitation. The wave of drowsiness generated by the readings of the works of Blackmore and Henley is represented as the spread of the ripples on a Dutch lake produced by the "dropping" of excrement, an allusion to the practice commonly attributed to the Dutch of using their lakes as common shores, just as Londoners placed their latrines over the shores of the tributaries of the Thames:

Who sate the nearest, by the words o'ercome,
Slept first; the distant nodded to the hum.
. . . .
As what a Dutchman plumps into the lakes,
One circle first, and then a second makes;
What Dulness dropt among her sons imprest
Like motion from one circle to the rest;
So from the mid-most the nutation spreads
Round and more round, o'er all the sea of heads.

(ll. 401–410)

The din from the noise contest pervades London in the same spreading ripples, a trope, in this poem, for the common shore:

Long Chanc'ry-lane retentive rolls the sound,
And courts to courts return it round and round.

(ll. 263–264)

In fact, the figure of the spreading ripples on the common shore is the
master metaphor for the reign of Dulness in book 2 and for the millen-
nial coming of the kingdom of Dulness at the close of the whole poem in
book 4, when the Queen interrupts her commencement address with a
final yawn:

> More she had spoke, but yawn'd—all Nature nods:
> What Mortal can resist the Yawn of Gods?
> Churches and Chapels instantly it reach'd;
> (St. James's first, for leaden Gilbert preach'd)
> Then catch'd the Schools; the Hall scarce kept awake;
> The Convocation gap'd, but could not speak:
> Lost was the Nation's Sense, nor could be found,
> While the long solemn Unison went round:
> Wide, and more wide, it spread o'er all the realm;
> Ev'n Palinurus nodded at the Helm.

(ll. 605–614)

The spreading ripples on the open conduits of the city sewer—round and
more round, wide and more wide—represent the irresistible force of
modernity.

We shall see in chapter 4 how the fluid and pervasive force of the sewer
enacts Dulness's power to shape the modern world in her own image, as a
"new world to Nature's laws unknown" (3.241). Ehrenpreis's sense of
Swift's relation to his urban scene in the *City Shower* might well be applied
to Pope's attitude toward Dulness's kingdom at its most lively, wild, and
exuberant. "Only an admirer," we might want to argue, could have written these vitally realized descriptions of the modern metropolis, and indeed a substantial and influential series of studies has emphasized the exuberance and energy of Pope's poetry in such passages.[37] But neither the
City Shower nor the *Dunciad* are limited to these effects; both participate in
closely connected fables of modern experience, in a vision of a new world
shaped by the irresistible energies of expansion and empire. In the very
force of their imagining, these energies evoke ambivalent and even contradictory responses: admiration, revulsion, exhilaration, anxiety, inspiration, or despair. The admiration Ehrenpreis locates in the apparently
derogatory neoclassicism of Swift's *Shower* is a facet of the paradoxical significance of these fables, whose complexities are expressed in the sus-

[37] See Emrys Jones, "Pope and Dulness," in *Pope: Recent Essays by Several Hands*, ed. Maynard Mack and James A. Winn (Hamden, Conn.: Archon Books, 1980), 612–651; and
Howard Erskine-Hill, "The 'New World' of Pope's *Dunciad*," *Renaissance and Modern Studies* 6
(1962): 49–67.

tained contemporary tropes of the flood, the torrent, the Thames, the ocean, the shower, and the city sewer.

IV

The *City Shower*, reread through the imaginative encounters with the city sewer that we have sampled here, enables us to track the local forms of this powerful contemporary fable in a compact, canonical text. In fact, those forms are highlighted by this poem's central pun, the conjunction of sewer and shower. First, in the convergence of effluent "from all Parts" of the city (l. 53), the *City Shower* demonstrates the universalizing impulse of this figure, an impulse that we have seen in the representations of geographical range so typical of urban local poetry. By this means, the *City Shower* seems to represent the city itself, in all its disparate reaches.

And relatedly, it seems to speak for all readers. Even Pope, whose poetic persona is often marginal to the worlds of his poems, thematizes this inclusiveness in the opening of book 4 of the *Dunciad*, when he anticipates his own incorporation in the "Universal Darkness" that "buries All" (l. 656) at the end of the poem:

Ye Pow'rs! whose Mysteries restor'd I sing,
To whom Time bears me on his rapid wing,
Suspend a while your Force inertly strong,
Then take at once the Poet and the Song.

(ll. 7–8)

In this sense the sewer reflects one of the central characteristics of bourgeois ideology in this period, its hegemonic quality. Like the *Spectator* or the *Tatler*, those early and powerful arbiters of the bourgeois public sphere, the fable of the sewer seems to condense or ventriloquize a truth that all of its audience already knows and lives. In the *Shower* this ventriloquization is expressed in the first stanza, in the repetition of the second person pronoun:

Returning Home at Night, you'll find the Sink [sewer]
Strike your offended Sense with double Stink.
If you be wise, then go not far to Dine,
You'll spend in Coach-hire more than save in Wine.
A coming Show'r your shooting Corns presage,
Old Aches throb, your hollow Tooth will rage.

(ll. 4–10)

"You" have already shared the experiences the poem recounts, even before they are described.

   Just as the sewer of this poem touches every urban landmark, it also absorbs the whole city into its stream. Its powers of association seem universal,
like the common shore where all sorts of waste may be deposited or where
all sorts may deposit their waste. In its initial form as a shower, it brings the
various kinds and classes of the London populace together to take shelter
from the deluge; in its final state as the torrent of Fleet Ditch, it mingles the
"Trophies" of all the regions of the city, including the "Drown'd Puppies"
and cats prominent in many other sewerscapes. Joined at the climax of the
flood with "Turnip-Tops," "Dung, Guts and Blood," this mingling of people, classes, species, and things echoes Rochester's account of the variety of
people to be seen at St. James's Park, Gould's description of the female
womb containing "Men, Dogs, Lions, Bears, all sorts of Stuff," or Swift's
representation of the mingling of the "Conflu'ents" of Celia's face. As we
have seen, however, the geographical, social, and physical inclusiveness
that marks this image does not have the effect of ordering, ranking, or even
simply connecting the disparate categories or objects it embraces. On the
contrary, the effect of the sewer's mixing is to emphasize heterogeneity
and diffuseness. The various social classes described in the *Shower*'s third
stanza—the women, the lawyer, the seamstress, the beau, and the members
of warring political parties—are mingled in a way that calls attention both
to their diversity and to the arbitrariness of their conjunction:

> Here various Kinds, by various Fortunes led,
> Commence Acquaintance underneath a Shed.
> Triumphant Tories, and desponding Whigs,
> Forget their Fewds, and join to save their Wigs.
>
>   (ll. 39–42)

This "joining" is emphatically accidental and deliberately trivialized—
only their wigs bring them together, and only in a shed—but at the same
time it is constitutive of the nature of the urban populace: unconnected
but intimately confluent, like its refuse. Swift's *Shower*, by superimposing
the social mingling of the shower upon the visceral mixing of the sewer,
makes this leveling effect central to its representation of the experience
of the city.

   This leveling function, as we have seen, characterizes both the image of
the sewer and the representation of the female body. Indeed, leveling is
such a powerful and defining effect for both images that it makes them almost interchangeable in the literary culture of this period: even when
they are not explicitly linked, one implies the other in the same way that,

in Swift's poem, the shower always implies the sewer. In Rochester's *St. James's Park* the mixing of people is ultimately associated with the image of Corinna's body as a "passive [chamber] pot"; in Swift's *Progress of Beauty*, though the woman melts and runs together apparently without the direct representation of the sewer itself, the "Conflu'ents" of her face connect her with those of Fleet Ditch; in *A Beautiful Young Nymph* the sewer is the subtext for the dispersal of Corinna's body; and in the *Dunciad* the sewer, the focal point for the indiscriminacy of the dunces, is a feminized space, consistently identified with a variety of female figures, not least Dulness herself. Both the sewer and the female body, by mingling, mixing, or joining, generate indiscriminacy, level hierarchy, repudiate genealogy, or overturn order.

Swift's *Shower* also feminizes the sewer, but by means of a simile centered on its phonetic equivalent and alter ego, the city shower. In fact, the shower is generated by a female force; the first drops of Swift's deluge are compared, in the first of the poem's two extended mock-heroic similes, to a sprinkling from a maid servant's mop:

> Such is that Sprinkling which some careless Quean
> Flirts on you from her Mop, but not so clean.
> You fly, invoke the Gods; then turning, stop
> To rail; she singing, still whirls on her Mop.
>
> (ll. 19–22)

From the context, the woman described here must be a maid servant, but a "Quean" could also denote a loose woman or a prostitute.[38] These lines evoke a representation of female promiscuity, reminiscent of Rochester's "lewd cunt" or Gould's "Whirl-pool Sluce," combined with an indirect allusion to the "Filth" that is the concomitant of the contemporary image of the insatiable whore, and that will be viscerally evident in the "Dung, Guts and Blood" of the fourth stanza. She sprinkles you with a filthy mop, which is still not so filthy as the feminized shower itself for which she stands. When you rail at her, presumably with the curses made familiar in the contemporary attacks on female promiscuity, she ignores you in a casual way that shows her imperviousness to your influence. She is not defiant; she is singing. While the male figure is flying, cursing, and ultimately stopped by the enjambment in the disrupted and attenuated rhythms of his lines, the female figure is singing and whirling her mop with a metric continuity, emphasized by the participial form of "singing" and the alliterative "s" that links it with "she" and "still," that matches her ineluctable

---

[38] On this woman, see Fischer, 25.

fluidity. This woman is the exuberant essence of Swift's shower at the point of its inception; she enacts that irresistible vitality that forms the enigmatic undercurrent of this urban local poetry.

This is one of the poem's two extended mock-heroic similes, in which the comparison introduced by "such" evokes the classical precedent of extended juxtaposition, where mortal events or characters were often likened to those of the gods. In the first book of the *Aeneid*, for instance, Virgil compares Dido with Diana; in Dryden's translation the simile resembles Swift's:

> Such on Eurotas' banks, or Cynthus' height,
> Diana seems; and so she charms the sight,
> When in the dance the graceful goddess leads
> The choir of nymphs, and overtops their heads:
> Known by her quiver, and her lofty mien,
> She walks majestic, and she looks their queen;
>
> . . . .
>
> Such Dido was; and with such becoming state,
> Amidst the crowd, she walks serenely great.
>
> (ll. 698–708)

Swift's use of this device seems designed to emphasize the tawdriness of the contemporary scene through a double deflation; the "Quean" takes the place of a goddess, and the shower—or sewer—takes the place of Dido, Queen of Carthage, at the height of her power and sexual irresistibility. And yet Swift's simile also works to evoke a quality of motion, energy, and music that could almost be read as a celebration of the singing, whirling woman. This fluid female energy gathers force in the course of the poem, as the shower increases in intensity, "threat'ning with Deluge" the doomed city and its populace (l. 32), "clatt'ring o'er the Roof" of the Beau's chair and terrifying him with its "frightful Din" (ll. 44–45), and finally emerging as the "Torrent" of the various London sewers, where all the disparate waste from all the parts of the city come together:

> Now from all Parts the swelling Kennels flow,
> And bear their Trophies with them as they go:
> Filths of all Hues and Odours seem to tell
> What Streets they sail'd from, by the Sight and Smell.
> They, as each Torrent drives, with rapid Force
> From *Smithfield* or St. *'Pulchre*'s shape their Course,
> And in huge Confluent join'd at *Snow-Hill* Ridge,
> Fall from the *Conduit* prone to *Holborn-Bridge*.

Sweepings from Butchers Stalls, Dung, Guts, and Blood,
Drown'd Puppies, stinking Sprats, all drench'd in Mud,
Dead Cats and Turnip-Tops come tumbling down the Flood.

(ll. 53–63)

This flood is the crescendo of the singing woman's irresistible vitality. It gives a concrete form to that peculiar intensity that characterizes the paradoxical subtext of the Augustan mock-heroic—its combination of deflation and admiration, indictment and celebration. Indeed, the flood enables us to locate the enigmatic "admiration" that Ehrenpreis finds in the *Shower*, and to see its connection with the fluid energy of the torrent in *Windsor*'s encomium to the *pax britannica*, or the arresting exuberance of Dulness's "new world" in the *Dunciad*. Danaë's shower is another name for this female force, as Rowe and Prior rightly felt. But the classical comparison, for all its elevation and authority, can only gesture at the potency of the contemporary deluge. The sewer's power is in the immediacy of its representation of modern urban experience; this immediacy is the vital quality that disorients the heroic juxtapositions of Augustan neoclassicism, paradoxically turning deflation to admiration.

The *City Shower* imagines modern life as a sewer. It records the essence of contemporary experience as an expanding vortex of heterogeneity, where hierarchies, structures, and genealogies are universally overturned by a force of boundless potency. And it understands this vitality and this disruption through the female body, using that body as the means of grasping and representing the transformative energies of modern culture. This poem gives us a picture of a vital, widely shared, cultural fable. If we reflect back from the *City Shower* to the collective story condensed there, we can unravel several strands of the historical significance of the fable of the city sewer. The geographical mapping and the social range connected with the sewer suggest that this fable expresses in part the demographic and geographic explosion of the capitalist metropolis, with its burgeoning administrative complexity, its mixing of humanity and objects, and its leveling of distinctions among classes, vocations, and genders. The *Dunciad*'s sordid energies suggest that this fable imagines in part the transforming powers of capitalism to make a new world in its own image, as it overturns categories of value and merit, and mixes people with books, concepts, noises, or things. The melting, dismembered, or dispersed female bodies of the misogynist poetry suggest that this fable confronts in part the effects of commodification, as the woman's identity disappears into indiscriminacy through its confusion with the veneer of her face, her make-up, her adornments, and the things she might put on or take off. The urban cataclysm of Gay's *Trivia* suggests that this fable understands the historical experience with which it is engaged in part as a kind of apocalypse, as the end of a world. And the woman herself, whose sexualized body subserves all these strands of significance, suggests that this fable makes history meaningful by seeing it as female.

The feminization of the forces of history is a striking characteristic of the cultural expression of this period. The figure of the woman is deeply bound up with various dimensions of modernity in the early eighteenth century: consumption, fashion, commodification, and even capitalism all find their most vivid forms in feminized images like those of the tea table, the hoop petticoat, the toilet scene, the hysterical vacillations of Lady Credit, or the transforming powers of Pope's Mighty Mother, Dulness. The fable of the city sewer suggests that the process by which modernity was imagined at this early stage of its development is deeply informed by the representation of women. And it points toward its generic counterpart—the corollary fable of torrents and oceans—in which the power of the flood carries with it not only the maritime commerce of an expansionist economy, but the meaning of human fate itself.

CHAPTER 2

Imperial Fate:
The Fable of Torrents and Oceans

SAMUEL Johnson's *Vanity of Human Wishes* (1749), the eighteenth century's most canonical poetic inquiry into the scope and efficacy of metaphysical explanation, opens expansively with an imaginative circumnavigation of the world:

> Let observation with extensive view,
> Survey mankind, from China to Peru;
> . . . .
> Then say how hope and fear, desire and hate,
> O'erspread with snares the clouded maze of fate.

This global inquiry comes to a problematic close in the poem's last verse paragraph, which begins with a figure that evokes a much more precipitous voyage:

> Where then shall Hope and Fear their objects find?
> Must dull Suspence corrupt the stagnant mind?
> Must helpless man, in ignorance sedate,
> Roll darkling down the torrent of his fate?[1]

The paired passions of hope and fear, which make a prominent appearance at this climactic moment in the *Vanity of Human Wishes*, were a fre-

---

[1] Samuel Johnson, *The Vanity of Human Wishes*, in *The Yale Edition of the Works of Samuel Johnson*, vol. 6, *Poems*, ed. E. L. McAdam Jr., with George Milne (New Haven: Yale University Press, 1964), lines 1–2, 5–6, 345–346. Subsequent references are to this edition; line numbers are given within the text.

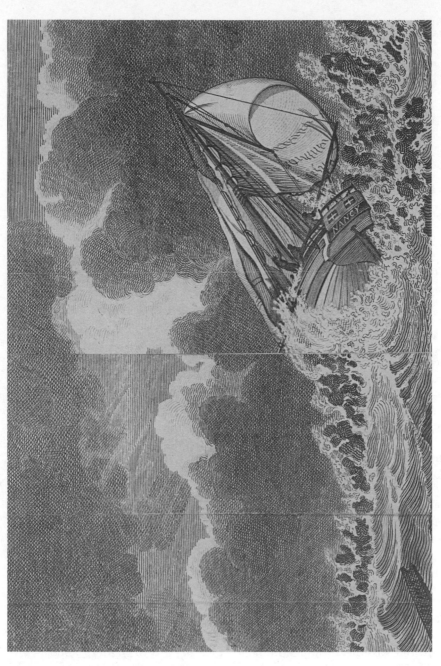

Samuel Atkins, *Bahama Banks* (1789). Illustration for vol. 2 of Olaudah Equiano's *Interesting Narrative*. By permission of the Photographs and Prints Division, Schomburg Center for Research in Black Culture, The New York Public Library, Astor, Lenox and Tilden Foundations.

quent point of reference in the period and commonly used in an attempt to develop a theory of the motive forces of human action in a society suddenly transformed by acquisition, exchange, and commerce.[2] Here "Hope and Fear" give rise to a sudden "torrent" that rushes the poem's subject and reader toward a seemingly irresistible fate. The following lines of the poem negotiate that destiny but without refuting its evocation of human helplessness or confirming any alternate notion of human agency. Through unassuming prayer, humankind can seek consolation in resignation, love, patience, and faith: "With these, celestial Wisdom calms the mind,/ And makes the happiness she does not find" (ll. 365–368). The "torrent" still carries us, with a force derived from an evocation of the powerful passions defined by contemporary social theory, but the poem gives us a means of constituting a faith whose main effect is to render that "torrent" as a beneficent "calm." The *Vanity of Human Wishes* provides an expansive survey of an unpredictable world that impels its occupants along a fluid and irresistible course toward an end beyond their agency or knowledge and that is conditionally, perhaps even ironically, ordered by powers of imagination.

Twenty-one years earlier, Edward Young's *Ocean: An Ode* (1728) depicts a similar scenario of hope and fear, of conditional consolation and fluid turbulence:

> How mixt, how frail,
> How sure to fail,
> Is every pleasure of mankind!
> A damp destroys
> My blooming joys,
> While Britain's glory fires my mind.

[2] One *locus classicus* for "hope and fear" for eighteenth-century print culture is the following well-known passage from Thomas Hobbes's *Leviathan*:

> When in the mind of man, Appetites, and Aversions, Hopes and Fears, concerning one and the same thing, arise alternately; and diverse good and evill consequences of the doing, or omitting the thing propounded, come successively into our thoughts; so that we sometimes have an Appetite to it; sometimes an Aversion from it; sometimes Hopes to be able to do it; sometimes Despaire, or Feare to attempt it; the whole summe of desires, Aversions, Hopes, and Fears, continued till the thing be either done, or thought impossible, is that we call Deliberation.

Leviathan, ed. Richard Tuck (Cambridge: Cambridge University Press, 1996), 44. J. G. A. Pocock uses the paired ideas of hope and fear in the context of his account of trade and credit in *The Machiavellian Moment: Florentine Political Thought and the Atlantic Republican Tradition* (Princeton: Princeton University Press, 1975), 452–461, and *Virtue, Commerce, and*

    For who can gaze
      On restless seas,
Unstruck with life's more restless state?
      Where all are tost,
      And most are lost,
By tides of passion, blasts of fate?

    The world's the main,
      How vext! how vain!
Ambition swells, and anger foams;
      May good men find,
      Beneath the wind,
A noiseless shore, unruffled homes![3]

Young's is an occasional political poem, written in direct response to an early speech praising British seamen by George II and expressing the characteristic themes of imperialist panegyric. Johnson's is a speculative moral work with no immediate occasion and no direct political or national referent. And yet these texts share a set of linked images: the conjunction of a conception of "fate" with the figure of a fluid waterway—a torrent, a tossing sea, a foaming main; the projection of a world of global compass within which that nautical fate is performed; the evocation of a contrastive structure of fear and hope, joy and frailty, glory and loss provoked by that fluid, rushing, or restless fate; and the conditional assertion of a state of tranquility in the midst of that headlong waterway—the wishful vision of a maritime calm. Unlikely cohorts, these poems share the same story of an experience that neither directly names. If we take seriously the notion that in this period "the world's the main," we can see a composite fable of powerful significance in the stock images of the poetic discourse of the first half of the long eighteenth century: the torrents, deluges, floods, rivers, seas, and oceans of Denham, Dryden, Tickell, Pope, Young, Johnson, and Goldsmith. But this fable is built upon the immediate liquid material of a vivid, contemporary economic and national experience. The literary evocation of torrents and oceans is an expression of that contemporary experience that gives it a specific meaning and structure, a structure that shapes a collective story about the nature of empire and human fate.

History: Essays on Political Thought and History, Chiefly in the Eighteenth Century (Cambridge: Cambridge University Press, 1985), chap. 6.

    [3] Edward Young, *The Poetical Works of Edward Young*, vol. 2 (London: Bell and Daldy, 1866), 165. Subsequent references to Young's poetry are to this edition; page numbers are given within the text.

I

The ocean was a foregrounded topic of national and cultural contemplation in this period. Commerce, both overseas and domestic, was first and foremost an ocean-going enterprise; its local site was the urban port, most notably the Port of London, though as the century progressed the major port cities of Liverpool, Bristol, and Whitehaven increased their contribution. In London, of course, the most visible locus of maritime contact was the Thames and the open sea beyond. The prominence of the sea and of shipping in English life is a distinctive development of the seventeenth and especially the eighteenth centuries. In the early seventeenth century, England was a rural and agricultural nation; in the course of that century, and especially after 1660, shipping emerged as one of the fastest growing industries: shipping tonnage increased seven times between 1560 and 1689, in a period when the population doubled.[4] And the decade of the 1660s represents the largest expansion of the English merchant fleet since the decade preceding the Spanish Armada a century earlier. Ships captured during the Dutch wars and added to the English fleet transformed both the size and the profile of the English merchant marine in the years from 1660 until 1688, leaving English shipping much better situated for long-distance overseas trade. Ralph Davis, a modern historian of the eighteenth-century shipping industry, describes this "spectacular" growth:

> The great expansion during this period took place among vessels for foreign trade. This may explain the common expression, at the end of the century, of the view that English shipping doubled between 1660 and 1688. This was an exaggeration, but one with a significant basis. It was the spectacular side of the shipping industry that progressed most rapidly in this period; the growth was in the number of large ships, and above all of London ships bound for Norway, the Mediterranean, Virginia, the West and East Indies, rather than in coasters and colliers, cross-channel traders of the south coast or fishing vessels of Cornwall or East Anglia. The frequenter of the Thames waterside may well have observed, over these twenty-eight years, a continuous increase, even a doubling, in the numbers of the big ocean-going vessels and the timber traders which towered above their fellows in the river. These would catch his eye and provide a basis for the impressions and reports which

[4] Ralph Davis, *The Rise of the English Shipping Industry in the Seventeenth and Eighteenth Centuries* (London: Macmillan, 1962), 388–389.

would give their own colour to the contemporary "statistics" of the industry. (16)

The consolidation of the overseas merchant navy thus took place before the turn of the eighteenth century, and the industry continued to expand, though at a less "spectacular" rate, in subsequent decades. But coastal shipping, and the English "coasting" trade, saw their major growth in the course of the eighteenth century. Coastal shipping, along with the improved road systems throughout the country, was a major basis for the stimulation of commercial circulation in the earlier half of the century and an essential dimension of industrial development in the latter. The Port of London was the center of the coasting trade. Coastal shippers brought provincial goods and raw materials—notably, for instance, coals from Newcastle—to the capital, and in turn distributed the various burgeoning imports from abroad to the provinces, and redistributed numerous raw materials such as leather, dyes, wool, alum, timber, lead, iron, tin, and copper, as well as the manufactured products of the city—among them the steam pumps needed to drain the northern coal mines.[5]

The volume of trade, both foreign and domestic, increased steadily from 1660 through the end of the eighteenth century, fed in part by the expanding commerce in the colonial products of tobacco, tea, and sugar, but supported as well by the importation of timber and shipbuilding materials from Scandinavia and the Baltic, the export of wool, metal, corn, and other domestic products, as well as the reexport of the colonial products throughout Europe. Trade volume of the Port of London increased threefold in the eighteenth century, producing visible, dangerous, and eventually intractable problems of overcrowding at the docks and in the Thames itself. In the course of this period, dock space became so limited that ships prepared to take on cargo could spend as much as a week waiting for admission to the dock areas, and vessels arriving to unload often spent longer. By the end of the century, in the Upper Pool, mooring space suitable for five hundred vessels was occupied by up to eighteen hundred. This situation gave rise to conditions so dangerous that legislation was finally introduced in the 1790s to expand the moorings and strictly control port entry. At the beginning of the eighteenth century the Port of London handled eighty percent of the national import business, sixty-nine per cent of the export business, and eighty-six percent of the reexports.

---

[5] T. S. Willan, *The English Coasting Trade 1600–1750* (1938; reprint, Manchester: Manchester University Press, 1967), 189–194; Roy Porter, *London: A Social History* (Cambridge: Harvard University Press, 1994), 136–149.

Though London remained the preeminent location for maritime trade, the other port cities increased their share throughout the period. Most notable was the growth of the Port of Bristol, a beneficiary of the "Americanization" of British foreign trade and a paradigm for the transforming powers of early modern capitalism.[6] Bristol owed its eighteenth-century expansion to the trade in colonial products, and especially in slaves, in which it dominated the commercial market. Kenneth Morgan, a recent historian of the Bristol trade, describes the appearance of the port:

> The considerable demand for shipping services in eighteenth-century Bristol meant that the wharves and quays in the centre of the city were thronged with many different types of wooden sailing ships—Severn trows, coasters, lighters, towboats and ocean-going vessels of various rigs and sizes. The miscellany of vessels can be glimpsed in Peter Monamy's contemporary painting of Broad Quay . . . or in the marine scenes painted by Nicholas Pocock, who had served as a master on several transatlantic voyages from Bristol. The striking visual effect of so many ships clustered together caught the attention of the poet, Alexander Pope. In 1739, on a visit to Bristol, he observed that on the quay there were "as far as you can see, hundreds of ships, their Masts as thick as they can stand by one another, which is the oddest and most surprising sight imaginable." (33)

Thus, the eighteenth century saw an explosion of naval traffic and related maritime industries that was highly visible in the port cities and especially on the Thames. Fielding's account in the *Journal of a Voyage to Lisbon* (1755) of the maritime activity to be seen on the Thames on his route from Redriffe to Gravesend evokes a nationalist admiration, centered on a resonant image of that river, typical of the period:

> Take it with all its advantages, particularly the number of fine ships you are always sure of seeing by the way, there is nothing to equal it in all the rivers of the world. The yards of Deptford and of Woolwich are noble sights; and give us a just idea of the great perfection to which we are arrived in building those floating castles, and the figure which we may always make in Europe among the other maritime powers. That of Woolwich, at least, very strongly imprinted this idea on my mind; for there was now on the stocks there the

[6] Kenneth Morgan, *Bristol and the Atlantic Trade in the Eighteenth Century* (Cambridge: Cambridge University Press, 1993), 1–6.

Royal Anne, supposed to be the largest ship ever built, and which
contains ten carriage guns more than had ever yet equipped a first
rate. . . .

Sure I am that . . . every inhabitant of this island, may exult in
the comparison, when he considers the king of Great-Britain as a
maritime prince, in opposition to any other prince in Europe.

Fielding's assertion of nationalist pride is located very specifically—in a
description of the particular vessels visible on the river:

Besides the ships in the docks, we saw many on the water: the
yatchts are sights of great parade, and the king's body yatcht is, I
believe, unequalled in any country for convenience as well as magnificence; both which are consulted in building and equipping her
with the most exquisite art and workmanship.

We saw likewise several Indiamen just returned from their voyage. These are, I believe, the largest and finest vessels which are
anywhere employed in commercial affairs. The colliers, likewise,
which are very numerous, and even assemble in fleets, are ships of
great bulk; and if we descend to those used in the American,
African, and European trades, and pass through those which visit
our own coasts, to the small craft that ly between Chatham and the
Tower, the whole forms a most pleasing object to the eye, as well as
highly warming to the heart of an Englishman, who has any degree
of love for his country, or can recognize any effect of the patriot in
his constitution.[7]

The image of the Thames, so crowded with ships that their masts make up
a "floating forest," becomes a trope for the river and, by association, for
the nation itself in the first half of the eighteenth century.

The sea was an immediate presence in English life in this period in
many other ways as well. At the end of the seventeenth century, the shipping industry maintained fifty thousand men in the service of the merchant marine, out of a national population of one and a half million.
Davis observes that "when we consider the rapid turnover in seagoing personnel, this suggests that a very substantial proportion of the men who
lived in the coastal counties and seaports must at some time during their
lives have gone to the sea" (389). Shipping generated other forms of em-

---

[7] Henry Fielding, *The Journal of a Voyage to Lisbon*, in *A Journey from This World to the Next
and The Journal of a Voyage to Lisbon*, ed. Ian A. Bell and Andrew Varney (Oxford: Oxford University Press, 1997), 149–151.

ployment as well. London was the nation's major entrepot, and the massive businesses of transshipment, distribution, repackaging, and warehousing were another prominent dimension of the port's presence. The Port of London was home to a myriad of related industries, including shipbuilding; rope, sail, and mast making; and sugar-refining and importing. At the beginning of the eighteenth century, as much as a fourth of the population of London was employed in trades related to the port and the business of shipping.[8] Attendant also upon the presence and growth of the port in the course of the century were the factors and brokers, not to mention the major trading companies situated in the City: the South Sea Company, the Russia, Levant and Hudson Bay Companies, the African Company, and the East India Company. And, designed to exploit the risk of maritime trade, the new business of marine insurance was established and instantly expanded in this period, so that by midcentury London was Europe's leading insurance center (Rudé, 32).

In a concluding assessment of the economic impact of the transformation of the English shipping industry in the eighteenth century, Davis raises the question of the role of the industry in relation to the largest economic, political, and social developments of the age. He concludes that the prominence of shipping in the English economy helped prepare the way for industrialization, in part by generating the massive accumulation of capital—in private fortunes and state revenues—upon which the industrial revolution was built, in part by sustaining colonial development through those major trade relationships with the new world, and in part by contributing through the profitable export business to the pace of development in those industries—especially iron and cotton—which were ripe for technological change (393–394). These economic roles were concurrent with prominent political changes. The Navigation Acts of 1660 to 1696, instrumental in shaping the relations of trade in the eighteenth century, were initially designed to assure the supply of ships and seamen for the British navy by protecting and building up the English merchant marine. But this legislation served also, and perhaps most significantly, to protect English colonial trade and to secure British power and profits in the new world by largely excluding foreign ships from carrying on trade with England.[9] In all these senses, the English shipping industry and maritime commerce served as central players in the dynamic historical transformations—economic, political, and imperial—that occupied the eighteenth century. Davis summarizes the situation:

[8] George Rudé, *Hanoverian London 1714–1808* (Berkeley: University of California Press, 1971), 20–33.

[9] For a summary of the Navigation Acts, see Davis, 305–314.

The needs of the state for naval power reinforced the demands of
the merchants and shipowners in securing legislation to preserve
the merchant marine, and so . . . preserved naval power and the
colonies; and colonial monopoly was one of the bases . . . for industrial expansion. When colonial monopoly was broken after 1776
the work was done; the wealth had been accumulated, and the
dependence of the American economy on England established too
firmly to be undone in less than another century. (393–394)

In this context, it is not surprising that the ocean pervades the popular
print culture of the eighteenth century. Philip Edwards provides a summary account of the cultural influence of the sea:

the reading public could not get enough in the way of accounts of
all the maritime activity involved in extending Britain's knowledge
of the globe and her control of territories old and new. (They liter-
ally could not get enough, so fiction writers supplied them with
more.) . . . . As early as 1710 the Earl of Shaftesbury drily noted
that voyage-narratives "are the chief materials to furnish out a
library . . . . These are in our present days what books of chivalry
were in those of our forefathers" [in *Advice to an Author*]. True
enough, voyage-narratives did have an impact on the imaginative
life of the eighteenth century comparable to the impact of the
world of chivalry on the imaginative life of the sixteenth century.
And just as the force of that earlier impact can be judged by the
epics of Ariosto and Spenser, so the force of the later can be found
in the fiction of Defoe and Swift, and the poetry of Cowper and
Coleridge. Even if writers show no direct influence in their work,
many of them acknowledge in one way or another the grip of voyages on their imagination.[10]

The sea is the ubiquitous fluid roadway of the travel narrative, a genre
that Edwards estimates included two thousand works in this period, from
William Dampier's *A New Voyage Round the World* (1697), to John
Churchill's *Collection of Voyages and Travels* (1732), John Atkins's *Voyage to
Guinea, Brasil, and the West-Indies* (1735), Thomas Astley's *New General Collection of Voyages and Travels* (1745–47), and James Cook's, Joseph Banks's,
and George Forster's journals of voyages in the Pacific (1768–1780). The
sea is the defining instrument of emblematic isolation in the eighteenth-

---

[10] Philip Edwards, *The Story of the Voyage: Sea-Narratives in Eighteenth-Century England*
(Cambridge: Cambridge University Press, 1994), 2–4.

century's single most influential vision of modern experience, *Robinson Crusoe* (1719), as well as in the subsequent castaway novels by Ambrose Evans, Penelope Aubin, and others. This is also the period of accounts of piracy, and the "high" seas of violent, communal, alternative heroism, compiled most notably by Charles Johnson in *A General History of the Pyrates* (1724), sometimes attributed to Daniel Defoe, and retailed prominently in Defoe's *Captain Singleton* (1720) and *Colonel Jack* (1722), as well as in the lively subgenre of piracy narratives written during the great age of English piracy following upon the demobilization of the navy after the Peace of Utrecht (1713). Naval adventure is a pervasive dimension of various forms of prose narrative in the course of the century, from Tobias Smollett's picaresque *Roderick Random* (1748) to Olaudah Equiano's autobiographical *Life* (1789). And, of course, Swift chooses the form of the ocean-going travel narrative as the frame of *Gulliver's Travels* (1726) and names Gulliver as a cousin of the well-known travel writer William Dampier and a traveler "instructed by the oldest mariners."[11]

This general cultural engagement with the ocean finds a special discursive focus in the many images of rivers, torrents, floods, oceans, and seas that in this period become a staple, especially, of poetic discourse. In the poetry, the evocation of these seas seems to condense a vital dimension of contemporary experience, to create a set of linked figures and narratives that reflect the particular qualities of fluidity and energy that characterize this experience and to shape from a material encounter with the river of English commerce—the Thames—and the oceans of the world to which it reaches, a cultural fable, a composite story that gives meaning to a complex historical moment.

II

In the decade of the 1660s, the sea becomes the national rhetorical topos. In this period, under the influence of Denham and Dryden, the image of the ocean takes the place of the isolated island as the basis for the representation of English nationalist identity. This change gives the early rhetorical appearance of seas and torrents a distinctive cast that shapes the significance of the representation of imperial waterways for a century beyond. Eighteenth-century representations of the sea have a vivid figurative predecessor in the isolationist images of England as a fortified island prevalent during the period of Elizabeth's reign, when early and ambivalent colonialist policies were muted by anxieties about English relations

---

[11] Jonathan Swift, *Gulliver's Travels*, in *Gulliver's Travels and Other Writings*, ed. Louis A. Landa (Boston: Houghton Mifflin, 1960), 5.

with the major European colonial powers. Shakespeare's well-known evocation of this edenic insularity in *Richard II* illustrates the subordinate
rhetorical position of the sea in the representation of the necessary political and religious distinctiveness and the military security of England, separating it as an island from the chaos and threat of Europe:

> This royal throne of kings, this sceptred isle,
> This earth of majesty, this seat of Mars,
> This other Eden, demi-paradise,
> This fortress built by nature for herself
> Against infection and the hand of war,
> This happy breed of men, this little world,
> This precious stone set in the silver sea,
> Which serves it in the office of a wall,
> Or as a moat defensive to a house
> Against the envy of less happier lands;
> This blessèd plot, this earth, this realm, this England,
> . . . .
> England, bound in with the triumphant sea,
> Whose rocky shore beats back the envious siege
> Of wat'ry Neptune . . . [12]

This sea belongs to a subordinate clause, dependent upon the representation of the land it defends; its triumph lies only in its role as a secure
barrier for the island of England. But the confluence here of fluidity and
power sets the scene for a much more concerted cultural focus on maritime waterways and provides for the imaginative transition from an insu-
lar to an imperialist politics.

John Denham's *Cooper's Hill* (1642, 1655, 1668), the first in a line of nationalist and imperialist local poems that extends through Pope, Tickell,
Thomson, and Young, makes the Thames the centerpiece of its claims to a
global vision of prosperity, exchange, and political stability. Here, as elsewhere, the Thames is England's and the poem's access to the larger ocean,
of which this river is a local manifestation and rhetorical synechdoche:

> My eye, descending from the hill, surveys
> Where Thames among the wanton valleys strays.
> Thames, the most loved of all the ocean's sons
> By his old sire, to his embraces runs;

---

[12] William Shakespeare, *Richard II*, in *The Norton Shakespeare*, ed. Stephen Greenblatt et
al. (New York: W.W. Norton, 1997), 2.1.40–63.

Hasting to pay his tribute to the sea,
Like mortal life to meet eternity.[13]

Denham's poem, like Johnson's *Vanity of Human Wishes*, connects the representation of this global waterway with an expansive "survey" that seems to extend to the whole world, and that evokes a notion of fate or destiny. The expansiveness of this image of the Thames projects the promise of a new style of mercantile imperialism: the world-benevolent mode of English commerce in which exchange brings prosperity, wealth, and civilization wherever it goes:

Nor are his blessings to his banks confined,
But free and common, as the sea or wind;
When he to boast, or to disperse his stores,
Full of the tributes of his grateful shores,
Visits the world, and in his flying towers
Brings home to us, and makes both Indies ours;
Finds wealth where 'tis, bestows it where it wants,
Cities in deserts, woods in cities plants.
So that to us no thing, no place is strange
While his fair bosom is the world's exchange.

(ll. 179–188)

This benevolent waterway—a rhetorical confluence of English river and global ocean—generates the famous lines that become the period's preeminent example of the neoclassical notion of *concordia discors*—unity in difference:

O, could I flow like thee, and make thy stream
My great example, as it is my theme!
Though deep, yet clear; though gentle, yet not dull;
Strong without rage; without o'erflowing, full.

(ll. 189–192)

No torrents here. This is the calm and glorious course of English national destiny, linked in Denham's poem to the political balance installed by parliamentary monarchy, and to the historical dialectic which produced an increasingly prosperous mercantile imperialist state out of absolutist

---

[13] John Denham, *Cooper's Hill*, in *The Poetical Works of Sir John Denham*, ed. Theodore Howard Banks Jr. (New Haven: Yale University Press, 1928), lines 159–164. Subsequent references are to this edition; line numbers are given within the text.

oppression and revolutionary excess. We might be surprised then, to see
this promise of "no unexpected inundations" (175) suddenly withdrawn
in the last lines of the poem, with a repudiation of precisely that evocation
of balanced tranquility:

> When a calm river, raised with sudden rains
> Or snows dissolved, o'erflows th'adjoining plains,
> The husbandmen with high-raised banks secure
> Their greedy hopes, and this he can endure.
> But if with bays and dams they strive to force
> His channel to a new or narrow course,
> No longer then within his banks he dwells:
> First to a torrent, then a deluge swells;
> Stronger and fiercer by restraint he roars,
> And knows no bound, but makes his power his shores.

(ll. 349–358)

Allegorically, the torrent is Denham's recollection of the revolution and
his warning to maintain political stability through parliamentary rule; the
poem does not name this fierce and uncontrollable river as the Thames.
But rhetorically this final figure makes conditional those earlier images of
calm. This is a waterway that has the power to impose the global destiny
that the poem evokes in its first account of the river on its way to meet
eternity. Indeed, this torrent could be said to have been conjured up by
that earlier evocation of a global fate: the scope of this fiercer river's
power is an appropriate counterpart to the extended compass and immortal claims of that impressive earlier stream, an answering note that
matches fate with apocalypse. The paradoxical conjunction of headlong
fluidity and conditional calm in Denham's rivers expresses—in a cultural
form more subtle and prescient than the poem's particular political allegories—a historical experience that we can find again, in different terms,
in Dryden's early poetry on the Stuart monarchy.

In the prefatory essay to his major maritime work *Annus Mirabilis. The
Year of Wonders, 1666* (1667), Dryden frankly acknowledges the sudden
prominence—rhetorical and material—of the sea in his writing and in
the world he represents: "For my own part, if I had little knowledge of the
Sea, yet I have thought it no shame to learn."[14] Indeed, in this "spectacu-

---

[14] John Dryden, "An Account of the ensuing Poem, in a Letter to the Honorable, Sir
Robert Howard," preface to *Annus Mirabilis. The Year of Wonders, 1666*, in *The Poems and Fables
of John Dryden*, ed. James Kinsley (Oxford: Oxford University Press, 1958), 45. Subsequent
references to Dryden's poems are to this edition; line numbers are given within the text.

lar" decade of nautical expansion, Dryden must have been speaking for
many other witnesses of the new preeminent industry of the nation. Not
surprisingly, then, the sea pervades Dryden's poetry of the 1660s; his celebratory works on the return of Charles II and the future of England
prominently feature invocations of bodies of water, which link maritime
events with historical and nationalist reflections, and in which we can locate the full cultural installation of this maritime fable. For Dryden as for
Denham, the sea is the medium of mercantile expansion, economic and
political, and this gives it a ubiquitous presence in imperialist apologia. Of
all Dryden's early poems, *Annus Mirabilis* expatiates most extensively
upon that imperialist panegyric, locating not only naval conquest—the
primary topic of the poem—but also global exploration, empirical science, the advances in chronometry that enabled the measurement of lon-
gitude, and even astronomy, not to mention commerce, in its representation of the sea:

> Of all who since have us'd the open Sea,
> Than the bold *English* none more fame have won:
> Beyond the Year, and out of Heav'n's high-way,
> They make discoveries where they see no Sun.
>
> But what so long in vain, and yet unknown,
> By poor man-kind's benighted wit is sought,
> Shall in this Age to *Britain* first be shown,
> And hence be to admiring Nations taught.
>
> The Ebbs of Tydes and their mysterious flow,
> We, as Arts' Elements, shall understand:
> And as by Line upon the Ocean go,
> Whose paths shall be familiar as the Land.
>
> Instructed ships shall sail to quick Commerce,
> By which remotest Regions are alli'd:
> Which makes one City of the Universe;
> Where some may gain, and all may be suppli'd.
>
> Then, we upon our Globes last verge shall go,
> And view the Ocean leaning on the sky:
> From thence our rolling Neighbors we shall know,
> And on the Lunar world securely pry.
>
> (st. 160–164)

This "British ocean" (st. 302), like Denham's, is an extension of the
Thames, "her own domestic flood" (st. 298), and it produces the same
global "emporium" (st. 302), the same benevolent system of commerce,
and the same conditional calm:

> Thus to the eastern wealth thro' storms we go,
> But now, the Cape once doubled, fear no more;
> A constant trade-wind will securely blow,
> And gently lay us on the spicy shore.

(st. 304)

This image has an allegorical significance: the voyage around the Cape of
Good Hope suggests the progress of England toward imperialist supremacy in Europe, and thus "Hope" forms an unstated but, to contemporary readers, clearly present contrast to "fear" in that line. Indeed,
hope and fear are so persistently counterposed in the many accretions of
this cultural fable that one inevitably implies the other. But despite the
hope and peaceful seas evoked here, "fear" is a powerful constituent of
this voyage, even as it anticipates future commercial "triumphs" (st. 302).
The calm of those gentle trade winds lies only in prospect. Indeed, the
poem celebrates a future prosperity that may have been in view, but was
hardly secured at the time of its writing. The result of the naval war with
Holland that the poem describes at length in its first half was still unde-
cided, and, as the second half recounts, the city of London had been devastated by the plague and leveled by the great fire.[15] Hope and fear con-
verge here in a striking defiance of fate—"the utmost malice of [the]
Stars" (st. 291)—with the effect of proposing a new destiny that extends
to "all the world" (st. 301). The fate evoked by the figure of the ocean in
this poem entails a metaphysical proposition, at the same time as it projects the global fate of an imperial vision.[16]

The complexity of Dryden's construction of the figure of the "*British
Ocean*" (st. 302) is even more fully evident in his earlier poems on the occasion of Charles's return. *To His Sacred Maiesty, A Panegyrick on His Coronation*
(1661) systematically identifies Charles II and his monarchy with the sea:

---

[15] Michael McKeon provides a full account of the poem's ideological function in presenting a vision of national unity and commercial power in the context of the political tensions
and economic debates of the moment. See *Politics and Poetry in Restoration England: The Case of
Dryden's* Annus Mirabilis (Cambridge: Harvard University Press, 1975), chaps. 1 and 3.

[16] McKeon documents the poem's adoption of the contemporary modes and assumptions of eschatological prophecy in a way that emphasizes the cultural codependency of
metaphysics and nationalist apologia that I am seeking to trace from this poem through to
the *Vanity of Human Wishes* (chap. 5).

Born to command the Mistress of the Seas,
Your thoughts themselves in that blue Empire please.
Hither in Summer ev'nings you repair
To take the fraischeur of the purer air:
Vndaunted here you ride when Winter raves,
With *Cæsar's* heart that rose above the waves.

. . . .

Beyond your Court flows in th' admitted tide,
Where in new depths the wondring fishes glide:
Here in a Royal bed the waters sleep,
When tir'd at Sea within this bay they creep.
Here the mistrustful [soul] no harm suspects,
So safe are all things which our King protects.

(ll. 99–116)

Significantly, though, the poem counterposes to this image of a controlled or calm sea an obsession with drowning. The historical cataclysm of the revolution is described in the opening couplet in terms of the biblical flood, the "Deluge where the World was drownd" (l. 1). But the return of the monarchy is also represented as another drowning, in which the revolutionary flood is redrowned by its own excess and replaced by a dubious and unsteady settlement: "Yet when that flood in its own depths was drownd/ It left behind it false and slipp'ry ground" (ll. 1–6). In Dryden's writings on the Stuart monarchy, the evocation of the sea seems symptomatically to call up attendant images of drowning in that fluid element of fate.

Most notably, in *Astrea Redux* (1660), Dryden's celebratory work on Charles II that immediately precedes the coronation poem, the sea presides with similarly paradoxical implications over the king's return across the Channel from France to Dover. This is of course a providential voyage, with "willing winds," "joyful" ships, "merry Seamen," and a sea that is itself personified as a benevolent goddess with a British identity:

The British *Amphitryte* smooth and clear
In richer Azure never did appear;
Proud her returning Prince to entertain
With the submitted Fasces of the Main.

(ll. 246–249)

But the representation of an obedient sea and a calm voyage is systematically complicated. The sea evokes dangers, reversals, and powers of rapidity and turbulence beyond human control:

> How easie 'tis when Destiny proves kind
> With full spread Sails to run before the wind,
> But those that 'gainst stiff gales laveering go
> Must be at once resolv'd and skilful too.
>
>   (ll. 63–66)

And the same sea can also signify change and loss, as in the fate of "Th'
Ambitious *Swede* like restless Billowes Tost,/ On this hand gaining what
on that he lost" (ll. 9–10). And it can even represent a force of destruction—here connected with the recent historical event of the revolution:
"The Rabble now such Freedom did enjoy,/ As Winds at Sea that use it to
destroy" (ll. 43–44). Charles's own fortunate voyage is constantly situated
against the "restless," tempestuous, doubtful trajectory of his and his father's recent history; he has been "toss'd by Fate, and hurried up and
down,/ Heir to his Fathers Sorrows, with his Crown" (ll. 51–52). Indeed,
in these figures of turbulence and disaster even Charles's homecoming
itself shades into shipwreck: "To all the Sea-Gods *Charles* an Off'ring
owes: . . . For those loud storms that did against him rore/ Have cast his
shipwrack'd Vessel on the shore" (ll. 120–124). We might even question
whether his welcoming country offers a secure future to the returning
monarch:

> Methinks I see those Crowds on *Dovers* Strand
> Who in their hast to welcome you to Land
> Choak'd up the Beach with their still growing store,
> And made a wilder Torrent on the shore.
>
>   (ll. 276–279)

Wild torrents are a signal of a force beyond the monarch's, or the poet's,
power to predict or control. Thus even as it seems to provide him calm
passage to the throne, the sea evokes for Charles the tragic fate of his father in that striking image of drowning that we have found elsewhere: "Secure as when the *Halcyon* breeds, with these/ He that was born to drown
might cross the Seas" (ll. 235–236).[17]

---

[17] Steven N. Zwicker provides a close reading of the "technique of denial and misrepre-
sentation" that for him defines Dryden's poetic form as well as his characterization of the
Stuart monarchy in these works. It is precisely this "denial" that seems to turn against the
poem's explicit celebratory and optimistic claims, notably in passages where the sea serves as
a figurative point of reference. See *Politics and Language in Dryden's Poetry: The Arts of Disguise*
(Princeton: Princeton University Press, 1984), 39–43. For a more extended reading of such
contradictory structures in Dryden's poetry, see Laura Brown, "The Ideology of Restoration
Poetic Form: John Dryden," *PMLA* 97 (1982): 395–407.

In the last verse paragraph of *Astrea Redux*, the prominent figure of the sea becomes the subject of proto-imperialist panegyric:

> Abroad your Empire shall no Limits know,
> But like the Sea in boundless Circles flow.
> Your much lov'd fleet shall with a wide Command
> Besiege the petty Monarchs of the Land:
> And as Old Time his Off-spring swallow'd down
> Our Ocean in its depths all Seas shall drown.
>
> (ll. 298–303)

It seems that this poem, like Charles himself, cannot escape the figure of drowning, no matter how optimistic its claims.

The nationalist histrionics of these poems are quickly to become the formulaic poetic rhetoric of the first era of English imperial expansion. We can find them again, with very few alterations, in Dryden's later political poetry, and in works of the next sixty years by Pope, Tickell, Thomson, and Young. But this early locus provides a striking glimpse of the complexity of the cultural fable of torrents and oceans, even as that fable, in its earliest iterations, is shaping imperialist apologia. Like that of Denham's *Cooper's Hill*, Johnson's *Vanity of Human Wishes*, and Young's *Ocean*, the sea of *Astrea Redux* is a figure whose amplitude and potency match the power of fate itself. It opposes optimism, promise, and limitlessness to uncertainty, risk, loss, and disaster—hopes to fears. It thus takes on the turbulence of contemporary English history, but in ways more complex than Dryden himself could have understood. On the one hand, this sea evokes a tension between the hopes raised by the Restoration settlement and the fears inherited from the revolution, and in that sense it reflects the ambiguous political and economic status of Charles II's reign. But the sea of *Astrea Redux* also reflects upon the boundlessness of the poem's projected imperial future, in which a headlong fate contends against a vision of global power.

Taken together, these representations of rivers and seas begin to develop a story with a form whose basic characteristics we can outline: a cultural fable that has both a protagonist and a narrative movement toward a climactic and surprising conclusion. It is a story that seeks to name and understand a powerful force by seeing it as a fluid entity, inexorable, expansive, exhilarating, and dangerous. It represents that force in motion, on a career characterized by radical irony or profound undecidability, conditionality or contradiction. And it projects the end point of this career as an unavoidable and apocalyptic fate in which triumph is matched with disaster, fulfillment with destruction, optimism with despair. This climax emanates from the specific character of the fable's fluid and complex protagonist, but it comes to include the whole world that this protagonist seems both to shape and to embody.

In defining this fable, we are examining the form of a cultural fiction, an imaginative creation that might at first seem peculiarly elusive. After all, this is not a story told by any particular individual, nor is it told in any particular text of Restoration or eighteenth-century print culture. Though it has a narrative form, it is never expressed formally as a narrative; and though it has a protagonist, that protagonist has no single name and no local or concrete identity. On the other hand, its constituents—the words and locutions, metaphors and images that surround the representation of rivers and seas—are a persistent dimension of the poetry of the Restoration, as we have already seen, and they will become a powerful rhetorical presence in the literature of the next several decades. These recurrent figures, though they have a specific relevance to the particular works in which they occur, overlap and intersect with one another in a way that projects a common set of reference points, affects, ironies, and contradictions and that constructs, through that intersection, a common story. This story's telling reveals a significant dimension of the cultural experience of mercantile imperialism, since it represents a collective imaginative rendering of that complex and cataclysmic historical event. We will see this fable of torrents and oceans expand in detail and significance over the next half century, as England moves to a secure place as the preeminent global colonial power.

III

In the two decades following the Peace of Utrecht (1713), the treaty that ratified British mercantile supremacy among the European powers, torrents and oceans are firmly installed as a ground of imaginative experience, first through the representation of the Thames, the "great Father of the *British* Floods,"[18] and then in the evocation of the ocean itself, the "watery kingdom"[19] of British imperial power. The cultural fable that these images adumbrate is prototypically problematic, alternately reflecting serenity and energy, subservience and overwhelming power. Further-

---

[18] Alexander Pope, *Windsor Forest*, in *The Poems of Alexander Pope*, vol. 1, ed. E. Audra and Aubrey Williams (London: Methuen, 1961), line 219. Subsequent references to *Windsor Forest* are to this edition; line numbers are given within the text.

[19] Thomas Tickell, *On the Prospect of Peace*, in *The Works of the English Poets* (London: C. Whittingham, 1810), 105. Subsequent references to Tickell's poem are to this edition; page numbers are given within the text.

more, as a figure for mercantile imperialism, the ocean comes in this period to embody a complex system that perfectly unites the physical and the metaphysical in a way that gives its evolving narrative glory, momentum, and expanse, reaching beyond political discourse to scientific inference, metaphysical supposition, moral contemplation, and even social criticism. This extension of the fable to include multiple dimensions of contemporary thought distinguishes these eighteenth-century iterations from the earlier forms that we have identified in Denham and Dryden. By the time of *The Vanity of Human Wishes*, the fable of torrents and oceans tells a rich, thick, multiply overdetermined story, with a shape that reflects a full imaginative engagement with a decisive moment in modern history, the transforming experience of mercantile capitalist expansion.

The Peace of Utrecht generated a set of celebratory works that develop the central claims of this story as we have already defined them in Dryden's nationalist poetry.[20] Thomas Tickell's *On the Prospect of Peace* (1712), for instance, follows its basic contours: the sea here is briefly described in terms of the Elizabethan figure of the fortifying moat, but more persistently it becomes an active projection of British imperial destiny. On the one hand, the ocean is a barrier to invasion:

> Amidst the world of waves so stands serene
> Britannia's isle, the ocean's stately queen;
> In vain the nations have conspired her fall,
> Her trench the sea, and fleets her floating wall.
>
> (104)

On the other hand, Tickell's sea is a "subject ocean" that represents a "watery kingdom" with a direct relation to the nationalist projection of a global empire:

> Great queen! . . .
> From Albion's cliffs thy wide-extended hand
> Shall o'er the main to far Peru command;

---

[20] The celebratory nationalist poetry common in the first half of the eighteenth century has been described as "Whig panegyric." See C. A. Moore, "Whig Panegyric Verse, 1700–1760," *PMLA* 41 (1926): 362–401. A full bibliography of poems on the Peace of Utrecht is available in David Foxon, *English Verse, 1701–50* (Cambridge: Cambridge University Press, 1975), 2: 296. David S. Shields describes a group of poems focusing specifically on the British "empire of the seas" in *Oracles of Empire: Poetry, Politics, and Commerce in British America, 1690–1750* (Chicago: University of Chicago Press, 1990), 25.

So vast a tract whose wide domain shall run,
Its circling skies shall see no setting sun.

. . . .

 Round the vast ball thy new dominions chain
Thy watery kingdoms, and control the main;

. . . .

On either bank the land its master knows,
And in the midst the subject ocean flows.

(105)

Here the ocean is the enabling figure for a global perspective that, by asserting a "watery kingdom," extends over the seas to "far Peru," laying
claim to the whole globe. This elusive and symptomatic rhetorical movement, in which intermediary and destination, fluid and firm, sea and land,
change places, substituting a "watery" empire for a solid one, is a persistent
constituent of the fable of torrents and oceans in this latter period of its
expression, generating a powerfully evocative expansionist fantasy which
represents an imperialism without geographical acquisition. We shall see
it further developed and extended in Young's ocean poems. For Tickell,
this superimposition of land and sea is linked to claims about the civilizing
and benevolent effects of British trade, a systematic global vision, centered
on the figure of torrents and oceans, that we can see most eloquently represented in Pope's poem on the Peace of Utrecht, *Windsor Forest* (1713).

The protagonist of *Windsor*, like that of Denham's *Cooper's Hill* to which
Windsor pervasively alludes, is the Thames. The centrality of the river ties
Pope's poem to a seventeenth-century subgenre of river poetry, another
literary strain of protonationalist celebration that forms an influential
source for the Whig panegyric of the early eighteenth century. As Pat
Rogers has shown, that earlier poetry serves as a precedent for the role of
the Thames, whose "swelling flood . . . as it flows towards the sea is an emblem of national well-being." But in Pope's poem, the marriage device
that usually provides the concluding affirmation in the river poetry is replaced with the imperialist image of the Peace of Utrecht.[21] The river, in
the persona of Father Thames, speaks the final lines of imperialist apologia that define the special properties and powers of this extraordinary
"Flood," beginning with an address to Windsor, calling out the British navy:

Thy Trees, fair *Windsor*! Now shall leave their Woods,
And half thy Forests rush into my Floods,

---

[21] Pat Rogers, "*Windsor-Forest, Britannia* and River Poetry," in *Essays on Pope* (Cambridge:
Cambridge University Press, 1993), 54–69.

Bear *Britain*'s Thunder, and her Cross display
To the bright Regions of the rising Day;

And moving directly to a contemplation of benevolent imperial trade:

The Time shall come, when free as Seas or Wind
Unbounded *Thames* shall flow for all Mankind,
Whole Nations enter with each swelling Tyde,
And Seas but join the Regions they divide;
Earth's distant Ends our Glory shall behold,
And the new World launch forth to seek the Old.
Then Ships of uncouth Form shall stem the Tyde,
And Feather'd People crowd my wealthy Side,
And naked Youths and painted Chiefs admire
Our Speech, our Colour, and our strange Attire!
Oh stretch thy Reign, fair *Peace!* From Shore to Shore,
Till Conquest cease, and Slav'ry be no more:
Till the freed *Indians* in their native Groves
Reap their own Fruits, and woo their Sable Loves,
Peru once more a Race of Kings behold,
And other *Mexico's* be roof'd with Gold.

(ll. 285–412)

Pope's sense of the sea is emphatically not the Elizabethan one of protective insularity.[22] The Thames is an active agent that carries the power of the British navy around the world. The sea, then, as the direct extension of the Thames, is not an interposing space or vacuum that separates the "regions" and "shores" of the world from one another, but a force that "joins" them together in an euphoric affirmation of peace and mutual benefit. The Thames thus purveys a benevolent world system, emanating from British mercantile prosperity, extending to "Earth's distant Ends," and bringing the *pax britannica* to "all Mankind." In demonstrating a strong resemblance between *Windsor* and *Annus Mirabilis*, Rogers has argued that, taken together, these two poems, though they are "not of the same poetic kind," enable us to "detect a convergence of the imperial theme with the providential."[23] This convergence, which extends beyond

[22] For another perspective that places a greater emphasis on isolationism in Pope's poem, focusing specifically on the animated forests that also preoccupy my reading, see Jeffrey Knapp, *An Empire Nowhere: England, America, and Literature from Utopia to The Tempest* (Berkeley: University of California Press, 1992).

[23] Rogers, "Trade and Dominion: *Annus Mirabilis* and *Windsor-Forest*," *Durham University Journal* 69 (1976): 14–20; these quotes, 16, 20.

these poems to the larger contemporary imaginative engagement with an expansionist culture, is effected by the formal structure of the fable of torrents and oceans as it projects the *pax britannica* toward a future fate.

Peru and Mexico, the only "nations" named in the global vision of Pope's poem, specifically exemplify the benevolent efficacy of the *pax britannica*: the Thames even has the power in this poem to rewrite the colonial past of Aztec and Inca civilizations, replacing brutal Spanish colonial conquest with the mutual "admiration" of British imperialism.[24] In this poem, as in Tickell's *Prospect of Peace,* and indeed throughout the literary culture of this period, "Peru" is the recurrent emblem of this transforming power, condensing in one geographical referent the world historical claims of British mercantile capitalism: to see the globe from the single perspective of Britain and to remake history in its own image.[25]

Windsor represents this transforming power with a matching rhetoric, an evocation of motion, energy, and even violence like that which we saw in the torrent of *Cooper's Hill* that made "his power his shores." The power of Pope's Thames, which also stretches "from Shore to Shore" of the globe, though apostrophized as "*Peace,*" is no less sudden and overwhelming than Denham's. In this final passage it comes as a tidal wave of expansionist strength, a kind of battle charge as the forests of Windsor, metamorphosed into the ships of the British navy, "rush" into the floods of the Thames and thence through the oceans of the globe, bearing "*Britain*'s Thunder . . . and Cross." The "Reign" of "fair *Peace*" is not necessarily a tranquil one.[26] This significant and paradoxical juxtaposition of tranquility and overwhelming energy is staged in the central section of the poem, following upon the myth of Lodona, where the shepherd contemplates the peaceful vision of the "watry Landskip" reflected in the stream of the Loddon, that feminized tributary of the Thames which sprang from the tears of Pope's nymph:

[24] In his reading of *Windsor,* Joseph Roach sees this as a recurrent trope "in the circum-Atlantic literature and orature of imperial surrogation, whereby the past and present must be reinvented to serve the needs of a hallucinatory future." *Cities of the Dead: Circum-Atlantic Performance* (New York: Columbia University Press, 1996), 139–144; this quote, 142.

[25] In their note to this line, David Nichol Smith and Edward L. McAdam establish the tropological role of "Peru" by citing other contemporary references: Sir William Temple, "in all Nations from *China* to *Peru*"; Soame Jenyns, "From frozen Lapland to Peru"; Thomas Warton the elder, "All human Race, from China to Peru." See *The Poems of Samuel Johnson,* ed. Smith and McAdam, 2d ed. (Oxford: Clarendon Press, 1974), 115n.

[26] The attention to empire in the eighteenth century in the last two decades has generated a critical debate about the status of *Windsor Forest* as an imperialist work. My earlier essay registers the violence of the *pax britannica*; see *Alexander Pope* (London: Basil Blackwell, 1985), chap. 1. For a deeply contextualized defense of Pope's poem as "anti-slavery," see Howard Erskine-Hill, "Pope and Slavery," in *Alexander Pope: Word and World,* ed. Erskine-Hill (Oxford: Oxford University Press, 1998), 27–54.

Oft in her Glass the musing Shepherd spies
The headlong Mountains and the downward Skies,
The watry Landskip of the pendant Woods,
And absent Trees that tremble in the Floods;
In the clear Azure Gleam the Flocks are seen,
And floating Forests paint the Waves with Green.

(ll. 211–216)

This pastoral scene supplies an almost static image of the British fleets as "floating forests" that "paint the Waves with Green." These are the oaks that Pope introduces in the opening lines of the poem, the trees that make up the forests of Windsor and that, in the form of the ships of the British navy, "command" all the realms of the world (l. 32). But here they are superimposed upon a tranquil stream, serving as emblems of maritime calm, though even in this state they seem barely contained, "trembling in the Floods" at the verge of animation, and poised to launch into the river and across the globe. And in the next couplet, dramatically, they are propelled into the familiar torrent of this maritime fable:

Thro' the fair Scene rowl slow the lingring Streams,
Then foaming pour along, and rush into the *Thames*.

(ll. 217–218)

This passage indicates the constituent counterposition of tranquility and energy, peace and power in the fable of torrents and oceans. But it also suggests the connection of that counterposition to a rhetorical and ideological superimposition of land and sea that becomes a fundamental undercurrent of this fable as it is developed in later poems by Young, Johnson, Pope, and Goldsmith.

IV

Even the understanding of the physical materiality of the ocean was a function of its role in this deeply significant story. Defoe in his *Review* entry for February 3, 1713, describes the behavior of the natural world in terms of British trade:

there is a kind of Divinity in the Original of Trade . . . How naturally does the Water, mov'd by the mighty winds, flow into every Hollow, and fill up every vacant Part in the Sea; the innumerable Particles diligently croud on the Heels of one another, to supply the Place of those forc'd away, and those that are forc'd from their Place by an

unusual Gust, immediately return to fill up the first Emptyness they
find? When the Ship, toss'd by the Fury of the contending Element,
and mounted on the Surface of a Rolling Body of disordered Water,
seems to be falling into a vast Gulph of Destruction, how do the
same Waves hurry into the Hollow Place, and Catching it in their
soft Arms, prevent its Descent to the Solid Bottom, where it would
be dash'd in a Thousand Pieces, and gently raise it up again by their
united Force, and having brought it to their Surface, launch it for-
ward to receive the same kind Usage from the next?

　　Thus obedient Nature, true to its own Laws, preserves the Com-
munication of one part of the World with another, and lays the
Foundation of Commerce, which would otherwise be altogether
Impracticable and Impossible.[27]

Here, in an empiricist and imperialist extension of early modern physico-
theology, Defoe proposes a physical science, which explains the tendency
of the crowded "particles" of the sea to "fill up" the empty space that would
otherwise stand between one part of the world and another, and also a
metaphysical system, which places the characteristics of the natural world
in the context of a benevolent providential plan.[28] These dual systems,
paired but distinct projections of imperialist apologia, are evoked regularly
in the poetry of the period. Young's two matched ocean poems, *Imperium
Pelagi* (1729) and *Ocean* (1728), written around the time of the accession
of George II and the signing of the Treaty of Seville, demonstrate both the
physical and the metaphysical significances of the figure of the sea.

　　Imperium Pelagi, "the empire of the sea," aims explicitly to raise the
"noble subject" (335) of trade to the status of the sublime through an imitation of Pindar, who provides the classical model for "the most spirited
kind of Ode" (336).[29] This "spirit" is in practice a rhetorical extension of
the identification of commerce and Britain with the geographical vastness, the mercantile significance, and the material immediacy of the
ocean. It is characterized by a repeated structure of apostrophe that leads
from "Britain!" to the sea itself, and that sees a physical and providential
ordering in that fortunate conjunction:

[27] Daniel Defoe, *Review of the State of the British Nation* (1706–1713), ed. Arthur Wellesley
Secord, Facsimile Text Society (New York: Columbia University Press, 1938) [9]:54, p. 107.

[28] On eighteenth-century physico-theology—the assumption that all creation was designed to serve man—see Arthur O. Lovejoy, *The Great Chain of Being: A Study of the History of
an Idea* (Cambridge: Harvard University Press, 1953), 186–189.

[29] Shields provides an account both of Young's classicism and his Christian sources in his
reading of *Imperium Pelagi* (23–26).

Britain! behold the world's wide face;
  Not cover'd half with solid space
Three parts are fluid, empire of the sea!
And why? For commerce, Ocean streams
For that, through all his various names:
And if for commerce, Ocean flows for thee.

(353)

For Young, as for Defoe, ocean is the material substance whose fluidity
makes possible both commerce and a global empire, the solid, land-based
British *imperium* that in this poem appears only as an "empire of the sea."
Ocean is the largest and most evident indication that "all Nature bends"
(344) to advance the exploitation of commerce, and, by the next step of
this expansionist logic, to promote British commercial supremacy:

Luxuriant isle! what tide that flows,
  Or stream that glides, or wind that blows,
Or genial sun that shines, or shower that pours,
But flows, glides, breathes, shines, pours for thee!

(342)

Providence shapes the laws of nature to encourage trade, but, as in *Windsor*, providence also operates through commerce to benefit all humankind, by circulating goods and materials among "different lands" to
which Heaven has imparted "different growths" and needs (344):

Britain! To these [different lands], and such as these,
  The river broad and foaming seas,
Which sever lands to mortals less renown'd,
  Devoid of naval skill or might,
  Those sever'd parts of earth unite:
Trade's the full pulse that sends their vigour round.

(368)

Here Young echoes the commonplace contemporary notion that trade
benefits the world by distributing goods and uniting people in its common
cause. Joseph Addison makes this argument often in the *Spectator* papers:

Nature seems to have taken a particular Care to disseminate her
Blessings among the different Regions of the World, with an Eye to
this mutual Intercourse and Traffick among Mankind, that the
Natives of the several Parts of the Globe might have a kind of

Dependance upon one another, and be united together by their
common Interest. . . . [Merchants] knit Mankind together in a
mutual Intercourse of good Offices, distribute the Gifts of Nature,
find Work for the Poor, add Wealth to the Rich, and Magnificence
to the Great.[30]

But these ideas are probably most eloquently expounded in George
Lillo's tragedy, *The London Merchant* (1731), one of the most popular dramatic works of the century, in which trade

keeps up an intercourse between nations far remote from one
another in situation, customs, and religion; promoting arts, industry, peace, and plenty; by mutual benefits diffusing mutual love
from pole to pole. . . . [teaching these nations] the advantages of
honest traffic by taking from them, with their own consent, their
useless superfluities, and giving them in return what, from their
ignorance in manual arts, their situation, or some other accident,
they stand in need of. . . . On every climate and on every country
Heaven has bestowed some good peculiar to itself. It is the industri-
ous merchant's business to collect the various blessings of each soil
and climate and, with the product of the whole, to enrich his native
country.[31]

"The empire of the sea" is in this popular construction at once the agent
of a providential system of distribution and a proxy for British global
power. Indeed, as we have seen in *Windsor*, the claims for the benevolence
of that system depend on that movement of superimposition of sea and
land, fluid and solid, that generates the displacement of power from the
"solid space" of the globe to the unsolid nonspace of the flowing, gliding,
rolling ocean. The representation of the solid *imperium* cannot be so pacific. By displacing imperial violence in this way, the fable of torrents and
oceans performs an essential service to the ideology of the *pax britannica*,
sanctioning its assertion of the peaceful imposition of empire on the
world.

This rhetorical superimposition expresses an ideological formation
that had a notable influence in the first half of the eighteenth century.
P. J. Marshall has described the role of this "empire of the sea" in con-

[30] Joseph Addison, *Spectator*, no. 69 (19 May 1711), ed. Donald F. Bond (Oxford: Clarendon Press, 1965) 1: 294–295. Subsequent references are to this edition; number, volume,
and page are given within the text.

[31] George Lillo, *The London Merchant*, ed. William H. McBurney (Lincoln: University of
Nebraska Press, 1965), 3.1.1–28.

temporary attitudes toward foreign war and national identity. British control over the seas was represented as a "peaceful enterprise," in keeping
with the notion of endemic British liberty and based in "free trade, not co-
ercion." But at the same time, such dominion was seen

> in extremely belligerent terms. It was an empire that rested not
> only on commerce but on naval power exerted over Britain's Euro-
> pean rivals. The trade of France, Spain, and the Netherlands was to
> be beaten off the oceans by force. Their colonies were to be sacked.
> Maritime wars of plunder were assured of enthusiastic support in
> eighteenth-century Britain. . . . Such wars were presumed to pay for
> themselves. They were fought by sailors, supposed to be the flower
> of English freedom, for the national objective of an expanded
> commerce. Continental wars, by contrast, were said to be waged for
> the narrow personal interests of the English monarchy, at great
> expense to the British taxpayer, and with standing armies, the
> instruments of despotism. . . . [Thus arose] the popularity of mar-
> itime war among a wide section of the population in London and
> in provincial English towns. . . . [whereas] even the most belliger-
> ent exponent of an "empire of the deep" could have serious reser-
> vations about territorial empire.[32]

But even in this euphoric poem, the sea is a complex protagonist. On the
one hand, ocean serves British trade and protects the island of England—
"The Servant Ocean for thy sake/ Both sinks and swells: his arms thy bosom
wrap" (342); in this sense, the sea seems a subordinate, obedient, even passive character. On the other hand, "the empire of the sea" is animated with
a distinctive presence and energy. It is not a static, defensive "wall" or
"moat" like the Elizabethan figure, nor is it an empty realm between the
"solid spaces" of the continents. Young's ocean is a vital repository of significance. It moves, flows, and glides with a kind of animation and autonomy
in keeping with Defoe's notion of the crowding and rushing of the water to
fill up every emptiness it finds on the globe; it is a strangely populous space,
a "peopled ocean," "swarming" with life (341); in fact, it is a thronging *imperium* of its own. In this sense, again, the ocean stands in for the vast global
empire that this poem proposes for Britain. Its thronging vitality is a de-
flected embodiment of the energy of the "solid" mercantile empire characterized by "Trade's swarming throng" (346) and represented in the metropolitan center of trade, the Port of London and the Royal Exchange:

[32] P. J. Marshall, introduction to *The Eighteenth Century*, ed. Marshall, vol. 2 of *The Oxford
History of the British Empire* (Oxford: Oxford University Press), 4–7.

> Vast naval ensigns [national flags] strew'd around
> The wondering foreigner confound!
>
> .   .   .   .
>
> At every port, on every quay,
> Huge mountains rise of cable, anchor, mast!
>
>
> .   .   .   .
>
> How earth's abridged! All nations range
> A narrow spot—our throng'd Exchange;
> And send the streams of plenty from their spring.
>
> (344)

These rising "mountains" of cable and mast and the adjacent image of the thronging port business present a similar impression of proliferation as *Windsor*'s floating and rushing forests, and they construct the same vision of animation and mobility. Indeed, the fable of torrents and oceans is notable for this striking rhetoric of animation: the image of trees rushing into the Thames—of forests as ships, or ships as forests. When James Thomson views the river in *The Seasons*, he too sees "On either hand,/ Like a long wintry forest, groves of masts."[33] And *Imperium Pelagi* specifically claims that trade can "Call forth . . . forests, [and] charm them into fleets" (361).[34] This figure reflects the felt presence of ships, shipping, and seas in contemporary experience, but in a manner that locates a distinctive sort of animation in the fluid medium of the river and the ocean. As the alter ego of the solid *imperium*, ocean contains all its energy and resistless activity.

And in the figure of the ocean, that image of the thronging, prosperous metropole is projected over the whole world:

> Hast thou look'd round the spacious earth?
> From Commerce, Grandeur's humble birth:
> To George from Noah, empires living, dead,
> Their pride, their shame, their rise, their fall,—

---

[33] James Thomson, "Autumn," in *The Seasons*, in *The Seasons and The Castle of Indolence*, ed. James Sambrook (Oxford: Clarendon Press, 1972), lines 123–124.

[34] For a vivid visual rendering of the ensigns, "forests," and "mountains" of the Port of London, see L. P. Boitard's engraving of the Legal Quays (1757). A comment from the end of our period describes this scene in the same language: "the whole river, from the bridge, for a vast way, is covered with a double forest of masts, with a narrow avenue in mid-channel." Thomas Pennant, *Some Account of London* (London, 1805), 269–279; quoted in Rudé, 30.

Time's whole plain chronicle is all
One bright encomium, undesign'd, on Trade.

(368)

The rhetoric of the global survey, as it figures here and elsewhere in its many manifestations in the fable of torrents and oceans, has two related implications. On the one hand, it contains, in a compact gesture, that movement of superimposition and consequent displacement of power that constitutes the formal and ideological complexity of this figure and that justifies the benevolence of the *pax britannica*. And as a consequence, on the other hand, it stands rhetorically as the site for metaphysical speculation and moral contemplation. To "look round the earth" in this period is to project a providential system defined by the physical nature of the ocean and located in the commercial preeminence of Britain. Such a system undertakes to account not only for the British empire, but also for reason, virtue, and human fate as well.

Thus in the last long section of *Imperium Pelagi* the man of reason, who is the incarnation of benevolent commerce, when faced with the "hopes and fears" (345) of fortune, puts his faith in the "empire of the sea," and expects to be launched on "the flood of endless bliss" (345) at the passing of the present day. This metaphysical assurance is derived from the boundless efficacy of Young's ocean, in which the image of the "streams of Trade" (368) is identical to that of fate itself:

Oh for eternity! a scene
To fair adventurers serene!
Oh! on that sea to deal in pure renown,—
Traffic with gods! What transports roll!
What boundless import to the soul!
The poor man's empire, and the subject's crown!

(371)

Here, in a rhetorical transport that reproduces the "rolling" of the torrents and oceans that we have seen throughout this poetry, human fate is a serene sea that sublimates trade into a "traffic with the gods," and that thus imagines a "pure" metaphysical realm in which rich and poor are common subjects of a higher national destiny where material are replaced by spiritual acquisitions.

Young's *Ocean* develops this metaphysical dimension of the story at greater length than *Imperium Pelagi*, though with the same rhetorical and ideological constituents. In this poem, too, the sea is a figure for poetic inspiration, imperialist celebration, and metaphysical fate, all at once. Greek poetry is a "torrent" that "roars" and "foams along" (142), and that therefore provides the appropriate model for the majestic, triumphant theme of ocean as the prerequisite of commerce and the proxy for *imperium*. The "wide prospect" and "boundless tide" (155) of ocean inspires the poet, who moves easily from the material vastness of the sea to its inevitable relation to British prosperity and power:

> Who sings the source
> Of wealth and force?
> Vast field of commerce, and big war,
>   Where wonders dwell!
>   Where terrors swell!
> And Neptune thunders from his car?
>
>   Where? where are they,
>   Whom Pæan's ray
> Has touch'd, and bid divinely rave?——
>   What! none aspire?
>   I snatch my lyre,
> And plunge into the foaming wave.
>   .   .   .   .
>
>   The main! the main!
>   Is Britain's reign
> Her strength, her glory, is her fleet:
>   The main! the main!
>   Be Britain's strain;
> As Tritons strong, as Syrens sweet.

(155–156)

In this poem, too, the ocean is a powerful and autonomous figure, but here Young elaborates more fully not only the vitality, but also the explicit dangers of such a force. In *Imperium Pelagi*, Young cautions abstractly that "Nations may thrive, or perish, by the wave" (352), like Tyre, which is destroyed by the seas of her own glory (350). But *Ocean* represents directly and repeatedly the perils of the sea in scenes of sudden reversal, in which serenity turns to destruction, peace to dread:

> Thro' nature wide
> Is nought descried
> So rich in pleasure or surprise;

When all-serene,
How sweet the scene!
How dreadful, when the billows rise.

(156)

Ocean is full of "storms" and "tempests," alternating with "peace" and "silence." The sea "tempts" sailors, then turns upon them, with "black'ning billows":

With terror mark
Yon flying bark!
Now center-deep descend the brave;
Now, toss'd on high,
It takes the sky,
A feather on the tow'ring wave!

(157)

The power of the ocean is an excessive, uncreating force: the power of "Chaos" to "blend . . . seas and skies" (157) in a repudiation of all order and structure. This is the same uncreating energy as that mobilized by Pope's Dulness, and, as we shall see in chapter 4, to the same imaginative end.

Young is alluding in these passages of terror to the developing notion of the Longinian sublime, a category expounded by Addison in the *Spectator* papers on the "Pleasures of the Imagination." In *Spectator* 489 (1712), Addison prints a response to his account of the sublime that attributes this status explicitly to the ocean:

Of all the Objects that I have ever seen, there is none which affects
my Imagination so much as the Sea or Ocean. I cannot see the
Heavings of this prodigious Bulk of Waters, even in a Calm, without
a very pleasing Astonishment; but when it is worked up in a Tempest, so that the Horison on every side is nothing but foaming Billows and floating Mountains, it is impossible to describe the
agreeable Horrour that rises from such a Prospect. A troubled
Ocean, to a Man who sails upon it, is, I think, the biggest Object
that he can see in Motion, and consequently gives his Imagination
one of the highest Kinds of Pleasure that can arise from Greatness.
(4:233–234)

The paradoxical contrast of calms and torrents, hopes and fears, is translated here from the metaphysical to the aesthetic. In Young's images of the destructive power of the ocean, we can see the cultural fable of tor-

rents and oceans, with all of its political, metaphysical, and historical significances, moving readily also into the realm of the aesthetic, and even
serving as a prototype of aesthetic pleasure.

Young is careful to exempt Britain from the "Chaos" of the uncreating
ocean, but only after the effect of those images of terror and shipwreck is
fully established in the poem:

>   Let others fear;
>   To Britain dear
> Whate'er promotes her daring claim;
>   Those terrors charm,
>   Which keep her warm
> In chase of honest gain, or fame.
>
>   (158)

Here the poem pursues the image of the ocean into the realm of moral
speculation. On the one hand, the "daring" enterprise of British imperialism proves a match for the destructive power of the sea, offsetting its
"terrors" with an equivalent energy—appropriately, since, as we have
seen, ocean is figured as the matching prototype of solid empire. On the
other hand, "virtue" is said to save Britain from the sea; the "generous passions," "public weal," and in this case the "grand design" of the construction of a hospital for seamen (161), which shape the providential rationale of the British *imperium*, exempt Britain from the dangers of the ocean.
In this sense, the self-fulfilling circularity of the interconnected physical
and metaphysical structures generated by the figure of the ocean both defines the virtuous system of British mercantile expansion, which gener-
ously distributes goods throughout the world and also confirms the reward for that virtue—safety and serene seas. This maritime calm, and the
virtue that earns it, guarantees that "the British flag shall sweep the seas"
(163) as long as stars and suns and the solid globe survive.

The conjunction of virtue, commerce, and empire in the image of the
peaceful sea directly inspires the metaphysical contemplation that opens
the concluding passage of *Ocean*:

>   How mixt, how frail,
>   How sure to fail,
> Is every pleasure of mankind!
>
>   (164)

These are the stanzas that see "the world [as] the main" in the passage
that we juxtaposed with Johnson's *Vanity of Human Wishes* at the outset of

this chapter. They propose an earthly state of hope and fear, a maritime scene in which "all are tost,/ And most are lost," but where "good men" may be rewarded with a "noiseless shore" and "unruffled homes" (165). This is the serenity of mercantile virtue, in which, as we have seen, both a morality and a metaphysics are generated from the material and commercial image of "the empire of the sea." But in *Ocean* it is a forced, conditional serenity, a hope rather than an assurance. This ocean, like the "mighty cause" (164) of the British empire that it embodies, is too close to "Chaos" itself to be so readily tamed. Thus, upon raising the question of the fate of "good men," this poem in its final stanzas repudiates the "public scene" (165) and embarks on a pastoral contemplation of the "humble life" (166), which ends with a familiar evocation of eternity:

> Unhurt my urn!
> Till that great turn
> When mighty nature's self shall die!
> Time cease to glide,
> With human pride,
> Sunk in the ocean of eternity.
>
> (168)

Like Denham's Thames, which flows to the sea "like mortal life to meet eternity," Young's ocean is nothing less than fate itself. But also much more. This metaphysical figure contains the whole of the ocean's complex character: its material vastness and physical ubiquity, its assertion of a national destiny, its projection of a moral system, its imposition of an expansionist global paradigm, and its ultimate power to overwhelm the speaker and the world. "Eternity" in this poetry is the product of an imaginative confrontation with the material forces of history. It is the climax of the fable of torrents and oceans, in which the complex and ambiguous character of that story's unnamed protagonist is finally uncovered.

The collective story whose strands we have gathered from its various manifestations in the poetry of this period addresses the transforming power of capitalist economic expansion, attempting to represent its nature and to project its effects. In its protagonist, the particular figure of torrents and oceans, this fable locates an examination of this historical force, its irresistible energy, its momentum, its danger, its promise, and its threat to overwhelm the world. In the shape of its action, the fable shows how this force makes the world over in its image, generating from its own nature a system whose logic reflects, explains, and justifies that nature. In the course of its unfolding, the fable enacts the contradictions attendant upon this historical moment, variously and paradoxically demonstrating the undecidable demeanor of its protagonist and the unpredictable effects of its action, alternating hope and fear, threat and subservience, unity and chaos, and mixing glory, peace, danger, and despair. But its final effort remains, throughout the vicissitudes of its plot, an attempt to come to terms with modern fate.

V

Johnson's poem is staged against this representation of fate. The passage from *The Vanity of Human Wishes* with which we began can be seen, from the hindsight of this reading of earlier torrents, as a metaphysical reflection upon the fable of torrents and oceans. Though the poem does not take up the themes of empire, ocean, or Britain as explicitly as Denham's, Dryden's, Pope's, or Young's works do, *The Vanity of Human Wishes* demonstrates the cultural pervasiveness and relevance of the story in a way that those more explicitly political works cannot. Its opening couplet—"Let observation with extensive view,/ Survey mankind, from China to Peru"—engages the same rhetoric of global survey that we have seen to be a central constituent of our fable. This "extensive view" is a projection of the theory of the physical propensity of water to fill the spaces of the globe and thus necessarily impel geographical expansion; it is the basis for the displacement of power from land to sea that produces the ideology of the *pax britannica* and the consequent denial of the political and the historical in this period of expansionism; and it serves as the systematic ground of metaphysical speculation, in which the assumptions of this global perspective are extended into the realm of moral inquiry. The specific naming of Peru, echoing Tickell's and Pope's global surveys, signals the historical underpinnings of this metaphysics: we are observing a world mapped out by the historical force of mercantile capitalist expansion, a world whose fate is framed within the moral system generated by that force, and whose reference points are the landmarks of that force's transforming power.

In this context, the subsequent couplet resonates with the ambiguous implications of the fable, which we have seen repeated in the literary culture of this period from Dryden to Young: "Then say how hope and fear, desire and hate, / O'erspread with snares the clouded maze of fate." Hopes and fears—abstractions from those images of drowning, shipwreck, storm, and flood, on the one hand, and of survival, daring, glory, the advances of navigational science, and even the Cape of Good Hope itself, on the other—signal the ambiguity of this cultural fable's implications, the mixed nature of the story's message, its tensions and contradictions with itself.[35] The "fate" that this poem evokes at its outset, then, projects the paradoxical outcome of the fable of torrents and oceans.

"Hope and fear" leads the poem to the central image of our fable, the "torrents" that we have seen in the representations of British imperial fate from Denham to Young, and, in the fable of the city sewer, the rushing, downstream images of urban experience from Rochester to Swift:

> Where then shall hope and fear their objects find?
> Must dull suspense corrupt the stagnant mind?
> Must helpless man, in ignorance sedate,
> Roll darkling down the torrent of his fate?

The fable of torrents and oceans comes full circle here: it belongs to the material world of ships and shipping, commerce and seas, and we have seen how that material category generates a science, a metaphysics, a morality, and a story with a climax corresponding to the ambiguous fate with which *The Vanity of Human Wishes* concludes. Here that very "fate" is self-consciously figured as a "torrent," in a metaphor that brings back the material experience of the fable as if it were an illustrative analogy. In fact, this circularity is a sign of the cultural fable's nature: language and material experience echo and corroborate each other in the collective imagination of literary culture.

The fable of torrents and oceans is rehearsed less readily after midcentury, when the first flush of the *pax britannica* and first era of English imperial expansion is complicated by the social, political, and cultural adjustments that emerge in the growing movements opposing the slave trade and advocating social and political reform, and in the nostalgic evocation of an ideal national past. The image of the ocean has a different valence in this period. No longer Britain's servant, it signifies a threatening force that seems to have the power to overwhelm the very shores which, in

[35] These tensions are evident also in the modern debate about *The Vanity of Human Wishes*, in which the poem is seen as either a Stoic satire or a Christian tragedy. For a compact summary of this critical history, see Leopold Damrosch Jr., *Samuel Johnson and the Tragic Sense* (Princeton: Princeton University Press, 1972), chap. 5. Damrosch cites this debate in relation to Johnson's use of hope and fear, which he sees as "not the vague, indefinite terms that they have become today" (156); he describes their reference to empiricist psychology and to the forces that impel human actions defined by that system. Damrosch observes that these terms, cited together at prominent moments in the opening and conclusion of the poem, seem to allude to a prominent contemporary formula. My reading provides a rhetorical and social-economic account of and context for that formula.

Shakespeare's figure, it served to protect:

> That trade's proud empire hastes to swift decay,
> As ocean sweeps the laboured mole away;
> While self-dependent power can time defy,
> As rocks resist the billows and the sky.[36]

These are the last lines of Oliver Goldsmith's *Deserted Village* (1770), composed for Goldsmith by Johnson. These couplets, following upon Goldsmith's attack on enclosure and emigration and his nostalgic evocation of a past rural simplicity, speak for a new isolationism, and for the rejection of commerce and expansion in favor of national self-sufficiency. The new maritime image of resisting "rocks" in the last couplet places the sea, in the form of the "billows," as the opponent of a solid locus of stable national power and identity. And the first couplet confirms this image of a destructive, overwhelming ocean. In this sense, Johnson's lines recall one dimension of the figure of the ocean that we have seen repeated in the poetry of the earlier part of the century: its dangerous and overwhelming power, fear in the absence of hope. In fact, Johnson's "laboured mole" or breakwater is the successor of the "dams" that instigate the concluding, destructive flood in *Cooper's Hill*:

> But if with bays and dams they strive to force
> His channel to a new or narrow course,
>
> . . . .
>
> Stronger and fiercer by restraint he roars,
> And knows no bound, but makes his power his shores.
>
> (ll. 353–358)

But Johnson's first couplet is strangely, and symptomatically, contorted, in its internal structure and in its relation to the following alternative image of the stable "rock" that resists the overwhelming "billows." In both couplets, the threat of the ocean is directed against the solid island of England. But in the first, "trade's proud empire"—the British empire as it is currently based on commerce—is slated for a hasty "decay," a self-contained and internal decline that alludes to the contemporary association of commerce with self-destructive luxury and corruption, a connection that had become increasingly frequent in the second half of the century. This notion of prospective "decay," however, is inconsistent with

---

[36] Oliver Goldsmith, *The Deserted Village*, in *The Poems of Gray, Collins, and Goldsmith*, ed. Roger Lonsdale (London: Longman, 1969), lines 427–430.

the simile that follows and illustrates it; there "the laboured mole"—one possible counterpart to "trade's empire"—does not decay through its own internal corruption, but is rather overwhelmed by a powerful and autonomous "ocean"—an ocean that is syntactically the proper counterpart to "trade" in the structure of the simile. In other words, on one hand, the "laboured mole" might be taken to stand for "trade's empire," since it is the object facing impending destruction; but on the other hand, the ocean that destroys the mole might also be taken to stand for trade, since it holds the analogous place in the structure of the simile. In the first case, trade—or the nation that embraces it—does not decay through its own corruption, but instead is overwhelmed by a massive external force, and in the second, trade is granted a power and autonomy that the first line would appear to deny to it. The effect is a shifting in the siting of trade in relation to ocean, a shifting that represents trade incoherently as both an active, destructive force and as a self-consuming sign of corruption, and England as both a victim of momentous energies external to itself and as a self-contained object of internal decay.

The confusion here is caused by the now vestigial rhetoric of the fable of torrents and oceans, upon which Johnson draws for his representation of trade's dangerous power. That fable, as we have seen, has installed in the literary culture of the first half of this century such a naturalized conjunction of ocean and commerce, and such a resonant characterization of ocean itself, that the prior significances of ocean shape these lines despite their explicit claims. Even at this climactic point of the *Deserted Village*, when Johnson and Goldsmith are explicitly repudiating British expansionism, attempting to separate Britain from identification with commerce, and refuting the allure of the power and prosperity conferred by trade, ocean's story can be heard: trade is still bound up with the representation of an ocean characterized by energy, power, and autonomy. These last lines of the *Deserted Village* suggest that the fable of torrents and oceans has a cultural momentum, a kind of literary afterlife, that carries it beyond the limits of its ideological relevance—an example, perhaps, of a kind of cultural canonization by which a mode of imaginative expression gains special power and permanence.

This moment of rhetorical anachronism provides an example of an individual author engaged in a struggle with a character created by the collective imagination out of a vivid material presence; Johnson's intentions vie with the ocean's venerable cultural identity, as he seeks to use the ocean in his own anti-expansionist simile. But the ocean makes a different claim for itself. Its assertion of autonomy in this concluding couplet, in spite of the poem's attack on commercial power, suggests the potency of our cultural fable, even after it ceased to be told. Like many engaging stories, it develops a life of its own; it transcends its time. Indeed, the fable of torrents and oceans tells us as much as it told its contemporary audience. It tells us how the distinctively modern experience of global economic expansion was understood at a time of dramatic and explosive growth. It demonstrates the intimacy of that experience with the material conditions of contemporary life. And it shows us how a culture might grasp the complexities and explore the contradictions of a historical transformation imaginatively, even as it clings to a simple, celebratory, or apologetic rationalization.

PART II : EXCHANGE

William Hogarth, *The Lottery* (1721). The Explanation reads in part: "*Upon the Pedestal* National Credit *leaning on a Pillar supported by* Justice. . . . Fortune *Drawing the Blanks and Prizes*. . . . *Before the Pedestal* Suspence *turned to & fro by* Hope & Fear." By permission of the Division of Rare and Manuscript Collections, Cornell University Library.

CHAPTER 3

Finance:
The Fable of Lady Credit

"TRADE IS an ocean," according to Daniel Defoe:

the best and most experienc'd Sailor needs his Pilot books, his navigating Instruments, his Cross-staff, Quadrant, Compass, &c. to steer by. . . . the various changes and turns that Trade takes in the nature and consequence of things, and by the length of time, are such, that the most experienc'd Tradesman may stand in need of new Instructions and Hints, and make daily discoveries of things, which he knew nothing of before. . . . the Tradesmen themselves . . . make new kinds of excursions out of their business, run new hazards and dangers, and are ruin'd by new and different ways than they did, or indeed than they could formerly.

In the good old days of Trade, . . . there were no Bubbles, no Stock-jobbing, no South-sea Infatuations, no Lotteries, no Funds, no Annuities, no buying of Navy bills, and publick Securities, no circulating Exchequer Bills; . . . Trade was a vast great River, and all the Money in the Kingdom ran down its mighty stream; the whole wealth of the Nation kept in its Channel . . . . Whereas now . . . half the stock of the nation is diverted from the channel of Trade to run waste, as I may say, and like a River without banks, to drown the flat country, and spoil the industry of the Plough and the Husbandman.[1]

---

[1] Daniel Defoe, *The Complete English Tradesman*, vol. 2, pt. 2 (London, 1726–1727), introduction, 2–8. Subsequent references are to this volume and edition; page numbers are given within the text.

In another passage from Defoe's economic writings, "Trade is a Mystery," whose ways

> will never be compleatly discover'd or understood; it has its Critical Junctures and Seasons, when acted by no visible Causes, it suffers Convulsion Fitts, hysterical Disorders, and most unaccountable Emotions——Sometimes it is acted by the evil Spirit of general Vogue, and like a meer Possession 'tis hurry'd out of all manner of common Measures; today it obeys the Course of things, and submits to Causes and Consequences; tomorrow it suffers Violence from the Storms and Vapours of Human Fancy, operated by exotick Projects, and then all runs counter, the Motions are excentrick, unnatural and unaccountable.[2]

According to another contemporary economic writer, Roger Coke, "Trade is . . . the Lady," who

> in this present Age is more Courted and Celebrated than in any former by all the Princes and Potentates of the World, . . . for she acquires not her Dominion by the Horrid and Rueful face of Warr, . . . but with the pleasant aspect of wealth and plenty of all things conducing to the benefit of Humane Life and Society, accompanied with strength to defend her, in case any shall attempt to Ravish or Invade her.[3]

Among these representations of modern trade, oceans and rivers, storms and hysteria, fancy and the female figure intersect in a complicated evocation of risk, loss, uncertainty, volatility, value, prosperity, modern finance, and historical change. But mystery is their mediating figure: in the collective imagination of the early eighteenth century, the mystery of trade seems to be assimilable both to the image of the ocean and to that of the lady. Though in the imperialist apologia that we examined in the last chapter oceans are not directly feminized, as we have seen they share the female energies of the city sewer and they play the same role as women in the discursive engagement with the forces of a modernizing, capitalist economy, evoking alternately ideas of power and fluctuation, dominion and contradiction, energy and ambiguity.

---

[2] Daniel Defoe, *Review of the State of the British Nation* (1706–1713), ed. Arthur Wellesley Secord, Facsimile Text Society (New York: Columbia University Press, 1938), 3:126, pp. 502–503. Subsequent references are to this edition; volume, number, and page numbers are given within the text.

[3] Roger Coke, *A Discourse of Trade* (London, 1671), vol. 2, sig. B2$^\text{V}$.

From this perspective, we can see the fables of expansion—torrents and oceans and the city sewer—as the counterpart of another group of cultural fables, centered upon the feminization of exchange. These two prongs of the contemporary representation of modernity together form a cultural genre, a group of fables with different structures and protagonists, but all drawing upon a similar imaginative relation to the experience of trade, expansion, commerce, credit, debt, and commodification. The "mystery" of this experience, as Defoe himself asserts, can only be grasped by participating in the collective stories that engage it: "If any Man requires an Answer [to these mysteries], they may find it in this Ejaculation——Great is the Power of Imagination!" (*Review* 3:126, p. 503).

The potent, changeable Lady who dominates the feminized representation of modern finance in the early eighteenth century, then, is the imaginative analogue of the protagonist of the cultural fable of torrents and oceans. This Lady takes many forms—sister, mistress, bride, wife, mother, whore, goddess, creator; she is an object of desire and revulsion, of transport and despair; her character and her fate implicate contemporary attitudes toward virtue, society, culture, aesthetics, and history; and her narrative describes the threat of change and the potency of creation. All these meanings have their point of reference in the female body. The Lady is understood in her various guises as the victim, agent, or embodiment of her own corporeality, which thus becomes the contemporary prototype for change and creation with all the historical implications of those ideas. In this regard, the figures of exchange that form the subjects of these two chapters are based upon the same premise that we have explored already in the fable of the city sewer: the idea that the female body is accountable for modernity. The fable of Lady Credit gives us a distinctive purchase on that claim and an indication of the scope of its relevance in this period. The fables of a new world that make up the *Dunciad* provide an entry into the feminized figuration of the mysteries of capitalism, its practices, its powers, and its consequences.

I

The early eighteenth century was the first age to live the immediate intensity of credit, loans, discounts, shares, futures, national debt, deficit spending, and the fascinating fluctuations of stock exchange in a way directly comparable to our own. An international money market and a futures commodity market were established in the first decade of the Restoration. Then, after the failure of the private goldsmith bankers during the financial crisis of Charles II's reign, national finances were fundamentally reconfigured. With the founding of the national banking system based in

the Bank of England in 1694, government deficit financing transformed
the financial world, through the institution of a national market in government securities and the resultant growth of speculation in government
funds. At the national level, these changes were influenced by the need to
finance the ongoing war on the Continent, which was supplied through
the selling of long-term bonds and the resulting growth of the national
debt. But foreign pressures were only one aspect of this transformation.
This was a period of rapid capitalization, where financial instruments,
means of exchange, and modes of production were reshaped as a response and encouragement to the continued growth of trade, manufac-
ture, and the investment that generates and stimulates them. P. G. M.
Dickson has described these changes as a "financial revolution," a fundamental and widespread transformation in the nature of exchange.[4] And
Larry Neal, in tracing the rise of capital markets in Europe from the late
seventeenth century, has emphasized "the modernity of their operations":

> Whereas the capital flows and price movements of that era have no
> direct bearing on today's events (although they can be used to test
> and refine modern economic and financial theories), the back-
> ground conditions that led to the development of the international
> capital markets of the eighteenth century do have some striking
> similarities to our modern adventures.[5]

The extensive engagement with credit and speculation was also mani-
fested domestically in the constantly increasing role of debt at all levels of
the economy. John Brewer observes that "public indebtedness, as every
politician and political pundit of the era complained, grew at a prodigious rate during the course of the eighteenth century," an increase made
possible, as Brewer shows, by the concomitant development of an effective tax system that "revolutionized eighteenth-century public finance."[6]
Private finance followed the same course. Defoe, the preeminent economic commentator of the early part of the century, felt the experience
of this financial revolution on his pulses:

> Some give Men no Rest till they are in their Debt, and then give
> them no Rest till they are out again; some will credit no body,

[4] P. G. M. Dickson, *The Financial Revolution in England: A Study in the Development of Public Credit 1688–1756* (New York: St. Martin's Press, 1967), 3–14. See also Charles Wilson, *England's Apprenticeship, 1603–1763* (London: Longman, 1974), chap. 10.

[5] Larry Neal, *The Rise of Financial Capitalism: International Capital Markets in the Age of Reason* (Cambridge: Cambridge University Press, 1990), 2.

[6] John Brewer, *The Sinews of Power: War, Money and the English State, 1688–1783* (New York: Alfred A. Knopf, 1989), 114, 89.

and some again are for crediting every body; some get Credit
till they can pay nothing, and some break tho' they could pay all.
No Nation in the World can show such mad Doings in Trade, as
we do. (*Review* 3:92, p. 365)

Because of the expanding economy, the increase in investment, and especially the shortage of specie resulting from the recoinage of 1696,
which undervalued British silver coin on the international market, indebtedness became so widespread that, according to Brewer, "even the
humblest of men found themselves enmeshed in the web of credit. Credit
and debt . . . were almost universal."[7] As a direct result of the specie shortage, workers were paid infrequently and indirectly, in the form of credit
with local tradesmen. Outside of London, the regional credit market was
based on the inland bill of exchange, a promise to pay a debt at a future
date. These bills were negotiable instruments, whose transfer enabled
businessmen, shopkeepers, and manufacturers to pay for goods without
exchanging specie. They quickly became the customary basis of exchange, generating extensive regional networks in which "producers, dis-
tributors and consumers were linked . . . by a highly elaborate (and extremely delicate) web of credit" (Brewer, "Commercialization," 205). The
inland bill of exchange itself became the basis of speculation and discounting, and a trade in these bills developed alongside that in government securities. On another front, credit was widely available and flexibly
negotiated for tradesmen and small manufacturers, who could readily obtain mortgages for business expansion. This expanded use of the mort-
gage led also to the growth of property insurance and the "widespread en-
tanglement of almost all tradesmen in the snares of trade indebtedness"
(Brewer, "Commercialization," 204).

Even the most venerable source of wealth and stability, landed property, came under the influence of modern finance in this period.
Through sales, mortgages, enclosures, innovations in agricultural production, and other means, land was tied increasingly to trade, innovation,
and speculation. John Barrell argues that

more and more landed estates were kept whole only by infusions of
money from the City . . . . the ownership of land was inevitably and
increasingly involved in an economy of credit, where values and
virtues were unstable, and where a man was estimated not by an
"objective" standard, but in terms of an opinion of his credit wor-

[7] Brewer, "Commercialization and Politics," in *The Birth of a Consumer Society: The Commercialization of Eighteenth-Century England*, ed. Neil McKendrick, Brewer, and J. H. Plumb
(Bloomington: Indiana University Press, 1982), 206–207.

thiness which was liable to fluctuate whatever the source of his income.[8]

In this period, the participation in exchange, rather than the possession of real property, became the preeminent basis of economic advancement.[9] Thus credit shaped a whole new world of political, social, and cultural ideas. The transition, as J. G. A. Pocock describes it,

> lay with the owner of capital, great or small, who invested it in systems of public credit and so transformed the relations between government and citizens, and by implication those between all citizens and all subjects, into relations between debtors and creditors. It was not the market, but the stock market, which precipitated an English awareness, about 1700, that political relations were on the verge of becoming capitalist relations. ("Mobility of Property," 110)

The proliferation of credit and debt stimulated business and encouraged expansion: "The entire credit system engendered a highly speculative and volatile economy, full of enterprise and initiative, open to an extraordinary degree to the vagaries of fashion and fad, encouraging quick returns and setting a premium on highly flexible and imaginative business strategies" (Brewer, "Commercialization," 213).

But the new system was also highly unregulated and extremely perilous for even the most secure. Liquidity crises were recurrent and constantly feared. Fluctuations, alarms, and crises of public credit were frequent and often arbitrary, generated by party struggles, foreign wars, the international market, domestic conflict, and sometimes by speculators themselves, whose trading patterns could stimulate a "bubble" which they sought to ride for profit. For small tradesmen and manufacturers, credit might be called in at any time, debt was determined solely by the word of the creditor, and businesses could be bankrupted on the basis of rumor or as a result of a deliberate conspiracy of competitors. According to Brewer's summary:

> In good times credit was easy, there was a marked proclivity for holding goods and securities, and the number of bills drawn would

---

[8] John Barrell, *English Literature in History 1730–80: An Equal, Wide Survey* (New York: St. Martin's Press, 1983), 39–40.

[9] See Brewer, "Commercialization"; and J. G. A. Pocock, "The Mobility of Property and the Rise of Eighteenth-Century Sociology," in *Virtue, Commerce, and History: Essays on Political Thought and History, Chiefly in the Eighteenth Century* (Cambridge: Cambridge University Press, 1985), 103–124.

multiply, thereby facilitating an increased volume of transactions. So-called bills of accommodation could be drawn to increase the funds available to an individual, commodities and securities would change hands as part of an accelerating speculative boom, and overall indebtedness would increase sharply. However, when the bubble burst—and it was almost certain to do so as long as there was a ceiling on interest rates, which meant an eventual check on credit of a rather unsatisfactory kind—a major liquidity crisis ensued. Speculators, bankers, merchants and tradesmen alike, they all tried to realize their assets: to convert from commodities to cash, from bills to specie, and from trade credit to hard currency. Credit became almost impossible to obtain precisely when it was needed most. Cash, silver and gold were at a premium because of the sudden and substantial demand for them. Simultaneously nearly everyone was demanding payment of their outstanding bills and being asked to pay off their own extant debts. ("Commercialization," 209–210).

This experience of credit and debt pervaded English life in this period, bringing with it an immediate sense of fluctuation, instability, and change, and enforcing at the same time a vital excursion into the realm of the imagination. As Defoe himself concludes, trade is a mysterious force, shaped not by the rules of logic, coherence, or order but by the "Power of the Imagination" to create a world of its own outside those rules. Pocock sees that force specifically embodied in the character of credit: "Credit . . . symbolized and made actual the power of opinion, passion, and fantasy in human affairs."[10]

The prominence of the "mystery" of trade and credit is registered in the proliferation of treatises and debates on money, bullion, credit, and stock jobbing in the print culture of the first half of the eighteenth century, from Defoe's *Villainy of Stock-Jobbers Detected* (1701) and *Essay upon Publick Credit* (1710) to Swift's account of the national debt in his *History of the Four Last Years of the Queen* (1758) and Hume's "Of Public Credit" (1741). Beyond these histories and treatises, credit can be seen to figure prominently in early eighteenth-century literary culture, as several recent critics have argued: Catherine Ingrassia sees Richardson's fiction as a "domestication of paper credit"; Colin Nicholson traces the theme of finance in Pope's poetry, *Gulliver's Travels*, and *The Beggar's Opera*; Patrick Brantlinger aligns "the question of epistemological credit" or "credulity,"

---

[10] Pocock, *The Machiavellian Moment: Florentine Political Thought and the Atlantic Republican Tradition* (Princeton: Princeton University Press, 1975), 452.

which he sees as constitutive of eighteenth-century literary discourse, with the problematic fluidity and insubstantiality of public credit, which lies "at the heart of the simultaneous financial revolution"; and Sandra Sherman, following the same track, sees credit as constitutive of "a new kind of narrativity" that can be used to understand Defoe's fiction.[11]

These critics are pursuing an avenue in recent studies of culture that has sought to link the cultural and the economic through the problematics of "belief"—viewed as a form of "credit." Thus Marc Shell has argued that "Credit, or belief, involves the very ground of aesthetic experience, and the same medium that seems to confer belief in fiduciary money . . . also seems to confer it in literature."[12] Another dimension of this argument offers yet another extension of the idea of credit, in which the epistemological issue of "belief" becomes a means of interpreting the economy. Recent critics engaged with the question of value—economic and cultural—have used the distinctively imaginative and affective implications of credit to propose a revisionist, antirationalist assessment of the financial revolution itself and, by implication, of liberal economic theory. According to these critics, the modern legacy of this period is not the rationalized system of capitalist exchange, but the flights of fancy and credulity of the free market and stock speculation.[13] Credit, from these perspectives, is a cornerstone of modernity. And Lady Credit, created in the first blush of the financial revolution, is the imaginative condensation of this economic phenomenon; her body shapes a cultural understanding of the economy and of womankind, together.

[11] Catherine Ingrassia, *Authorship, Commerce, and Gender in Early Eighteenth-Century England* (Cambridge: Cambridge University Press, 1998), 138; Colin Nicholson, *Writing and the Rise of Finance: Capital Satires of the Early Eighteenth Century* (Cambridge: Cambridge University Press, 1994); Patrick Brantlinger, *Fictions of State: Culture and Credit in Britain, 1694–1994* (Ithaca: Cornell University Press, 1996), chap. 2; these quotes, 78, 75; and Sandra Sherman, *Finance and Fictionality in Early Modern England: Accounting for Defoe* (Cambridge: Cambridge University Press, 1996), 5. See also Simon Schaffer, "Defoe's Natural Philosophy and the Worlds of Credit," in *Nature Transfigured: Science and Literature, 1700–1900*, ed. John Christie and Sally Shuttleworth (Manchester: Manchester University Press, 1989), 13–44; and Julian Hoppit, "Attitudes to Credit in Britain, 1680–1790," *Historical Journal* 33 (1990): 305–322.

[12] Marc Shell, *Money, Language, and Thought: Literary and Philosophical Economies from the Medieval to the Modern Era* (Berkeley: University of California Press, 1982), 7. Here Shell cites Fernand Braudel, *Capitalism and Material Life, 1400–1800*, trans. Miriam Kochan (New York: Harper and Row, 1973), whose notion of the confusion of money and writing—in the form of fiduciary money and scriptural money—provides an early model for this exploration of the idea of credit (357–358).

[13] See, for instance, Mary Poovey, *A History of the Modern Fact: Problems of Knowledge in the Sciences of Wealth and Society* (Chicago: University of Chicago Press, 1998); Terry Mulcaire, "Public Credit; or, The Feminization of Virtue in the Marketplace," *PMLA* 114 (1999): 1029–1042; and Sherman, *Finance and Fictionality*. These new assessments of the affective

II

Lady Credit is a product of the periodical press in the first decade of the eighteenth century, a period when the debate on credit is especially colorful, varied, and heated. She is described most frequently by Daniel Defoe, whose *Review of the State of the English Nation* (1706–1713) develops her genealogy, character, and day-by-day behavior over at least fourteen separate numbers.[14] But her story is taken up in various other periodical essays of the time, including one in *The Moderator* (1710) entitled "The False Fits of Whiggish Credit Discovered; or, An Account of the Turns and Returns, Comings and Goings, Visits and Departings of that Subtle Pharisaical Lady Call'd Whiggish Phanatical Credit" (1710),[15] and most notably in Joseph Addison's *Spectator* paper (no. 3, 3 March 1711) on the Bank of England.[16] This was a period of intense partisan debate on the economy, and especially on the complex issues of credit and national deficit spending, caused by the economic demands of the war on the Continent and the political instability of the last years of Anne's reign. The Tory position tended to attack the national dependence on the sale of government securities by associating it with Whig financial policies. Whig supporters claimed, among other things, that public credit was damaged by Tory threats to the succession and schemes to repudiate the national debt and the financial system that supported deficit spending. Lady Credit, then, is the exfoliation of a heated contemporary economic and political dispute.[17] But though she is frequently cited in partisan argumentation, Lady Credit is not a simple political emblem. Her story complicates and ex-

---

and imaginative dimensions of the financial revolution are all indebted, as I am, to Pocock's various accounts of the strange status of credit—its versions of irrationality, reification, speculation, and imagination. See *Machiavellian Moment*, chap. 8; and "Mobility of Property."

[14] Lady Credit has recently received critical attention as a progenitor of Defoe's novelistic characters. Sherman observes that she "was the first female narrative subject that Defoe created, the one which . . . obsessed him the longest" (*Finance and Fictionality*, 40). And John F. O'Brien sees her as "a fairly complicated character . . . [who] resembles the kinds of figures we are familiar with from reading novels"—in his case, notably, *Roxana*; "The Character of Credit: Defoe's 'Lady Credit,' *The Fortunate Mistress*, and the Resources of Inconsistency in Early Eighteenth-Century Britain," *ELH* 63 (1996): 603–631; this quote, 619.

[15] *The Moderator*, no. 28 (25 August 1710). Subsequent references are to this edition; column numbers are given within the text.

[16] See Sherman, *Finance and Fictionality*, 53–54; and Ingrassia, 17–39, for additional examples of representations of a feminized credit or trade.

[17] For an account of the relevant political history and a summary of Defoe's engagement with these issues, see Paula R. Backscheider, "Defoe's Lady Credit," *Huntington Library Quarterly* 45 (1981): 89–100. O'Brien also places Lady Credit in the context of Defoe's complicated political position during these years (613).

ceeds the claims of Whig and Tory, partly because that debate over modern finance was far too complex to line up against partly politics,[18] and partly because, like the phenomenon of credit which she embodies, she occupies a world of imagination that takes on a life of its own.

In Defoe's various versions of the story,[19] Lady Credit is pervasive, powerful, and ubiquitous, the object of admiration, desire, and dismay. The current fluctuations in the financial market, the frequent crises of liquidity, and the political debates around these events are Defoe's direct political concern in his description of her character, and these reflections on the immediate problems of national finance occupy at least five numbers (6:32, 7:58, 7:59, 7:102, 7:134), in which Defoe uses the changeable behavior of Lady Credit to upbraid the Tories for their financial policies, to attack the stock speculators for self-interested profiteering, to urge the nation to maintain peace and order, and to implore the public to avoid divisiveness and unrest. But these direct political lessons do not account for the complexities and mysteries that develop around the character of Lady Credit in the *Review*. Her story exceeds Defoe's economic advice, through its attempt to know her, genealogically and viscerally, to assess her powers, and to imagine their creative force.[20]

Lady Credit is everywhere and everything to the English nation. She can occupy many places and many times at once. In Defoe's account of her at the peak of her current power, she appears to be ubiquitous, mapping with her presence the urban financial geography of London:

> 'Tis all CREDIT, she sits upon the Door of the Bank, and waits at the Levee of my Lord *Treasurer*; she dwells in the Exchequer, and has her Rich Appartment in the Offices of every Fund; she shews her Face at every Call, and her Image is stampt upon every Fund; my Lord *H—x* (one of her especial Favourites) stamps her Beautiful countenance upon the Exchequer Bills——The Directors of the Bank, her Menial Servants, have her Warrant, and act by her Commission; she seals all their Specie-Bills, Signs all their Current

[18] Mulcaire also argues, in detail, that Lady Credit cannot be lined up with partisan positions in this period (1031).

[19] The *Review* essays that develop the story of Lady Credit are as follows: 3:5 (10 January 1706), 6:31 (14 June 1709), 6:32 (16 June 1709), 7:55 (1 August 1710), 7:56 (3 August 1710), 7:57 (5 August 1710), 7:58 (8 August 1710), 7:59 (10 August 1710), 7:102 (18 November 1710), 7:115 (19 December 1710), 7:134 (1 February 1711), 7:135 (3 February 1711), 7:136 (6 February 1711), 8:38 (21 June 1711).

[20] Sherman responds to this inconsistency by arguing that Lady Credit represents a site of discursive instability that can be read against Defoe's authorial identity. "Lady Credit No Lady; or, The Case of Defoe's 'Coy Mistress,' Truly Stated," *Texas Studies in Literature and Language* 37 (1995): 185–214.

Notes, and in short, all the Money-Business in the Nation, is done in her Name. (7:58, p. 226)

Even when she suffers a decline, and rumors circulate of her death, the narrator makes the same financial tour—from the Bank, to the coffee houses, to the Exchequer—to hear the reports and give advice on her recovery (7:59). Her absence as well as her presence is felt throughout the city; indeed, it defines the city, in the same way—but without the pungency—in which the sewer defines the city in that parallel fable.

Just as Lady Credit seems to sum up the geography of the modern metropolis, she is also held accountable, anachronistically, for all of British history. In several numbers, Defoe uses Lady Credit to outline the political situation of the monarchy from the time of King Henry V to the present day (3:5, 6:31, 6:32, 7:55, 7:57). Through these appearances, Defoe constructs a comprehensive history of England, in which politics is determined by finance and directed by the behavior of Lady Credit, who becomes, in turn, a coy virgin, a kept mistress, a prisoner, an eloping bride, and a victim of rape. "King *Harry* V. brought her over from *France*, she hid herself in the Broils of *Harry* VI. She shun'd the Crooked Tyrant *Richard* III. for fear he should Ravish her" (7:57, p. 222). Henry VII "began to invite her," but lost her through his "immoderate Avarice" (6:31, p. 123). Henry VIII "quite disobliged her, and being grown wayward, peevish and cruel, she took a long Leave of the Court" (6:31, p. 123). Queen Elizabeth

> quickly found the want of her; but having rummaged all *Europe* for her, there was no finding her high nor low; her *Dudly* sought her in *Holland*, but lost more of her than he carried over——The Queen sent over to K. *Henry* IV. of *France* for her, but she was not there; ESSEX Rummag'd *Ireland*, Invaded *Spain*, Plunder'd *Cadiz*, Insulted *Lisbone*, but got no Credit there; Sir *Francis Drake* sailed round the World, and yet came Home without her——At last she was brought Home in a Great Ship of Silver, taken from the *Spaniards*, and the Queen Coin'd her into broad Shillings. (7:57, p. 222)

James I, "being neither fit for Peace nor War, but wholly bent upon the oppressing of his own People, . . . had no great Occasion for her" (6:31, p. 123). Charles I "stood fair for enjoying this coy Mistress," but she fled the country when he sought to raise "his Funds by Extra-Parliamentary Methods" (6:31, p. 123). Then,

> when the War broke out——She went over to the Parliament—— They Hugg'd and Embrac'd her, carry'd her into the City, and

plac'd her in the *Guild Hall* there, in great Pomp and State; immediately the Thimbles and Bodkins, the Plate, the Money, came tumbling in so fast, that it was no Wonder the Parliament was too hard
for the King. (7:57, p. 223)

But when Cromwell came to power he "took her Prisoner, and when he
had her in his Clutches, he kept her by Force——And whether for Fear of
his High-Commission Court, or for Fear he should commit a Rape upon
her——She stay'd with him to the Day of his Death" (7:57, p. 223). At the
Restoration, Charles II

> got her once for his Mistress, and she was very kind to him a great
> while; what vast Anticipations did she bring him, upon every Act of
> Parliament: what a Height did she run up his *Exchequer* too? That,
> had he gone on, he might in time, meerly by this Jades Assistance,
> have got all the Mony in the Nation into it: But he . . . thinking he
> had got her fast in his *Exchequer,* claps upon her, and shut up the
> Place; but she was too nimble for him: he got the Money indeed,
> *but he lost the* CREDIT; away she flew, and she never came near him
> again as long as he liv'd. (3:5, p. 18)

In these historical passages, Lady Credit's agency gives Defoe the opportunity to reflect repeatedly upon English political history. He tells
the story of Charles II again, a few years later, with some different details:

> It was expected, that at the Restoration she would come over from
> *Holland* with their young King *Charles* II. and indeed she was some-
> where *incognita* in his Retinue——For it was plain, as this was a
> trading thriving Nation, she had a great Mind to dwell here; but
> that king disgusted her several Ways, as in his selling *Dunkirk* for
> *French* Money, next in his Attempt upon the *Dutch Smirna* Fleet, and
> at last in shutting up his Exchequer, which she took so heinously,
> that she declar'd open War against him, and withdrew her Concur-
> rence from every Action of his Life. (6:31, p. 124)

Defoe's characterization of Lady Credit actually obscures the history of
modern English finance, and this account of Charles's financial arrangements provides a case in point. Charles's suspension of loan repayment in
the "Stop of the Exchequer" of 1672 broke the grip of the private goldsmith bankers who had funded the monarchy and opened the way for the
transformation of national finances and the establishment of the Bank of

England in the 1690s.[21] But Defoe's account of the history of public credit deplores that event in order to focus on the representation of Lady Credit's volatile affections. These affections dictate Defoe's interpretation of English history. Charles's successor, James II, courted Lady Credit but was never able to make her fully his friend: "she began to come to hand in a few Matters, but never to be wholly at his devotion" (3:5, p. 18). Next King William refers her to Parliament, which offers her various funds, securities, duties, and other schemes, but:

> the Government however meaning well, gave her whole bundles of Tallies [wooden sticks used as receipts], like *Bath-Faggots* [kindling] upon these Funds; but Deficiencies happening, and the Supply not coming in, she was fain to make vast Discounts with the greedy Banks and Brokers, to answer her Foreign Demands; and having no Satisfaction, she took it so ill, that she made a second Elopement, and away she run and left us. (3:5, p. 18)

At this point, Defoe describes the founding of the Bank of England, the result of the promise of a "Knot of her Friends" to "establish a General Fund for running Cash, that should at any time furnish what quantity of Money she should have occasion for" (3:5, p. 18). But despite the benefits of this proposal, Lady Credit remains coy and difficult. In a later number, the history is brought up to the present day, and we learn that in the time of Queen Anne, "my lord *T—r* has brought her new Cloaths, dress'd her up like a Princess—And now she is as Gay and as Bright as ever she was, and is become the whole Nation's Mistress" (7:58, p. 225). Indeed, more than a mistress:

> It is now *seven Year* that she has liv'd here, in this glorious posture; you never met her, but she was always Smiling and Pleased, Gay and in Humour——Her walk was daily between the Bank and the Exchequer, and between the Exchange and the Treasury; she went always Unveil'd, dress'd like a Bride; innumerable were her Attendants, and a general Joy shew'd itself upon the Faces of all People, when they saw her. (7:58, p. 226)

This dimension of the fable serves to establish Lady Credit's identification with the nation, by defining British history in terms of her varying, vexed, and changeable relationship with the monarchy. Paula Backscheider suggests that with Lady Credit "Defoe may have intended to create a

---

[21] For a full account of this event, see Wilson, 206–225.

new emblem for England's rising numbers of merchants and tradespeople," an "economic, everyday Britannia" based on the Roman Britannia that had become the familiar sign of the rising British empire (97–99). Even the contemporary Tory attack on the "False Fits of Whiggish Credit" in the *Moderator* essay by that title, which counters Defoe's allegory with a much less flattering representation of Lady Credit as a monstrous and hypocritical force, accepts this notion that the course of English history is determined by her influence. For a large contemporary audience, Lady Credit stands for modern Britain—geographically, historically, and emblematically. But her intimacy with the nation goes deeper than this. In the imaginary world of this cultural fable, she is the motive power of British history. In this sense, she represents a historical force, a force associated with volatile change. Lady Credit's characterization is an imaginative examination of this force.

III

Defoe demonstrates his concern with the question of Lady Credit's character through various constructions of her genealogy. The earliest description of Lady Credit begins by giving her a familial rationale:

> Money has a younger Sister, a very useful and officious Servant in
> Trade, which in the absence of her senior Relation, but with her
> consent, and on the Supposition of her Confederacy, is very assis-
> tant to her; frequently supplies her place for a Time, answers all the
> Ends of Trade perfectly, and to all Intents and Purposes, as well as
> Money her self; only with one Proviso, That her Sister constantly
> and punctually relieves her, keeps time with her, and preserves her
> good Humour . . . Her Name in our Language is call'd CREDIT.
> (3:5, p. 17)

Later on, she is identified in a different way:

> *Prudence* and *Vertue*, were two Sisters, and had each of them Hus-
> bands; *Prudence* was married to *Probity*, and *Vertue* to *Wisdom* by
> whom they had each of them among other Children, one Daughter,
> so like one another, in Feature, Shape, Voice, and Temper, that a
> Man can hard[ly] speak of one, but he must give some Description
> of the other——*Vertue*'s Daughter was called *Reputation*, and the
> Daughter of *Prudence* was called Credit. (7:55, p. 215)

Meanwhile, in another number, which contains a long genealogy of Trade, Credit is the daughter of Trade and Mrs. Punctual, in "the Line of the Male Branch of the great and Ancient Family of NECESSITY" (8:38, p. 156). Thus, Lady Credit is the younger sister of Money or, alternately, the identical cousin of Reputation; and she is the daughter of Prudence and Probity (7:55), or, inconsistently, of Trade and Mrs. Punctual. These abstract and incoherent efforts to locate Credit in an allegorical system, to give this elusive nonentity a family, a past, and a logical connection with the present, are quickly superseded, though, by much more concrete images. Central to almost every redaction of her character in the *Review* is the threatening volatility of her behavior. The causes and meanings of this volatility form the central problematic of her fable.

One cause lies in her body itself. Lady Credit is the victim of hysteria, the female ailment of the age. She is subject to fits of melancholy, "spleen," or "vapours": "if she be never so little disappointed, she grows sullen, sick, and ill-natured, and will be gone for a great while together" (3:5, p. 17). Her disease and its cure are common topics of the *Review* essays. In 6:32, Defoe describes the fluctuations of Credit in the current year:

> However, Credit receiv'd a Shock, that some Folk thought had given Her a Disgust to us in general: My *L. H.*——— told us she was sick of the Disorder, and had not recover'd Her self yet, nay, and being a Physician skillful in those Things, talk'd as if he had some Reason to doubt, whether she would ever come to her self again:———But the Policy of the Government chear'd her up again; and my *L. Treasurer*, Her old *Physician*, gave her a *Cordial*, compos'd of a very High extracted Spirit, or rather Tincture, called *New Subscription*, and the quantity very great too. (6:32, p. 127).

The male characters surrounding Lady Credit, as well as the narrator himself, are occupied in ministering to her health, shielding her from shock and disturbance, regulating her diet, and administering cordials to revive her spirits. But rude treatment, public unrest, and attempts at ravishment on the part of the stock jobbers, the Tories, the French, or rich merchants (7:102, 6:32, 7:115) bring on her fits again. The narrator laments her weakened state: "But poor CREDIT! What shall we do for this poor distres'd Lady, CREDIT; she was Weak enough before, and ill prepared to meet with such a shock . . . how it will go with her, *as to her Distemper*, I know not" (7:59, p. 230). Any setbacks produce grave turns in her health. Defoe describes the consequences of one period of public unrest: "But the *publick Divisions* since this, *Encreasing*, has very unhappily endanger'd her again, and she is fallen into a Relapse——She has for some time kept her Chamber, and as I am told, her Distemper is turn'd into the *Falling-Sickness*" (7:58, p. 227). This new turn brings her to the point of death.

These recurrent "Convulsion Fitts, hysterical Disorders, and most un-
accountable Emotions" (3:126) shape Defoe's representation of Lady
Credit's character and determine both her historical role and her contemporary political effect. Indeed, extrapolating from Defoe's female
protagonist to the larger context over which she presides, the fable of
Lady Credit makes the British nation itself the victim of female hysteria.
The complex implications of this disease, for the representation of
women, of value, and of change, provide a distinctive purchase on the
story of Lady Credit. The pathology of Lady Credit's fluctuations distinguishes her from her precursors, the Renaissance neoclassical goddesses
of changeability and instability—Fortuna, Occasione, and Fantasia.[22] The
eighteenth-century goddess has a visceral cause for her inconstancy.

Defoe's detailed account of his female protagonist's behavior coin-
cides precisely with the publication of one of the earliest works defining
the physiological theory of hysteria, Bernard Mandeville's *Treatise of the
Hypochondriack and Hysterick Passions* (1711). "Hysteria" was an ancient female disorder centered in traditional theories of the womb; in the eighteenth century, the idea of hysteria absorbed the influential new theories
of sensationalist physiology, and became a prominent dimension of the
contemporary medical understanding of the female nervous system.[23]
Accounts of this disease proliferate in the course of the eighteenth century, accumulating details and examples, and progressively pervading literary culture. Mandeville is an early exponent of a theory that comes to
dominate the understanding both of female physiology and of female
character in the eighteenth century, a theory that attributes to the female
body a peculiar relation to fluctuation, irregularity, excess, passion, and
imagination. Most basically, hysteria is attributed to a supersensitive constitution and heightened passions, which were consistently connected
with female reproduction and thought to generate physiological symptoms of weakness, weeping, fainting, fits, and even death. According to
Mandeville,

> Women are not of that robust Constitution as Men are, they are
> sooner offended by, and more impatient of, Heat, Cold, and other
> Injuries; they have not that Constancy, Resolution, and what we call
> Firmness of the *Mind*, . . . Grief, Joy, Anger, Fear, and the rest of
> the Passions, make greater Impressions upon them, and sooner
> discompose their Bodies. . . . Their Frame . . . is more delicate, and

---

[22] Pocock describes these figures in *Machiavellian Moment*, 453.
[23] For a summary account of the development of the new physiology of sensibility and
the place of hysteria in that system, see G. J. Barker-Benfield, *The Culture of Sensibility: Sex and
Society in Eighteenth-Century Britian* (Chicago: University of Chicago Press, 1992), chap. 1.

themselves more capable both of Pleasure and of Pain, tho'
endued with less Constancy of bearing the Excess of either. . . . the
Weakness of the Contexture of the Spirits . . . renders all Women
more or less liable to become Hystericks."[24]

The special sensitivity of the female constitution is a common refrain
in the medical literature of this period. Nicholas Robinson, in his *New System of the Spleen, Vapours, and Hypochondriack Melancholy* (1729), finds that
"those Fits, vulgarly call'd the Hysterick Disease, are more frequently ob-
serv'd to affect [the Fair Sex], either from a stronger Impulse of their Passions, or a finer texture of their Nerves."[25] Such heightened sensitivity was
connected in this literature with a greater vulnerability to disease of all
sorts. Richard Manningham in *The Symptoms, Nature, Causes, and Cure of the
Febricula, or Little Fever* (1746) finds that "The *chief* of my Practice, indeed,
has been among the *Female* Sex, who are generally of more *tender* and delicate Constitutions; and therefore such as are always *most* liable to this Sort
of Fever."[26] Hysteria, however, supersedes all other diseases to which
women might be subject, defining a physiological base line of susceptibility in the female body.

The female reproductive system was seen as the ultimate source of this
special sensitivity, serving in this respect as the determinant of a woman's
health, behavior, and nature. Thus Robert James in his *Medicinal Dictionary* (1743–45) defines hysteria as a "spasmodico-convulsive Affection of
the nervous Kind, proceeding from a Retention or Corruption of Lymph,
or Blood, in the uterine Vessels, which . . . influences all the nervous Parts
of the Body."[27] John Purcell's *Treatise of Vapours, or, Hysterick Fits* (1707) asserts that "the reasons why women are more subject to *Vapours* than Men,
are first because their *Menses* is an Excrement more apt to cause Obstruc-
tions than any Recrement or Excrement whatsoever in Man's body; and

[24] Bernard Mandeville, *A Treatise of the Hypochondriack and Hysterick Diseases* (1711), 3d
ed. (1730), in *Collected Works of Bernard Mandeville*, facsimile editions prepared by Bernhard
Fabian and Irwin Primer (Hildescheim: Georg Olms Verlag, 1981), 2: 246–250. Subsequent
references to Mandeville's treatise are to this edition; page numbers are given within the
text.

[25] Nicholas Robinson, *New System of the Spleen, Vapours, and Hypochondriack Melancholy*
(London, 1729), 212. Subsequent references are to this edition; page numbers are given
within the text. This passage is also cited in John Mullan, *Sentiment and Sociability: The Language of Feeling in the Eighteenth Century* (Oxford: Clarendon Press, 1988), 222. My discussion
of the medical discourse around hysteria is indebted throughout to Mullan's account.

[26] Richard Manningham, *The Symptoms, Nature, Causes, and Cure of the Febricula, or Little
Fever* (London, 1746), iv–v. Cited in Mullan, 222.

[27] Robert James, *A Medicinal Dictionary* (London, 1743–1745), s.v. "HYSTERICA." Subsequent references are to this edition; the entry title is given within the text.

being retain'd produces more various and dismal Accidents."[28] And even Mandeville, though he argues that hysteria and its male counterpart, hypochondria, are caused by the failure of the stomach to generate sufficient "Spirits" to supply the blood, finds that the peculiar vulnerability of women to this disease arises ultimately and inevitably from the nature of the female organs of generation:

> the Want of Spirits in Hysterick Women may often be imputed to their Diet; in which the generality of them commit so many Errors: But besides these their idle Life, and want of Exercise likewise dispose them to the Disease, but above all the innumerable Disorders, which upon account of the menstrual Flux, and the whole *Uterus*, they are so often subject to. (244)

John Mullan, in his summary of the medical discourse of hysteria in the period, shows that "the primary fact in the aetiology of hysteria is menstruation." Though the status and significance of the uterus itself decreases in the course of this century, menstruation remains the sign and cause of hysteria, its irregularity according with and generating a "nervous disruption" in the female constitution. In Mullan's words:

> The association between menstruation and hysteria is exactly that: not a clearly defined causal sequence, but an area of susceptibilities and equivalences. Menstruation is represented as an irregularity which takes the guise of a regularity; it is especially likely to signify a precarious condition in the bodies of those for whom womanhood does not mean the life of the fertile, domesticated, married female. (225–226)

The result is chronic and endemic changeability. Nicholas Robinson argues that women subject to the "Hysterick Disease" are "wavering and unsteady in their judgments .... Now they love a Person to Excess, presently they hate him in the other Extreme" (214). John Purcell finds that "the least Contradiction to their Will casts them into violent Passions; they are fickle, wavering, and unconstant, now resolving on one thing, and immediately changing to something else" (13). And Robert James's *Medicinal Dictionary* asserts that women thus affected "indulge Terror, Anger, Jealousy, Distrust, and other grievous Passions .... They know no Moderation, and are constant only in Inconstancy. Those of

---

[28] John Purcell, *A Treatise of Vapours, or, Hysterick Fits* (London, 1707). Subsequent references are to this edition; page numbers are given within the text.

whom they are one Minute extravagantly fond, the next they will abhor" (HYSTERICA).

In the course of the century, hysteria is canonized, not only medically as the preeminent female disorder, but also culturally, as the sign of personal, aesthetic, and even moral distinction. Hysteria is the physiological counterpart and groundwork of sensibility. Lady Credit's changeability, then, anticipates a major new cultural norm, projected from the female body, embracing female character, and extending ultimately to a standard of behavior, a system of valuation, and a theory of sociability. In literary culture this heightened sensitivity becomes a visible sign of moral superiority and a definitive criterion of virtue, female or male.

Richardson's Clarissa is the period's canonical prototype of this construction of virtue through the constitutional delicacy of the female body, but these qualities of supersensitivity, sympathy, and "elevation of the mind" (Mullan, 229) largely preside over narrative characterization in the novel, the drama, and periodical fiction in the second half of the eighteenth century. The attribution to these sentimental protagonists of an elevated sensibility, an especially vivid imagination, a highly tuned sympathy, and a susceptibility to narratives of misfortune and suffering illustrates the fluid integration of the literary and the medical representation of women in this period. These characterological traits are all grounded physiologically in the theory of hysteria, where the female nervous system, thought to be "more moveable than in men," sensitizes the whole organism.[29] In this way, the medical theory of hysteria grows into a system of valuation and significance, based upon the privileged accession of sensibility and constituted through the female body. Such a construction of virtue is intimately tied to a theory of society, since one function of sensibility is its constitution of sociability through its distinctive responsiveness to the suffering of others, a social theory canonized in part in David Hume's *Treatise of Human Nature* (1739).

Lady Credit's story, then, forms one dimension of the unfolding and extended cultural event that has come to be called the cult of sensibility. In this conjunction both credit and sentiment take on new meanings. The appearance of Lady Credit at this early moment in the development of the discourse of hysteria suggests an affiliation between Defoe's protagonist and the sentimental heroines of later narratives. Both are tied to the diffuse phenomenon that we have learned to call the cult of sensibility, whose extended and uneven development includes the physiological ideas connected with female hysteria as well as the aesthetic structures

[29] Robert Whytt, *Observations on the Nature, Causes, and Cure of those Disorders which have been commonly call'd Nervous, Hypochondriac, or Hysteric* (Edinburgh, 1765). Cited in Mullan, 217.

that suggest the representation of complex character. Not that Lady Credit embodies the standard of virtue that Clarissa promulgates; rather, she and the sentimental female protagonist implicate the figure of woman in a powerfully realized and influential cultural expression of fluctuation and excess, distinctive aspects of the experience of modernity, and they both place these effects within the grasp of the collective imagination by locating them in the female body. Indeed, we can find these effects in various forms throughout the sentimental fiction of the second half of the eighteenth century.[30]

The charged psychic dynamic that marks Clarissa's erotic engagement with Lovelace, and the verbal battles between Pamela and Squire B, both depict an intense exchange structured around the potential for a feminized, sexual changeability. Clarissa's attraction to Lovelace makes her flee from him, Pamela's seduction of B makes her defend herself from him. These canonical sentimental narratives, like the story of Lady Credit, are driven by the alternation of female attraction and aversion. The dangerous and volatile power of female sensibility is the focus of Charlotte Lennox's *Female Quixote* (1752), in which Arabella's imagination seems to enable her to remake the world in her own image. And in Oliver Goldsmith's *Vicar of Wakefield* (1766), excessive female passion, in the form of the illicit alliances of the Vicar's daughters, threatens to destroy the pastoral world of the family unit. In the *Vicar*, female sexuality is closely connected to capital, and the project of the novel is to bring both safely under the control of the "good man." Laurence Sterne's *Sentimental Journey* (1768) also joins women and capital in its representation of an exemplary sensibility. The diffuse sources of sentiment that fill this text—the Franciscan monk, the dead ass, the caged starling—are focused in the figure of the suffering woman—Maria or Madame de C—with whom Yorick mingles his tears, and in the corollary figure of the sexually available woman—the Grisset, the *filles de chambres*—with whom Yorick mingles something else. At the same time, sensibility is represented in terms of money and exchange, and repeatedly enacted in the financial exercise of charity. Yorick's sensibility is defined by the financial representation of his identification with female passion.

In short, Lady Credit helps to inaugurate a mode of representation that becomes dominant in eighteenth-century prose fiction. She is part of an evolving engagement with the experience of a feminized volatility. In this sense, the fable of Lady Credit can be understood, in part, in terms of

[30] For a different perspective on the parallel femininization of financial and literary markets, based on an analogy between the paper credit of the financial revolution and the figurative credit and debt projected in the commercialization of literary production, and on the claim that both realms are dominated by women or gendered as female, see Ingrassia.

the evolution of the culture of sensibility. Modern finance, in this collective story, is grasped through the evocation of female nature. But reciprocally, the fluctuations of modern finance that stand behind Lady Credit's story can also be seen as the generative precursors of sentiment. In other words, finance might make sensibility possible; Clarissa might be the long lost daughter of Lady Credit.

IV

The evocation of female hysteria produces Defoe's most intensely imagined portrayal of Lady Credit, which extends over three numbers of the *Review* in 1711 (7:134, 7:135, 7:136). In the first of these, we find the Lady in a "dejected" state, sadly fallen from a previous "Glory and Splendor," which in this essay is only retrospective. The narrator engages her in an intimate debate in a private place:

> POOR CREDIT! Sunk and dejected, sighing and walking alone; I met her t'other Day in the Fields, I hardly knew her, she was so lean, so pale; look'd so sickly, so faint, and was so meanly dress'd. (534)

Upon hearing of her plans to leave England, the narrator begs her to stay, attempting to answer her complaints about the ill usage she has suffered and to counter her views of the current state of politics and the economy. This scene develops not only the Lady's precarious emotional state, but the sexual dimension of her relation to her male observer. The narrator describes himself as the Lady's "humble Votary," "start[ing]" at her words of rejection, throwing himself at her feet, begging "the Liberty to speak to her," and after she "returns short" upon him, asking where she intended to go, so that he might follow her: "For having still a Trading Inclination, I resolv'd to begin again somewhere, but it should be no where but where she was pleas'd to appear; for What is Commerce? What Invention? What Stock? What Industry, without Credit? ———." He "beg[s] she would give me leave to make one Proposal to her," that she might "delay so fatal a Resolution." But she responds with a barrage of "killing words," detailing her mistreatment. Their discussion is marked by the repeated breaking off of the syntax—typographically signaled by the long dash—that later in this period becomes a sign of the affective intensity of the cult of sensibility: "She told me, if ever she return'd to *England* again, she would———I started at the Word, threw my self at her Feet, and beg'd I might have the Liberty to speak to her———" (534–535).

In this segment of the story, Lady Credit's ailment makes her an object of desire, on the part of the narrator, but also, by extension, on the part of the reader and the nation, for whom the narrator courts her.[31] We are all desperately in love with this Lady, all hanging upon her every move, all modeling our judgments on her demeanor. In short, she is the period's prototypical heroine, the suffering and innocent female victim, whose changeableness is attributed to a heightened sensibility that confirms her moral and aesthetic value, and that simultaneously makes her a standard of virtue and taste. At this point, by means of the female body, the imaginative experience of modern finance merges with the moral assumptions of the cult of sensibility. Defoe notes in *The Complete English Tradesman* that "the credit of a tradesman . . . is the same thing in its nature as the virtue of a Lady" (1:229).[32] The fable of Lady Credit takes on that claim and projects it beyond the simple analogue of invaluable and elusive reputation. Superficially, credit is like virtue in that it is hard to win and easy to lose, it requires the "utmost vigilance to preserve it"(1:132), it depends on and generates confidence, and it defines the tradesman's and the woman's character. But within the fable of Lady Credit, those local parallels are superseded by a larger frame of reference: the feminized figure of credit becomes a cultural arbiter, measuring value, determining judgment, and conferring meaning. Credit is not just like virtue, credit is virtue itself.

Much like credit, female virtue is also a profoundly unstable category in the cultural imagination of the early eighteenth century. The figure of woman is problematic in every era of literary history. In this period, however, images of women play a particularly intense and specific role in the representation of questions about character and identity that develop around the new images of accumulation, adornment, and commodification that reflect the burgeoning consumption of an expanding mercantile capitalist economy.[33] This affecting anecdote of the narrator's meeting in the lonely field with "poor" Lady Credit illustrates the implication of the fable of finance in the contemporary ambivalence about female character.

---

[31] O'Brien sees Lady Credit as a figure designed to generate male desire in order to make an appeal that could bridge the party divisions over national finance produced during the political crisis of the change in the ministry (617). Sherman's reading emphasizes Lady Credit's sexuality, her problematic alternation from virgin to whore, and Defoe's identification with these epistemological uncertainties. Sherman thus "assimilates Defoe to Lady Credit's . . . epistemological opacity," taking Lady Credit as a progenitor and emblem of Defoe's relationship to fictionality (*Finance and Fictionality*, 40–54).

[32] Shawn Lisa Maurer provides a description of this connection of trade and female virtue in *Proposing Men: Dialectics of Gender and Class in the Eighteenth-Century Periodical* (Stanford: Stanford University Press, 1998), 82.

[33] See Laura Brown, *Ends of Empire: Women and Ideology in Early Eighteenth-Century English Literature* (Ithaca: Cornell University Press, 1993).

Here, Lady Credit's most pointed complaint introduces the image of a "sponge," an image that is specifically tied to the problem of female identity in contemporary writing through the figure of the lady's toilet. First, the Lady canvasses for the narrator her many recent services to the nation:

> She began to recapitulate and run back into her own History for
> about 16 Years here, ever since the Year 96——She hinted how she
> Coin'd Paper, Money, and gave the Exchequer Credit for five Mil-
> lions of Bills, only with the Breath of her Mouth; how she alter'd
> the Coin of *England* at a time of such extremity, that if it had not
> been for her, the Nation had sunk in the Attempt; she told me how
> she resettled the Bank, took in all the Bankrupt Tallies, and their
> own Notes at *Par*, when the last were at 20 *per Cent*. Discount, and
> the first at above 40; how she United the *East India* Companies,
> when that Faction in Trade bid fair not to Ruin themselves only,
> but to Stock-Jobb the whole Nation——She bid me look back upon
> the Funds Mortgag'd to her for Annuities, and ask'd me how the
> War had been carry'd on, but for her? (535)

Then she describes the crisis that has brought about her current despair: "And now my Face is Threatened to be wash'd with a Spunge" (535).

Historically, this image alludes to the rumor, groundless in the event, that Parliament might postpone or stop the payment of interest on governmental securities (a "Parliament spunge"). The level of public anxiety about the economy was high in 1710 and 1711, at the time when Defoe was publishing these numbers of the *Review*, as a result of the unsuccessful pursuit of the war on the Continent and the growing national debt to support that war, as well as the political tensions around the change to the new Tory ministry. This ministry, under the financial leadership of Robert Harley, began to initiate innovations in national financial policy, aimed especially at funding the ongoing war, schemes which issued in the successful establishment of the South Sea Company, but which, in the interim, gave occasion for doubt, confusion, and rumor (Dickson, 62–75). In the next number, Lady Credit elaborates this specific concern—that she will be "washed with a sponge"—by emphasizing, in the first two items of the list of conditions upon which she would continue to live in England, the stability of the Parliamentary funds at stake:

> 1. That the vile and barbarous Suggestion of a PARLIAMENT
> SPUNGE, however in itself Ridiculous, and in its very Notion *Foolish*,
> yet being in its Suggestion Malicious, and improv'd Wickedly, to
> shock the Confidence and Satisfaction of the People, in the Verac-

ity, the Steadiness, and Honour of Parliament Securities, may receive some *publick stigma,* and be *damn'd by Parliament,* so, as it never shall and never can be brought to a Question in the Houses . . . .

2. That some such other Vote in Parliament, may pass for declaring the Sacred Stability of all Parliamentary Securities, (and that no Necessity shall prevail upon the Houses, either to Vacate or *postpone* the Establish'd Payments of Interests on Money Advanc'd) as to that Honourable Assembly shall seem meet. (7:136, p. 543)

Defoe plays upon the two current uses of the word "sponge"—as a porous toilet accessory and as the revocation of a debt. Rhetorically, the word perfectly links the worlds of finance and female identity. The financial act of canceling interest payments is described in the same way as the physical one of washing the face, a constituent feature of the female toilet, and in that context an image specifically relevant to the complex issues of painting, commodification, and the questions about female identity implicated by those themes in this period. The same image occupies a central role in Defoe's representation of the identity of his female protagonist in *Roxana* (1724), a character whose nature and career is so closely linked to the contemporary complexities of commerce and finance that Patrick Brantlinger describes her as "a realistic incarnation of such allegorical figures as Lady Credit" (76).

This novelistic character provides a more extended occasion to explore the questions of female identity raised by the image of the woman washing her face with a sponge. Both Lady Credit and Roxana regard the exercise of washing their face as a radical activity, fundamental to their identity. But whereas Lady Credit sees the threat of having her face washed as an insult to her character, Roxana, as the mistress of the "French Prince," uses the washing of her face as the means to prove her authenticity:

> As he saw the Tears drop down my Cheek, he pulls out a fine Cambrick Handkerchief, and was going to wipe the Tears off, but check'd his Hand . . . I took the Hint immediately, and with a kind of pleasant Disdain, *How, my Lord!* said I, *Have you kiss'd me so often, and don't you know whether I am Painted, or not? Pray let your Highness satisfie yourself, that you have no Cheats put upon you; for once let me be vain enough to say, I have not deceiv'd you with false Colours:* With this, I put a Handkerchief into his Hand, and taking his Hand into mine, I made him wipe my Face so hard, that he was unwilling to do it, for fear of hurting me.

He appear'd surpris'd, more than ever, and swore . . . that he cou'd not have believ'd there was any such Skin, without Paint, in the World: *Well, my Lord,* said I, *Your Highness shall have a farther Demonstration than this; as to that which you are pleas'd to accept for Beauty, that it is the Meer Work of Nature,* and with that, I stept to the Door, and rung a little Bell, for my woman, *Amy,* and bade her bring me a Cup-full of hot Water, which she did; and when it was come, I desir'd *his Highness* to feel if it was warm; which he did, and I immediately wash'd my Face all over with it, before him; this was, indeed, more than Satisfaction, that is to say, than Believing; for it was an undeniable Demonstration, and he kiss'd my Cheeks and Breasts a thousand times, with Expressions of the greatest Surprize imaginable.[34]

Roxana demonstrates that she is not painted, but that proof does not confer authenticity; quite the opposite. As an acknowledgment of her per-formance, the French Prince gives her a diamond necklace: "I love, Child, *says he,* to see every thing suitable; a fine Gown and Petticoat; a fine lac'd Head; a fine Face and Neck, and no Necklace, would not have made the Object perfect" (73). Even in the act of asserting her authenticity, Roxana is confirmed as an "Object" to be obtained for money and to be adorned by and identified with the signs of material property. Far from revealing an authentic woman and confirming a stable female identity, this scene highlights the absence at the core of Roxana's character, as it defines her, with or without paint, solely as an object to be acquired or adorned. In the course of the novel, Roxana turns the tables on the problem of female identity by becoming an acquiring agent on her own behalf, a move that does not resolve but rather raises to a higher level the question of com-modification that her character engages.

Using Roxana's toilet scene as a gloss on Lady Credit's, we can pursue the contemporary question of female identity into this cultural fable. In evoking the image of washing her face with a sponge, Defoe places Lady Credit in the context of another well-developed contemporary fable, the fable of commodification. In the cultural imagination of the early eigh-teenth century, the experience of commodification was often staged through the representation of the female toilet—in the lady's dressing room itself or through the evocation of a list of objects with which the fe-male body might be adorned. These figures open up the question of fe-male character and raise the possibility that it is unknowable or absent—

---

[34] Daniel Defoe, *Roxana,* ed. Jane Jack (Oxford: Oxford University Press, 1969), 72–73. Subsequent references are to this edition; page numbers are given within the text.

that it is subsumed by the objects with which it is associated.[35] Pope responded to this question by proposing that "most women have no characters at all," Swift by stripping the female body to a "nauseous, unwholesome, living carcass" in pursuit of its soul.[36] Lady Credit sees the "sponge" as a fundamental affront to her female nature, a repudiation of her value, an attack on her identity. By raising these questions, Defoe places his protagonist at the center of that contemporary speculation on female character. Though she is our mistress, our bride, our historical touchstone, our fictional heroine, our standard of virtue, Lady Credit remains unknowable throughout Defoe's stories of her career. Indeed, Defoe tells us repeatedly that she is a phantom, a "Non-Entity," a "nothing," a breath of air, a gust of wind, "neither a Soul or a Body," "neither visible or invisible," "a Being without Matter, a Substance without Form," "a perfect free Agent" (6:31, p. 122). Even when he constructs a genealogy to tie her to a knowable order, her families are incoherent and contradictory, and her relationships lead nowhere. In this sense, Lady Credit exemplifies the problematic of female identity in the period as it is rendered through its implication in the issue of commodification.

The conjunction of credit and commodification—like the coincidence of the theorization of hysteria with the representation of the fluctuations of modern finance, and the affiliation of Lady Credit with the sentimental protagonist—suggests that the fable of Lady Credit plays a part in a larger cultural engagement with the representation of the female body, an engagement that takes the figure of the woman as the paradigm for a current historical or ideological problematic. Even the diagnosis of hysteria, specific as it is to the female constitution, is generalized within this fable, serving as a means of translating the health of the female figure into that of the nation at large, or confounding the two. Though the Lady is most directly represented as the victim of hysteria, in a reciprocal arrangement her condition reflects and is reflected in the anxieties of the nation; her "Fitts [and] hysterical Disorders" become indistinguishable from the "Vapours of Human Fancy" that possess the tradesmen and stock-jobbers in the grip of the fluctuations of a volatile economy.

The same language that describes Lady Credit's "vapours" character-

---

[35] I have described the tropes typical of the contemporary representation of commodification elsewhere, though without the formal and ideological notion of the cultural fable. See Laura Brown, *Alexander Pope* (Oxford: Basil Blackwell, 1985), chaps. 1 and 2; and *Ends of Empire*, chaps. 4 and 6.

[36] Alexander Pope, "Epistle to a Lady," in *The Poems of Alexander Pope*, vol. 3.2, ed. F. W. Bateson (London: Methuen, 1951) line 2. Subsequent references to Pope's poems are to this edition; line numbers are given within the text. Jonathan Swift, "Answer to Several Letters from Unknown Persons," in *Prose Works*, ed. Herbert Davis (Oxford: Oxford University Press, 1951), 12:80.

izes the nervous disorder that was seen to afflict the real people—men and women—who were caught up in contemporary booms and busts. One treatise advertises this correspondence in its title: John Midriff writes *Observations on the Spleen and Vapours: Containing Remarkable Cases of Persons of both Sexes, and all Ranks, from the aspiring Directors to the humble Bubbler, who have been miserably afflicted with those melancholy Disorders since the Fall of South-Sea and other publick Stocks* (1721).[37] Indeed, as Catherine Ingrassia has shown, much of the imagery around the South Sea Bubble focused on iconographic female figures like Lady Credit—for instance, the Lady of the South Sea, or the Lady of the Bank.[38] The physiology of Lady Credit is both a personal and a national phenomenon, with

> infinite Branches; the secret Springs and Streams which maintain
> it's Variety and Circulation, by which, as by Veins and Arteries, it
> conveys its quickning Spirits to all the remotest Parts of that Poli-
> tick Engine, the constitution; and by which it likewise receives its
> own Nourishment and Supply from the Heart. (6:32, p. 125)

The idea of the nation as a physiological body is a familiar one, of course; in this period it stands beside the figure of the family as a means of representing the dynamic logic of political structures. But in the context of the intense engagement with the female body that pervades Lady Credit's story, this generalization has the effect of calling attention to the process of feminization that the fable of Lady Credit enacts. The female body is evoked as an explanation for the forces of contemporary economics. When that explanation is extended into an image of the national body, then by association even the body politic becomes female. In this sense, the cultural fable of Lady Credit has the power to recreate the world in her own image.

V

Though the evocation of a specific female ailment pervades the fable of Lady Credit, its protagonist's character is not exhausted by these allusions to disease. Defoe's female protagonist is not only weak, melancholy, "sunk and dejected" (7:135, p. 534), a victim, a patient, or a "Menial Servant" (6:32, p. 127). She is, often in the same essay, fickle, jealous, despotic, and perverse:

[37] Midriff, *Observations* . . . (London, 1721).

[38] Ingrassia, chap. 2. Ingrassia discusses the appearance of the Lady of the South Sea and the Lady of the Bank in a contemporary commentary on the crisis by James Milner, *Three Letters, Relating to the South-Sea Company and the Bank* (1720) (25–26).

If once she be disoblig'd, she's the most difficult to be Friends
again with us, of any thing in the World; and yet she will court
those most, that have no occasion for her; and will stand at their
Doors neglected and ill-us'd, scorn'd, and rejected, like a Beggar,
and never leave them: But let such have a Care of themselves, and
be sure they never come to want her; for, if they do, they may
depend upon it, she will pay them home, and never be reconcil'd
to them, but upon a World of Entreaties, and the severe penance of
some years Prosperity.
   'Tis a strange thing to think, how absolute this Lady is; how
despotickly she governs all her Actions: If you court her, you lose
her, or must buy her at unreasonable Rates. (3:5, 17–18)

She always loves to give her Attendance, when People have no need
of her. . . . the Management of our Treasury in *England*, has . . .
retriev'd the Favour of this Coy Dame, by that very Method, *viz. Not
having occasion of her*; and the way to keep her, is to keep up that
Condition; that not having any need of her Assistance, you may
always have her at Command. (3:5, p. 19)

This practice of appearing only when she is not needed represents a perverse autonomy that serves as the ultimate measure of Lady Credit's despotism. Indeed, in the history of her relations with the monarchy and
ministry, she asserts a singular energy and self-sufficiency, effecting a
"nimble" escape from Charles II (3:5, p. 18), leaving her friends at the
Bank of England "in a Huff," and resisting every self-sacrificing entreaty
they make for her return (3:5, p. 19). This obdurate and tyrannical Lady
Credit must be courted and flattered, placated and persuaded. My Lord
Treasurer treats her as a difficult mistress, making her compliments
(6:32). The narrator makes love to her, throwing himself at her feet and
begging to be allowed to follow her (7:134). In these passages, Lady
Credit governs her actions vengefully and "despotickly," resisting all entreaties, bribes, or force. Indeed, this tyranny is made even more explicit
in the behavior of the Lady Credit of the contemporary Tory essay on
"Whiggish Credit" in the *Moderator*; her aspiration in setting up the Bank
of England is

to grow Great and Topping; nay, so Towering and Aspiring was she,
that she was thinking every day to set up for herself, and had the
Impudence to tell the Q—n, *That she made Her what She was* . . . .
And this is the true Fits of *Whiggish Phanatical* CREDIT in all its Rise
and Changes. (col. 4)

Lady Credit's character, then, combines infirmity and impotence with assertiveness and power. On one hand, she seems the passive object of the machinations of the Tories, the ministrations of the Whigs, the anxieties of social disorder, the incursions of the French, or her own diseased physiology, but on the other, she reigns despotically on her own behalf. She is both the victim and the agent of her history. This arrangement is central to the structure of her fable, and to its extension into the imaginative life of the age.

Despotism and disease are often linked in contemporary accounts of female identity in this period. Lady Credit is a misogynist type. In fact, Defoe observes in his historical account that her despotic and changeable behavior "has been seen by manifold Experience, among a great Variety of Ladies" (3:5, p. 18), of which she is only the worst example. Defoe is here evoking the contemporary tradition of misogynist satire, which we have already sampled in Rochester's, Gould's, and Swift's poetry of the feminized sewer. This tradition consistently presents female sexual inconstancy as a form of tyranny over men, and describes the womb as a site of corruption and disease. The *Moderator* essay on "Whiggish Credit" gives Lady Credit the same misogynist label, seeing her as a female "Monster" set upon the destruction of men (col. 3). This attack on women also depends, as we have seen at length, on the representation of the female body as a locus of prolific and indiscriminate generation. In Defoe's story, too, the agency of the female protagonist is seen as a creative force, "a thing of [such] Immense Value and Infinite consequence, that I dare not Write, what to me seems contain'd in the Teeming Womb, of this Mother of Great Designs. What cannot CREDIT do?" (3:5, p. 20). Defoe's awestruck contemplation of his protagonist here situates the Lady outside the normal order of things: she "has strange Qualities" like the "best Philosophers Stone in the World"; she "has the best Method for Multiplication of Metals" and "the effectual Power of Transmutation," turning "Paper into Money, and Money into Dross" (6:31, p. 122). Pope, in a satiric attack on credit in his *Epistle to Bathurst* (1733), makes the same conjunction of finance, magical transformation, and, ultimately, female sexuality:

Blest paper-credit! last and best supply!
That lends Corruption lighter wings to fly!
Gold imp'd by thee, can compass hardest things,
Can pocket States, can fetch or carry Kings;
A single leaf shall waft an Army o'er,
Or ship off Senates to a distant Shore;
A leaf, like Sibyl's, scatter to and fro
Our fates and fortunes, as the winds shall blow:

Pregnant with thousands flits the Scrap unseen,
And silent sells a King, or buys a Queen.[39]

These figures of female procreative power—of multiplication, preg-
nancy, and the "Teeming Womb, of this Mother of Great Designs"—recall earlier images that consistently joined finance and the female body:
the sixteenth and seventeenth-century critiques of usury. Ann Louise Kibbie has argued that Defoe's representation of capital should be seen in
the context of earlier anti-usury rhetoric, in which the fecundity of capital—the power of money to generate money—was represented as a threat
to natural and moral order.[40] In this discourse, the female body served
both as the moral example of a natural, self-limiting procreative power, and
as an admonitory metaphor for the threatening, insatiable self-generative
energies of money when it is set out at interest. A sixteenth-century tract
suggests both of these aspects:

> What is more against nature, than that money should beget or
> bring forth money, which was ordeined to be a pledge betwixt man
> and man, in contracts and bargayning, . . . and not to increase it
> self, as a woman dothe, that bringethe forthe a childe. . . . such
> money which bringeth forth money is a swelling monster, waxing
> everye moneth bigger one than another.[41]

Though the woman is the explicit moral norm here, the "swelling monster"
of usury bringing forth money is also clearly a feminized metaphor: both
sides of the story seem to be located in the female body. But as Kibbie shows,
in the sixteenth and seventeenth-century accounts of usury these two sides
are kept separate; money increases only through the exploitative intervention of the usurer, not through the autonomous activity of female fertility.

In anathematizing the usurer and objectifying his money, anti-usury
discourse indicates its allegiance to a precapitalist economy: "By separating the usurer and his capital and by presenting money as inert, these
works allow money to be liberated from the usurer and returned to a
purer relation of precapitalist exchange" (1032). Lady Credit's "Teeming
Womb"—and, as we shall see, Dulness's maggots, spawn, and monsters—
radically revise this earlier financial discourse, while they build upon its
engagement with the female figure. In these modern fables of capitalism

[39] Alexander Pope, *Epistle to Bathurst*, lines 69–78.

[40] Ann Louise Kibbie, "Monstrous Generation: The Birth of Capital in Defoe's *Moll Flan-
ders* and *Roxana*," *PMLA* 110 (1995): 1023–1034.

[41] Thomas Wilson, *Discourse upon Usury* (1572), ed. R. H. Tawney (New York: Kelley,
1963), 286–287. Quoted in Kibbie, 1025.

and finance, capital—with all its promising and threatening procreative energy—is wholly situated in the female figure: as Lady Credit, money cannot be returned to a prior or a purer state, and its increase is not the result of any agent's immoral machinations, but an internal quality emanating from the procreative and transforming powers of the woman. In Kibbie's words: "the fate of the antiusury doctrine in the eighteenth century is not so much extinction as metamorphosis, and at the center of the transformation is the woman whose body becomes the body of capital" (1024).

For Defoe, the effects of these transforming powers are radically open-ended.[42] Defoe's question, "What cannot CREDIT do?" indicates again Lady Credit's significance in this fable as a historical force—past, present, and future. Just as she accounts for the past, Lady credit projects the future; she can create a new world out of the proliferative energy of her own body.[43] And her womb is at once the cause, the site, and the source of this transformation. As the organ that defines her being and generates her hysterical condition, it accounts for her arbitrary fluctuations. As the locus of her creative energy, it absorbs that cause into itself, making the woman both object and agent of change. And as the "teeming" image of generation, the womb represents transformation as a creative force, indiscriminate, random, beyond logic or control, and ultimately unknowable.

VI

Only a few weeks after Defoe's series in the *Review* on "poor" Lady Credit and the Parliamentary sponge, and just a month before the contentious election of April 1711 in which the Tories sought to unseat the Whig directors of the Bank of England and thereby reverse current financial policy based upon a national debt, Joseph Addison made his contribution to this fable of fluctuation and change (*Spectator* 3, 3 March 1711). Addison's is the most canonical and literary of the contemporary images of Lady Credit, and it lays out some of the central complexities and implications of her characterization. The essay is constructed as a dream vision allegory, in which a daytime visit to the Bank of England and a consideration of "the many Discourses which I had both read and heard concerning the Decay of Publick Credit, with the Methods of restoring it" stimu-

---

[42] Sherman shows in detail the complexity and "tension" in Defoe's participation in the discourse of credit. His promotion of credit and the imagination was matched by his anxiety about their irrationality: "Defoe's configuration of credit . . . transits between gothic horror and mercantile soundness" (*Finance and Fictionality*, 40).

[43] Here I join with Mulcaire in finding in Lady Credit a new resource of "desire" with profound implications for an understanding of value and exchange in the eighteenth century, that of "the fecundity or creative power of the imagination" (1033).

lates a "Methodical Dream" about the "beautiful Virgin," "*Publick Credit,*" who presides over the Bank and seems to control its funds.[44]

The following vision contains all the basic formulae of this engaging story. It begins by pointing to the recent legislation that had established the modern financial instruments of credit and debt: "Both the Sides of the Hall were covered with such Acts of Parliament as had been made for the Establishment of publick Funds" (15). It locates its protagonist in relation to a global economy: "There sat at her feet a Couple of Secretaries, who received every Hour Letters from all Parts of the World, which the one or the other of them was perpetually reading to her" (16). And, most centrally, it focuses on the sudden fluctuations that constitute Lady Credit's identity in all her manifestations. First, when a group of allegorical "Phantoms" representing contemporary political crises—"Tyranny," "Anarchy," "Bigotry," "Atheism," and the "Genius of a Common-Wealth [the Pretender] . . . holding a Spunge in his left Hand"—enter the Hall in "a kind of Dance," the Lady "fainted and dyed away at the Sight" (16–17).[45] At once:

> there was a great a Change in the Hill of Mony Bags, and the Heaps of Mony, the former shrinking, and falling into so many empty Bags, that I now found not above a tenth Part of them had been filled with Mony. The rest that took up the same Space, and made the same Figure as the Bags that were really filled with Mony, had been blown up with Air, and called into my Memory the Bags full of Wind, which *Homer* tells us his Hero receiv'd as a Present from *Æolus*. The great Heaps of Gold, on either side the Throne, now appeared to be only Heaps of Paper, or little Piles of Notched Sticks [receipts], bound up together in Bundles like *Bath*-faggots [kindling]. (17)

As soon as these "hideous Phantoms" are replaced by "a second Dance" of "amiable Phantoms"—"Liberty," "Monarchy," "Moderation," "Religion," Prince George," and "the Genius of *Great Britain*"—"the Lady reviv'd, the Bags swell'd to their former Bulk, the Piles of Faggots and heaps of Paper changed into Pyramids of Guineas," and at this point the narrator, "transported with Joy," awakes (17).

---

[44] Joseph Addison, *Spectator,* no. 3 (3 March 1711), ed. Donald F. Bond (Oxford: Clarendon Press, 1965), 1: 14–15. Subsequent references are to this edition; page numbers are given within the text.

[45] Mulcaire sees this attack on Credit with the "sponge" as "by far the more terrifying weapon," since it threatens "the financial and legal codes that are Credit's indispensable supports" (1038).

Addison's version of the story provides the same medical diagnosis of Lady Credit's vacillations as Defoe's: she is the victim of hysteria, of a supersensitive constitution that reacts suddenly and violently to even the slightest provocation. This behavior is evident in her opening description:

> She changed Colour, and startled at every thing she heard. She was likewise (as I afterwards found) a greater Valetudinarian than any I had ever met with, even in her own Sex, and subject to such Momentary Consumptions, that in the twinkling of an Eye, she would fall away from the most florid Complexion, and the most healthful State of Body, and wither into a Skeleton. Her recoveries were often as sudden as her Decays, insomuch that she would revive in a Moment out of a wasting Distemper, into a Habit of the highest Health and Vigour. (15–16)

The familiar female "distemper" evoked here, in Lady Credit's hysterical inconsistency, seems to be offered as a way of accounting for the contemporary experience of economic volatility. The problem is that modern finance is impossible to explain or predict; the answer is that it is like a woman. But Addison stages that answer with a directness that betrays the nature of its inefficacy, in his own allegory and in the other stories of Lady Credit as well. In this essay, the Lady and the gold are immediately and physically contiguous with one another. Their joint rising and falling calls attention to their reciprocity, rather than to the way in which the metaphor of the Lady might illuminate the experience of the economy. Their comparison only registers more decisively the extent to which both remain mysteries, beyond explanation. The incoherence of Defoe's complex genealogies demonstrates this same aspect of the Lady's rhetorical status and her fable's imaginative significance: the story of Lady Credit does not explain the world of modernity to her dazzled and disoriented audience. She does not stabilize, organize, or rationalize it. She makes it.

This creative energy can be felt directly in Addison's depiction of the Lady as King Midas, making gold:

> Behind the Throne was a prodigious Heap of Bags of Mony, which were piled upon one another so high that they touched the Ceiling. The Floor, on her right Hand, and on her left, was covered with vast Sums of Gold that rose up in Pyramids on either side of her: But this I did not so much wonder at, when I heard, upon Enquiry, that she had the same Virtue in her Touch, which the Poets tell us a *Lydian* King [Midas] was formerly possess'd of; and

that she could convert whatever she pleas'd into that precious
Metal. (16)

This passage accords the Lady a magical power, not only over the instruments of finance, but over the world around her, any object of which she can absolutely and instantly transform.[46] Indeed, it is this power, rather than the fainting and fading of the Lady at her moments of weakness, that provokes the "transport" that shapes the narrator's response to Lady Credit throughout his account of her changes, his "wonder," "dizziness," and ultimate euphoria. Even when she is dying, Lady Credit is a marvel of transformation. She is Addison's representation of the power of the imagination.[47]

Defoe, as we have seen, claims "the Power of the Imagination" as the only means of approaching the "mystery" of the experience of modern finance. His invention of Lady Credit is an attempt to utilize this power. And her story, reciprocally, points beyond itself to the intangible experience that it attempts to render. The "Power of the Imagination" links the literary and the intellectual: it demonstrates the relation between the expressive artifacts featuring Lady Credit and her realm, on the one hand, and the larger structures of thought brought to bear on contemporary finance, on the other. Pocock describes for us the functioning of that larger world:

> Government stock is a promise to repay at a future date; from the
> inception and development of the National Debt, it is known that
> this date will in reality never be reached, but the tokens of repay-
> ment are exchangeable at a market price in the present. The price
> they command is determined by the present state of public confi-
> dence in the stability of government, and in its capacity to make
> repayment in the theoretical future. Government is therefore main-
> tained by the investor's imagination concerning a moment which
> will never exist in reality. The ability of merchant and landowner
> to raise the loans and mortgages they need is similarly dependent

[46] Erin Mackie describes the power of Addison's feminized version of credit, juxtaposing it to the image of the hoop petticoat; see *Market à la Mode: Fashion, Commodity, and Gender in The Tatler and The Spectator* (Baltimore: Johns Hopkins University Press, 1997), chap. 3. Mulcaire cites this passage to support her idea that Lady Credit represents "virtue defined in explicitly irrational and magical terms" (1033).

[47] Mulcaire offers a strong reading of Addison's treatment of Lady Credit's powers of transformation, which differs from mine. She sees Addison as an unqualified advocate of the imagination, and his essay as an argument for the "liberation" of the "fantastic potential" of the new market in the form of Lady Credit (1039).

upon the investor's imagination. Property—the material foundation of both personality and government—has ceased to be real
and has become not merely mobile but imaginary. (*Machiavellian
Moment*, 112)

Imagination enters the realm of economic calculation at the same moment that finance enters the world of the contemporary imagination.

In this sense, Addison's Lady Credit is an imaginative, rather than an
allegorical or emblematic figure; she does not explain, rationalize, or sim-
plify the problem of modern finance for her own audience or for us. In
fact, Addison's characterization of Lady Credit enables us to see how her
failure to explicate modern finance matches her capacity to elaborate it.
The figure of Lady Credit deepens the mystery for which she is a
metaphor. Defoe makes this dimension of her presence explicit when he
emphasizes that the "greatest alchymists" can never comprehend credit
(6:31), and when he delineates her ubiquitous and marvelous effects:

> What has this invisible Phantosm done for this Nation, and what
> miserable Doings were there here before without her?——She cuts
> all the Notches in your Tallies, and the obedient Nation takes them
> for Money; your Exchequer Bills have her Seal to them, and my
> L— H—x sets his Hand to them in Her Name; 'tis by Her you raise
> Armies . . . , and in short by Her you found your grand Alliances
> have supported the War, and beat the *French*: By this Invisible, *Je ne
> scay Quoi*, this Non-natural, this Emblem of a something, tho' in it
> self nothing, all our War and all our Trade is supported. . . . Pay
> Homage to her Image. (6:31, p. 122)

The elusive nature, or non-nature, of Lady Credit bears out, at every turn,
Defoe's assertion that "Trade is a Mystery." But at the same time, her story
gives that mystery—the irrational, unpredictable, disorienting experience
of contemporary finance—a distinctive resonance. The fable of Lady
Credit opens up for the contemporary imagination the transforming powers of the volatile new forces of exchange.

VII

In one sense, the fable of Lady Credit is a minor cultural event with a
short history and a limited frame of reference. But in another sense this
story reaches across modes of discourse and embraces cruxes of contemporary thought in a way that gives it an unexpected and extensive cultural
purview. Most broadly, the "mystery" that this fable assigns to modern fi-

nance, its evocation of the "Power of Imagination" and the creative, transforming energies of proliferation, reflects the new relationship to the
economy and to value itself that takes shape in the eighteenth century
and that Mary Poovey defines as constitutive of the "modern fact":

> Credit, credibility, credentials, and credulity . . . each of these terms
> implies something about people's willingness (or need) to believe,
> but the range of the terms—from credit to credulity—also takes us
> from activities that seem to be merely economic to attitudes that
> seem exclusively psychological . . . . even behaviors that seem to
> be "merely" economic have always depended upon mechanisms
> that solicited belief . . . . Thus all the terms that circulate around
> "credit" call our attention to the leaps of faith that underwrite both
> the modern economic infrastructure and the knowledges with
> which we enable this infrastructure to support our lives. (27)

The "Power of Imagination" penetrates even to the nature of knowledge.

The distinctive character of Lady Credit is also relevant to eighteenth-
century literary culture. Sandra Sherman and Catherine Ingrassia have
separately explored this connection through a sustained analogy between
contemporary finance and contemporary fiction, or between financial
credit and the figurative "credit" required by the new genres of prose narrative. Such parallels indicate the prevalence of "credit" as a common cultural parlance in this period. More specifically, but no less significantly,
our account of the fable of Lady Credit suggests that she is an early prototype for the sentimental female protagonist of eighteenth-century literature. Excessively sensible and intensely desirable, she enters the canon of
the novel with Richardson's fiction, and she shapes the future of the form
for a century to come: she represents a major cultural investment of identification. Seen through this lens of female sensibility, Lady Credit—in her
shifting passions and her imaginative energy—is canonized as an object of
desire, a standard of value, a mode of thought. And through the representation of modern finance—specifically the peculiarly modern experience
of the volatile, immaterial, excessive, and transformative energies of public credit—she enters the culture's imaginative life. But reciprocally, this
representation of finance also reflects upon the sentimental female protagonist who dominates the literature of this century and the next. The
fable of Lady Credit suggests that this long lived fictional heroine is partly
the product of an early confrontation with the experience of modernity.

Lady Credit prepares the way for another sort of literary heroine, as
well—the misogynist, burlesque, or problematic female figure who represents the contemporary cultural engagement with consumption, commodi-

fication, and capitalism. As we have seen, Lady Credit raises those fundamental questions about female character, or absence of character, that are
in this period tied to the fetishism of the commodity. In this regard, the
fable of Lady Credit makes a connection between the mystery of modern finance and that of the commodity, a connection that posits a relationship
between separate dimensions of the experience of modernity. Here we can
see the collective imagination of eighteenth-century culture in the process
of analyzing the structures of modern experience through the resonant
evocation of the figure of the woman. The *Dunciad* extends the terms of that
analysis, while unleashing that female figure's most ungovernable energies.

Cooper half-pence (1772). By permission of the Division of Rare and
Manuscript Collections, Cornell University Library.

CHAPTER 4

Capitalism:
Fables of a New World

Though Dulness, the Mighty Mother of Alexander Pope's *Dunciad*, has her own genealogy as "Daughter of Chaos and eternal Night,"[1] the troping of the female body in the cultural imagination of the early eighteenth century suggests another heritage. Dulness might well be none other than the daughter of Lady Credit. Following Defoe's various versions of Lady Credit's ancestry, this would make her the niece of Money, the granddaughter of Trade, and the last and greatest descendent of the family of Necessity and Invention, whose progeny include Projector, Industry, Ingenuity, Merchant, and Shopkeeper.[2] As we have seen, Defoe's genealogies are symptomatic in their failure to explain the nature of Lady Credit. But in the case of the *Dunciad*, this lineage helps to place Dulness's character within a resonant and fertile cultural fable. Like Lady Credit, Dulness is a personified abstraction with a concrete female body that becomes a site of generation; she is a phantom, a shadow, an emptiness, a gust of wind; she presides over an urban landscape that stands for the city of London; she authorizes a detailed historical narrative of which she comprises the motivating force; she is surrounded by a population of

---

[1] Alexander Pope, *The Dunciad*, 1.12. All references to the *Dunciad* are to *The Poems of Alexander Pope*, vol. 5, ed. James Sutherland (London: Methuen, 1943). References to the 1729 variorum edition are indicated within the text by that date, followed by book and line numbers. References to the four-book version of 1743 are indicated by book and line numbers alone.

[2] Daniel Defoe, *Review of the State of the British Nation* (1706–1713), ed. Arthur Wellesley Secord, Facsimile Text Society (New York: Columbia University Press, 1938), 3:5, 7:55, and 8:38. Subsequent references are to this edition; volume, number, and page numbers are given within the text.

ardent followers; she is attended by dances of antic figures: she privileges gold over truth; she generates a teeming progeny; and she magically transforms the world.[3]

Both Dulness and Lady Credit are emblematic figures from an established seventeenth-century literary and graphic tradition of moral and political allegory, a tradition that frequently characterized these emblematic figures as classical deities.[4] Such prosopopoeia is a prominent aspect of eighteenth-century neoclassical rhetoric, prevalent in prose as well as poetry. Earl Wasserman finds allegories of personified abstractions to be common practice in the periodical essay;[5] in that context Lady Credit is only one such character among many. An increasingly prominent member of this neoclassical pantheon was the Roman figure of Britannia, who in the eighteenth century became the preeminent allegorical representative of the nation. She was installed on English coinage in 1672, seated and holding the emblematic lance, shield, and olive branch. By the 1740s, in a period of imperialist apologia, she was a graphic and literary commonplace, associated with the sea and with maritime power and frequently accompanied by the corollary figures of Liberty, Justice, Religion, and Plenty. Relatedly, she could be used for satiric purposes; according to Herbert Atherton, "the medallic history of Britannia begins with a Dutch satiric piece of 1655 . . . showing Cromwell kneeling before Britannia, his head in her lap, and his arse exposed for a Frenchman and Spaniard to kiss."[6]

We have already seen how Defoe's Lady Credit might have been received as an "everyday Britannia" by her contemporary audience, a character who was identified with the new era of British economic and mercantile expansion.[7] Dulness has the same emblematic progenitors and the same political and moral genealogy. Sitting in her temple with her chosen son, Colley Cibber, dreaming in her lap at the opening of book 3, confer-

---

[3] Colin Nicholson also sees Dulness as a manifestation of the "Queen of Credit," an embodiment of "public credit as cultural agency." *Writing and the Rise of Finance: Capital Satires of the Early Eighteenth Century* (Cambridge: Cambridge University Press, 1994), 183, 10.

[4] See Jean H. Hagstrum, *The Sister Arts: The Tradition of Literary Pictorialism and English Poetry from Dryden to Gray* (Chicago: University of Chicago Press, 1958).

[5] Earl R. Wasserman, "The Inherent Values of Eighteenth-Century Personification," *PMLA* 65 (1950): 435–463.

[6] Herbert M. Atherton, *Political Prints in the Age of Hogarth: A Study of the Ideographic Representation of Politics* (Oxford: Clarendon Press, 1974), 90–91.

[7] Paula Backscheider, "Defoe's Lady Credit," *Huntington Library Quarterly* 45 (1981): 99. For the history of personified abstraction in moral and political allegory, see Backscheider; Dorothy George, *English Political Caricature to 1792: A Study of Opinion and Propaganda* (Oxford: Clarendon Press, 1959), 1:44–61; Hagstrum, 147–148; Atherton, 89–96; and Wasserman.

ring orders and degrees from the height of her throne in book 4, or exposing "all below" (1.18) to our view as she climbs up to her seat for that degree-conferring ceremony, Dulness resembles the graphic figures of Britannia that were commonplace in the period. Like Lady Credit, Dulness evokes an emblematic female figure that claims to register the contemporary sense of the nation—its character, its history, and its destiny.

Most evidently and visibly, then, the *Dunciad* absorbs the cultural fable of Lady Credit. But not that fable alone. This "everyday Britannia" emanates, like Swift's Corinna, from the "common shore" of Fleet Ditch and presides over the same heterogeneity and exuberance that we have found in the fable of the city sewer. She launches an "empire over seas and lands"(3.68) that participates in the fluid potency and the ideological inversions that characterize the fable of torrents and oceans. And her anarchic realm is constituted through the indiscriminate lists, the objectification, and the magical transformations that define the fable of commodification, in which the female body is mystified by the objects with which it is adorned. The *Dunciad* integrates this group of fables in a way that enables us to trace the rhetorical and formal relationships among various imaginative encounters with the experience of capitalism. In this sense, the poem is a composite cultural event, a proving ground for the generic affiliations among the fables of a new world.

In her explicit materialism, Dulness is like Addison's Lady Credit, weighing "truth with gold . . . / and solid pudding against empty praise" (1.53–54) in the scales of Poetic Justice, in the same way that Lady Credit turns all she touches to gold. Dulness, however, unlike Lady Credit, is tied directly to the materialism of the printing industry, and to the transformation of literature into an enterprise of profit and commerce.[8] The immediate material referent of *The Dunciad* is the contemporary book trade—emblematically figured in this period in terms of the geographical site of Grub Street in Cripplegate parish—whose writers, printers, and booksellers make up the personnel of the poem.[9] The publication history of the *Dunciad* reflects its ongoing engagement with the materials and practices of modern publishing. The poem was issued first in three books in 1728 in a form that was clearly designed to incorporate the hostile responses that it was to evoke among the writers and printers against whom

---

[8] Materialism is a prominent dimension of Helen Deutsch's reading of Pope's poetry, centrally informing her understanding of Pope's "poetics of deformity" as a "contagion of embodiment." *Resemblance and Disgrace: Alexander Pope and the Deformation of Culture* (Cambridge: Harvard University Press, 1996), 178.

[9] For an extended account of contemporary cultural reflections of and upon Grub Street and the bookselling trade, see Pat Rogers, *Grub Street: Studies in a Subculture* (London: Methuen, 1972).

it was directed. It was reprinted in 1729 as an annotated "Variorum" edition with a lengthy apparatus mimicking and citing the individuals it attacked. More than ten years later, in 1742, Pope published a new, more apocalyptic book of the poem under the title of *The New Dunciad* in which the literary personnel of the first three books are replaced by allegorical figures of broader cultural relevance—in education, science, and religion. And lastly, the whole was revised to produce the final, four-book *Dunciad*, published in 1743, the year before Pope's death. This version brings the poem's engagement with Grub Street up to date, replacing Lewis Theobald with Colley Cibber as Dulness's favorite son.

The *Dunciad* is a directory of the contemporary book trade. Randomly and repeatedly, it names dozens of contemporary printers and authors, among them: Edmund Curll, Bernard Lintot, Jacob Tonson, John Dennis, Ambrose Philips, Nahum Tate, Daniel Defoe, Elkanah Settle, Lewis Theobald, James Ralph, George Ridpath, Abel Roper, Nathaniel Mist, Thomas Shadwell, Elizabeth Thomas, Thomas Cook, Matthew Concanen, John Tutchin, Edward Ward, John Ozell, James Moore Smythe, Eliza Haywood, Thomas Osborne, Leonard Welsted, John Breval, Besaleel Morris, William Bond, William Webster, Thomas Blackmore, John Oldmixon, Edward Roome, William Arnall, Benjamin Norton Defoe, Jonathan Smedley, James Pitt, Susanna Centlivre, Bernard Mandeville, William Mears, Thomas Warner, William Wilkins, Thomas Durfey, Giles Jacob, William Popple, Philip Horneck, Edward Roome, Barnham Goode, Charles Gildon, Thomas Burnet, George Duckett, Thomas Hanmer, William Benson, Richard Bentley, and Joseph Wasse. These names are not mere topical allusions; they are the rhetorical raw material of the first three books of the poem and the discursive foundation for the allegorical figures that dominate book 4.

The weighty textual apparatus of the *Dunciad* is concerned mainly with parodies, quotes, personal quarrels, and attacks involving these individuals and their writings, attacks that emphasize their self-interest and their prolific production of mindless materials. The long opening note, for example, signed "Theobald," disputes the spelling of "dunciad" without an "e," and raises the example of Bentley's edition of Shakespeare, in which the "e" is preserved. This is answered by another note signed "Bentley," taking further the argument about the spelling of "Shakespeare." In other notes, Pope launches direct attacks on "the presumptuous Critics of our days" (1.134n.), or quotes directly from their works to demonstrate their various absurdities. Cibber, in his *Life*, provides Pope with several opportunities to illustrate folly and especially bad taste and conceit: "My muse and my spouse were equally prolific; that the one was seldom the mother of a Child, but in the same year the other made me the father of a Play"

(1.228n). Elsewhere, Pope cites personal and professional attacks made upon himself and describes his own injuries and injustices. In one long and famous note, Pope cites John Dennis's description of him at length: "A young, squab, short gentleman, whose outward form, though it should be that of a downright monkey, would not differ so much from human shape as his unthinking immaterial part does from human understanding.——He is as stupid and venomous as a hunch-back'd toad" (1729: 1.107n). In short, and as every reader can readily perceive, the *Dunciad* documents the contemporary experience of the literary marketplace. But that documentation launches a much larger vision, which uses Grub Street as a rhetorical springboard to assimilate a variety of contemporary responses to its analysis of the modernizing powers of capitalism.

I

Publishing was a rapidly growing and transforming trade in the eighteenth century; its new products, markets, and structures of value had a direct impact upon the accessibility and forms of print culture. But indirectly these innovations also served as a showcase for the broader cultural implications of modernity. According to John Feather's *History of British Publishing*,

> By the middle of the eighteenth century, the British book trade
> had taken on many of the characteristics which continue to distin-
> guish it. . . . [It had become] a highly developed free-enterprise
> trade, working to the demands of a diverse and growing market,
> and generating substantial profits for the many who were involved
> in the long chain of supply from author to reader.[10]

This growth is evident in the rapid rise in the number of presses, the increase in publishing booksellers, the substantial expansion of edition sizes, and the proliferation of forms of printed materials. It is clear also from the dramatic shift in the scale of employment within the printing houses from the sixteenth and seventeenth centuries to the eighteenth. In the earlier period, the trade was characterized by small houses often served by a single printer and apprentice. The eighteenth-century houses were large enterprises with substantial salaried workforces: in 1730 Tonson and Watts employed about fifty workers in their printing house, and

[10] John Feather, *A History of British Publishing* (New York: Methuen, 1998), 105. My account of the trade is indebted to Feather throughout, especially 67–125. See also Marjorie Plant, *The English Book Trade: An Economic History of the Making and Sale of Books*, 3d ed. (London: George Allen and Unwin, 1973); and P. M. Handover, *Printing in London: From 1476 to Modern Times* (Cambridge: Harvard University Press, 1960).

in the 1750s Richardson employed more than forty workers in three separate houses (Feather, 94). The changes in the trade that correspond
with this growth were based on a process of restructuring, set in motion in
the last decade of the seventeenth century with the lapse of the Printing
Act, and the consequent reorganization of the trade in response to this effectual end of official control over publishing. This decade saw the institution of a new wholesaling mechanism by which copyright-owning publishers established a network of "trading booksellers" who marketed their
books directly. The new structure protected the risk capital of the publishers by discouraging piracy and supplying a source of revenue in anticipation of retail sales, and was both a result and in turn a stimulant to the
expansion of the trade, since under this arrangement publishers were better able to answer the rising demand for printed materials by purchasing
copyrights and financing long print runs.

Throughout this period, rising consumer demand, answered by dramatic increases in production, were the joint forces behind the structural
transformation of the trade. The distinctive social and economic features
of the first half of the eighteenth century—literacy, leisure, innovation,
imperialism, economic expansion, and political debate—variously generated a need for books and periodicals that could supply entertainment,
practical information, commercial and political news, travel accounts, history, and opinions. And as James Raven shows, the "commercially alert
and financially successful band of booksellers" that "relaunched the
trade" both attended to and shaped these needs.[11]

The novel is obviously the most prominent product of this historical
conjuncture, fueling the growth of the trade through its ephemeral nature and its consequent requirement for continuous resupply. And the
new forms of periodical literature played a similar role, contributing simultaneously to current profits and to the further expansion of a burgeoning market. Feather shows that "by the middle of the eighteenth century, the periodical was as familiar in the publishing world as it is today,
and was of great economic importance to publishers and booksellers
alike" (113). The magazine or miscellany, with its diffuse mixture of materials—from literature and music to news, reviews, and history—was a
major innovation in print culture specifically designed to respond to the
omnivorous tastes of this growing audience. Essay periodicals on political
or cultural topics like Defoe's *Review* or Addison and Steele's *Spectator* also
found large readerships and achieved substantial and, in the case of the
Spectator, even spectacular commercial success. Number books, the instal-

---

[11] James Raven, *Judging New Wealth: Popular Publishing and Responses to Commerce in England, 1750–1800* (Oxford: Clarendon Press, 1992), chap. 2; this quote, 32.

ment publication of works on various topics, suddenly became numerous and highly profitable in the third decade of the century; serial publication made texts more affordable to the audience and more profitable for the publisher, who could be assured of sales along the whole course of publication, even for an expensive and substantial book.[12]

And of course the trade was transformed by the rise of the newspaper, the major event in the print culture of the first decades of the century. This phenomenon was variously stimulated: by the end of pre-publication censorship, the development of a new and widespread interest in public affairs and politics, the immediate appetite for reports of the conduct of the war in Europe, and the ever more essential requirement for information regarding the changing conditions of commerce. According to Feather,

> The freedom to read a book or a newspaper, and to read there a vitriolic attack on the ministers of the crown and their policies, was soon seen as an integral part of [the Englishman's] birthright. Taken together with the idea of free trade, untrammelled by gild regulation and outmoded protective legislation, the idea of a free press created a situation in which the book trade could flourish as never before. (91)

In this period, relatedly, arose the practice of the paid political use of newspapers as direct mouthpieces of the parties and the government (Handover, 138–140). The Stamp Act of 1712, which imposed a tax upon the periodical press, led to an even greater dependence upon political subsidy, and a general assumption of political bias, so that, in this period, "to be described as a journalist was not a compliment."[13]

Periodical publication played a direct structural role in the growth of the trade. The organizational skills required to put together and distribute a daily, biweekly, or weekly paper must have augmented management capacities within the business (Feather, 110). More importantly, periodical publication provided a model of national distribution which was essential to the restructuring of the trade in this period. The periodical market, and ultimately the book market at large, owed a substantial part of its expansion to the provinces, where new demands and hitherto untapped audiences created an appetite for newspapers and, eventually, magazines and books of all sorts. In the first years of the century, provincial demand generated a network of newspaper printers and delivery

---

[12] See R. M. Wiles, *Serial Publication in England before 1750* (Cambridge: Cambridge University Press, 1957).

[13] On the periodical press in general, see Handover, chap. 5.

agents throughout the countryside with the ability to circulate printed materials over a large area. These provincial printers had direct ties to the London papers from which they derived their news and, more importantly, to the London suppliers of the stamped paper required for newspaper printing. Feather explains:

> Thus the provincial newspaper owners established contacts and, crucially, lines of credit, with the London paper merchants, and through them were able to develop links with the London book trade. . . . The provincial newspaper owners represented a means of deep penetration of the provincial market; the newspaper owners themselves, and many of their agents, became booksellers, and by the middle of the eighteenth century there was no town of any significance which did not have at least one "bookseller" . . . [who] could order books from the London publishers, which, through the same system, the Londoners were able to supply. (98)

This provincial network was instrumental in the distribution of trade catalogues, a form of advertising designed to further extend the market; individual publications were also advertised in increasing numbers in the periodical press. Similarly, the newly created circulating library was influential, especially in the provinces, as a means of expanding the market, particularly for the novel. The extension of the London trade into the provinces thus made possible the establishment of a large national market, resulting in increases in production and profits.

With major growth and restructuring of the publishing trade came dramatic changes in the practice and culture of writing. Perhaps most significant was the rise of writing on demand for direct payment. The practice of paid political writing for the periodicals, established in the first years of the century, generated a stable of authors who were next called upon by the publishers to produce essays and books on subjects newly in demand. The burgeoning market, then, came to exert new pressures upon authors, even as it rewarded them with increased opportunities and income. Feather summarizes this reciprocal arrangement:

> The magazines, as they grew both in numbers and popularity, were always in need of material to publish, and they needed writers who could be trusted to meet a deadline. Although the newspapers had produced the first generation of journalists in Queen Anne's reign, it was the magazines which provided an outlet for the talents, great and small, of writers who could not support themselves by writing for the booksellers. These writers, contributing essays, reviews, epit-

omes, news reports and the like, were able to support themselves by their periodical writing, and the magazines thus played a crucial role in helping authors to establish a stronger position *vis-à-vis* the book publishers in the middle of the eighteenth century. (111)

The profession of writing, the practice of writing for the market, and the new social phenomenon of the self-supporting author, are thus all consequences of the growth and restructuring of the publishing trade. Pope was one of the first of these professional authors, defensive of his rights over his copies, active in pursuing his interests and profits, and directly involved with the trade, helping to establish three separate publishers— Robert Dodsley, Lawton Gilliver, and John Wright—in profitable businesses (Feather, 103). In fact, Pope exemplifies the modern, self-interested, profit-oriented professional; in Brean Hammond's words: "Pope embodied the direction taken by progress."[14] A progress embodied, however, in a complex, even contradictory manner. Several recent critics have shown that Pope's attitude toward the printing industry and toward the institutionalization of literature and learning in the library and the archive, as well as his situation as a beneficiary of mediated forms of patronage, reveal a deep structural ambivalence in his relation to these forms and institutions of modernity, and even a willingness to profit from and further their development while attacking their cultural, political, and moral effects.[15] Margaret J. M. Ezell, for instance, believes that Pope's literary production, throughout his career, is "nourished" by his commitment to the practices of manuscript circulation.[16] And Dustin Griffin has

[14] Brean S. Hammond, *Professional Imaginative Writing in England 1670–1740: "Hackney for Bread"* (Oxford: Clarendon Press, 1997), 2.

[15] The matter of Pope's ambivalent material implication in modernity—in the forms of the printing industry, the decline of patronage, and the library and archive—has been an important dimension of recent work. See David Foxon, *Pope and the Early Eighteenth-Century Book Trade* (Oxford: Clarendon Press, 1991); Joseph M. Levine, *The Battle of the Books: History and Literature in the Augustan Age* (Ithaca: Cornell University Press, 1991); Hammond; Catherine Ingrassia, *Authorship, Commerce, and Gender in Early Eighteenth-Century England: A Culture of Paper Credit* (Cambridge: Cambridge University Press, 1998), chap. 2; Colin Nicholson, *Writing and the Rise of Finance: Capital Satires of the Early Eighteenth Century* (Cambridge: Cambridge University Press, 1994); and James A. Winn, "On Pope, Printers, and Publishers," *Eighteenth-Century Life* 6 (1980–81): 93–102. My account is particularly indebted to J. Paul Hunter, "From Typology to Type: Agents of Change in Eighteenth-Century English Texts," in *Cultural Artifacts and the Production of Meaning: The Page, the Image, and the Body*, ed. Margaret J. M. Ezell and Katherine O'Brien O' Keeffe (Ann Arbor: University of Michigan Press, 1994), 41–70; and Harold Weber, "The 'Garbage Heap' of Memory: At Play in Pope's Archives of Dulness," *Eighteenth-Century Studies* 33 (1999): 1–20.

[16] Margaret J. M. Ezell, *Social Authorship and the Advent of Print* (Baltimore: Johns Hopkins University Press, 1999), chap. 3; this quote, 83.

argued, in regard to Pope's relationship to patronage, that "as always Pope tries to have it both ways" in public appeal and elite affiliation,[17] a position that captures the characteristic tensions that we will see in the *Dunciad*'s engagement with modern letters.

Expanded, restructured, and reconceived in these ways, the eighteenth-century business of bookselling displayed in a highly visible public arena the power and effects of the capitalist development of an industry: the exploitation of free enterprise, the trajectory of an expanding trade, the growth of productivity, the development of a national market, the centrality of consumer demand, the proliferation of advertising, the preeminence of profit, the commodification of the printed text, and the professionalization of the author. In the case of the book trade, such economic changes intersect with cultural production in a way that brings the power of capital into an unusually close proximity with the imaginative constructions of literary culture. The modernization of the eighteenth-century printing industry provides a template for the imaginative experience of the effects of capitalism. The *Dunciad* constructs its integration of the contemporary fables of a new world upon that template.

II

By beginning with the most visible connections between the *Dunciad* and the fable of Lady Credit, we can assess the ways in which the poem expresses that fable's cultural engagement with finance, but also the rhetorical means by which it integrates Lady Credit's story with a series of other cultural fables.[18] Like the fable of Lady Credit, the *Dunciad* explores the elusive character and the physical body of its female protagonist—who shapes its people, places, events, visions, and outcome. The poem takes up four books: book 1 introduces the Goddess and describes her choice of Cibber as her chosen son and poet laureate; book 2 contains the heroic games, which Dulness stages for the competition of her dunces; in book 3 Dulness gives Cibber a vision of the past, present, and future of her empire; and in book 4 she confers degrees upon a succession of academics, scientists, virtuosos, and aristocrats, and sends them out into the world, bringing "universal darkness" to all learning, civilization, and culture.

Dulness has a corporeal presence in the poem—a large, unwieldy, sexualized, female body. In the opening genealogy, she is introduced as a "fair Ideot," "Laborious, heavy, busy, bold, and blind" (1.15). When she

[17] Dustin Griffin, *Literary Patronage in England, 1650–1800* (Cambridge: Cambridge University Press, 1996), 144.

[18] For the detailed context of the *Dunciad*'s engagement with the local politics of contemporary finance, which my reading does not explore, see Nicholson, chap. 6.

first appears to Cibber in book 1—"Her ample presence fills up all the place; / A veil of fogs dilates her awful face: / Great in her charms!" (1.261–263). These are specifically female "charms," even coquettish ones, like those of Lady Credit, evident again when she contemplates her chosen laureate: "Dulness with transport eyes the lively Dunce, / Remembring she herself was Pertness once" (1.111–112). And throughout that first book we see the Mighty Mother or, in her stead, her chosen son, constantly surrounded by maggots, spawn, monsters, "Sooterkins," and shapeless embryonic progeny (ll. 59, 61, 83, 102, 121, 126), projections of a perverse female procreative energy like that of Lady Credit's "Teeming Womb." Dulness's body is visible again in book 4, when at the start of the degree ceremony "She mounts the Throne: her head a Cloud conceal'd, / In broad Effulgence all below reveal'd" (4.17–18). These images of Dulness's obscene corporeality are typical of the contemporary literary image of the prostitute; we have already encountered one such example in Rochester's *Mrs. Willis*—"Her belly . . . a bag of turds, / . . . her cunt a common shore." And Pat Rogers has demonstrated at length the connection between Grub Street and prostitution, or the Grub Street hack and the prostitute (*Grub Street*, 219). The female body, and its reproductive capacity, is a central dimension of Dulness's characterization.[19]

Just like Lady Credit, Dulness lays claim to the geography of the metropolis—in the dunces' own words: "what street, what lane but knows, / Our purgings, pumpings, blankettings, and blows?" (2.153–154). But the presence of the city is much more fully developed for Dulness than for Lady Credit. As we have seen in chapter 1, in the *Dunciad* urban geography is elaborated through another cultural fable, distinct from the fable of Lady Credit but intimately integrated with it in this poem, that of the city sewer. Dulness's connection with Grub Street prostitution, and with the image of the "common shore" that pervades the *Dunciad*'s representation of London, evokes those effects of leveling, heterogeneity, and exuberance that we have found to emanate from the experience of urban expansion. These effects, as we shall see, tie the fable of the city sewer to that of Lady Credit, and both to the fable of commodification, in a complex interchange of mutual tropes.

[19] Feminist critics have taken up Pope's or the poem's attitude toward women. See, for instance, Susan Gubar, "The Female Monster in Augustan Satire," *Signs* 3 (1977): 380–394; Valerie Rumbold, *Women's Place in Pope's World* (Cambridge: Cambridge University Press, 1987), 161–167; Catherine Ingrassia, "Women Writing/Writing Women: Pope, Dulness, and 'Feminization' in the *Dunciad*," *Eighteenth-Century Life* 14 (1990): 40–58, and *Authorship, Commerce, and Gender*, chap. 2; and Marilyn Francus, "The Monstrous Mother: Reproductive Anxiety in Swift and Pope," *ELH* 61 (1994): 829–851. Ingrassia's *Authorship, Commerce, and Gender* provides a detailed summary of the *Dunciad*'s many imaginative and historical references to women.

Again like Lady Credit, Dulness is made the motive cause of English history. In fact, geography is blended with history in an expansionist trajectory that rhetorically melds the fable of Lady Credit with that of torrents and oceans. The whole of book 3 is occupied with Dulness's historical claims. Here, Dulness puts Cibber to sleep and gives him a historical dream vision, narrated by his underworld guide, the dunce Elkanah Settle:

> For [thee], our Queen unfolds to vision true
> Thy mental eye, for thou hast much to view:
> Old scenes of glory, times long cast behind
> Shall, first recall'd, rush forward to thy mind:
> Then stretch thy sight o'er all her rising reign,
> And let the past and future fire thy brain.
>
>   (3.61–66)

This history, unlike Lady Credit's, is framed by the rhetoric of the "empire of the seas" that we have seen to be central to the fable of torrents and oceans:

> Ascend this hill, whose cloudy point commands
> Her boundless empire over seas and lands.
> See, round the Poles where keener spangles shine,
> Where spices smoke beneath the burning Line,
> (Earth's wide extremes) her sable flag display'd,
> And all the nations cover'd in her shade!
>
>   (3.67–72)

In this troping of the image of "extensive view," the *Dunciad* extends its own purview to the global prospect of British imperial identity, at the same time as it extends its historical reach beyond the English past to the ancient world. As Cibber learns, Dulness has shaped history at all points of the compass. In the East, in ancient China, "Emperor Chi Ho-am-ti" caused "whole ages [to] perish" when he "destroyed all the books and learned men of that empire" (3.75n., 77). In the south, where "rival flames with equal glory rise" (3.80), Cibber sees the burning of the Ptolemaic library. From the north, the nomadic tribes come to overwhelm the arts of Italy, Spain, and France. The "western world," which includes the cultures of the middle east, is put to sleep by Moslem evangelism. And in the south, the medieval Church systematically destroys classical Roman arts and sculpture.

The narrative next turns to England, Dulness's "own" island, where religious conflicts once prevailed, but which Dulness now holds through influence rather than war:

In peace, great Goddess, ever be ador'd;
How keen the war, if Dulness draw the sword!
Thus visit not thy own! On this blest age
Oh spread thy Influence, but restrain thy Rage.

(3.119–120)

Whereas Defoe represents Lady Credit's historical power through her vexed relations with the British monarchy, reflecting the topical relevance of monarchs and ministers to financial policy, the *Dunciad* stretches the trope of history to include the whole globe, and extends the idea of its protagonist's power to the projection of a national imperialist destiny. In this sense, the image of Dulness's "boundless empire over seas and lands" integrates the expansionist rhetoric of the fable of torrents and oceans with the historical trope of the fable of Lady Credit, in a way that emphasizes the unprecedented extent of the modern claim to power. References to Dulness's empire occur throughout the poem, but this allusion to its excess recurs, as a facet of the fable of torrents and oceans, in the apocalyptic encounter with the vision of the new world of modernity that ends book 3.

When Dulness's empire comes to England, the "extensive view" of the fable of torrents and oceans is mixed with a much more local reference:

And see, my son! the hour is on its way,
That lifts our Goddess to imperial sway;
This fav'rite Isle, long sever'd from her reign,
Dove-like, she gathers to her wings again.
Now look thro' Fate! behold the scene she draws!
What aids, what armies to assert her cause!
See all her progeny, illustrious sight!
Behold, and count them, as they rise to light.

(3.123–130)

England's present—seen as the imperial army of Dulness's cause—is represented by an extended list of Grub Street authors, which follows upon these lines and includes Theophilus Cibber, Edward Ward, Giles Jacob, Barnham Goode, and many others, "nameless name[s]" (l. 157) convened "to crown Britannia's praise" (l. 211). This unflattering juxtaposition—between an imperial destiny and the trivial personnel of Grub Street—is a mock-heroic gesture, which links the largest economic and social effects of modernity with the immediate, local instance of the capitalization of the printing industry. Rhetorically, the connection demonstrates the way in which the poem typically associates its broadest range of reference with its most concrete cultural material, its various fables of a new world with the template of Grub Street.

III

Dulness differs from Lady Credit in that she is not an hysteric, plunged as Lady Credit is into fits of fluctuation. But Dulness demonstrates the same inscrutable and shifting nature that generates Lady Credit's changeability. She too is represented as "Emptiness," and consistently connected with specters, phantoms, shadows, hollow winds, and empty air. Her genealogy, with which the poem begins, sets up this identification with "Nothing":

> In eldest time, e'er mortals writ or read,
> E'er Pallas issu'd from the Thund'rer's head,
> Dulness o'er all possess'd her ancient right,
> Daughter of Chaos and eternal Night:
> Fate in their dotage this fair Ideot gave,
> Gross as her sire, and as her mother grave,
> Laborious, heavy, busy, bold, and blind,
> She rul'd in native Anarchy, the mind.
>
> (1.9–16)

The opening description of Dulness's throne in Bethlehem Hospital introduces the image that comes to define her and her realm. We first encounter her in the "Cave of Poverty and Poetry" where "Keen, hollow winds howl thro' the bleak recess, / Emblem of Music caus'd by Emptiness" (1.34–36).

This "Emptiness," in the form of empty air, empty sound, and empty phantoms, pervades the poem. Later in book 1, Cibber calls upon Dulness for inspiration by the name of "Emptiness" (185). Empty noise echoes through the city during the noise contest of book 2. And empty air is all the well-bred gentleman of book 4, back from the grand tour and a candidate in Dulness's degree-conferring ceremony, can claim for his education:

> . . . he saunter'd Europe round,
> And gather'd ev'ry Vice on Christian Ground;
> .   .   .   .
> Dropt the dull lumber of the Latin store,
> Spoil'd his own language, and acquir'd no more;
> All Classic learning lost on Classic ground;
> And last turn'd *Air*, the Echo of a Sound!
>
> (4.311–322)

Empty phantoms and shadows like this one populate the poem. At the end of book 4, all of modern youth—"trifling," "narrow'd," and "contracted" by corrupt education—is shrunk down to Dulness's "gentle shadow" (ll. 504–509).

In the same way that Addison's Lady Credit is visited repeatedly by dances of "Phantoms," Dulness is attended frequently by emblematic specters and dancing abstractions. As she sits on her throne in book 1, she is entertained by a dance of "Metaphors" (l. 67). For the games of book 2, she herself creates the "phantom" of a poet, a "tall Nothing" formed of "well-body'd air," to whom she gives "A brain of feathers, and a heart of lead; / And empty words . . . and sounding strain" (ll. 44–45, 50, 110). When at the end of the game this phantom poet melts into the air "Like forms in clouds, or visions of the night" (l. 112), Dulness creates other empty figures out of her own dunces and sets the contestants running after them:

> Three wicked imps, of her own Grubstreet choir,
> She deck'd like Congreve, Addison, and Prior;
> Mears, Warner, Wilkins run: delusive thought!
> Breval, Bond, Besaleel, the varlets caught.
> Curl stretches after Gay, but Gay is gone,
> He grasps an empty Joseph for a John.
>
> (2.123–128)

In this case the phantoms are so numerous they must be run together in a list. And in the last couplet here, Pope even refers to a ghost created by the printing industry; as he says in his note, Joseph stands for "Joseph Gay, a fictitious name put by Curl before several pamphlets, which made them pass with many for Mr. Gay's" (2.128n.). In the course of her conferring of degrees in book 4, Dulness is visited by a long parade of phantoms, each representing a different aspect of the depravity of modern culture. The "soft sliding" form of Opera and the "Spectre" of the oppressive schoolmaster Richard Busby (ll. 45, 139) are explicitly named as phantoms in this passage, but all these figures reflect the abstract, empty nature of Dulness's empire and its constituents, and echo the essential "Non-entity" at the center of Dulness's character.[20]

The development of the idea of Dulness's "emptiness" emerges directly from the descriptions of credit that Defoe elaborates in his accounts of Lady Credit and in his contemporary *Essay upon Publick Credit* (1710). As

---

[20] Nicholson also engages with these phantoms, which he describes as a theme of "fraudulent equivalencies," a form of the "promissory note" of contemporary stock jobbing (192, 194, 198).

we have seen, for Defoe credit embodies the "Mystery" of modern economics; it is an "invisible Phantosm," an "Emblem of a something, tho' it self nothing" (*Review*, 6:31, p. 122). He explains this notion in vivid detail in the *Essay upon Publick Credit*. Credit is

> like the Wind that blows *where it lists*, we hear the *sound* thereof, but hardly know *whence it comes*, or *whither it goes*.
>   *Like the Soul* in the Body, it acts all Substance, yet is it self Immaterial: it gives Motion, yet it self cannot be said to Exist; it creates *Forms*, yet has it self *no Form*; it is neither Quantity or Quality; it has no *Whereness*, or *Whenness*, *Scite*, or *Habit*. . . . It is the essential Shadow of something that is Not . . . . To come [at a] direct and clear Understanding of the Thing, the best Method will be to describe its *Operations*, rather than defining its *Nature*: to show *how it Acts* rather than *how it Exists*, and *what it does*, rather than *what it is*. . . .
>   CREDIT is . . . the quickning SOMETHING, that gives Life to *Trade*, . . . 'tis the . . . *Spirits* in the Heart of all the Negoce, Trade, Cash, and Commerce in the World.[21]

This issue of the immateriality of modern financial arrangements returns repeatedly in Defoe's writings on credit:

> That substantial Non-Entity call'd CREDIT, seems to have a distinct Essence (*if nothing can be said to exist*) from all the Phaenomena in Nature; it is in it self the lightest and most volatile Body in the World, moveable beyond the Swiftness of Lightning; the greatest alchymists could never fix its Mercury, or find out its Quality; it is neither a Soul or a Body; it is neither visible or invisible; it is all Consequence, and yet not the Effect of a Cause; it is a Being without Matter, a Substance without Form—A perfect free Agent acting by Wheels and Springs absolutely undiscover'd. (*Review*, 6:31, p. 122)

John F. O'Brien describes Defoe's *Essay* as a "riot of figurative language," a proliferation of metaphors that demonstrates a distinctive imaginative approach to the representation of modern finance.[22] In these passages, winds, shadows, phantoms, and insubstantiality figure forth, for Defoe,

---

[21] Daniel Defoe, *An Essay upon Publick Credit* (London, 1710), 6, 9.
[22] John F. O'Brien, "The Character of Credit: Defoe's 'Lady Credit,' *The Fortunate Mistress*, and the Resources of Inconsistency in Early Eighteenth-Century Britain," *ELH* 63 (1996): 603–632; these quotes, 612–613.

the nature of public credit.[23] Defoe's account, applied to the phantoms and winds of the *Dunciad*, enables us to see the cumulative significance of those images both for the characterization of Dulness and for the poem's encounter with modernity. The endemic "Emptiness" of the *Dunciad* is systematically built upon the contemporary imaginative encounter with modern finance in the fable of Lady Credit, an encounter consistently figured through the female body.

Regularly, in the literary culture of this period, such emptiness is represented as a female quality. The possibility that woman herself is unknowable, that she can only be known by the objects with which she is adorned, or that she is an empty vessel, a painted surface with nothing beneath, is a central constituent of another cultural fable, the fable of commodification, which we have already seen to be evoked briefly in Defoe's representation of Lady Credit's toilet scene, where she must wash her face with a sponge. In the case of Defoe's *Review* essay on the parliamentary sponge, the evocation of the fable of commodification is a gesture, based on a local parallel with an event within the fable of Lady Credit. In the *Dunciad* these two fables are closely interwoven. Through its intersection with the rhetoric of commodification, Dulness's insubstantiality extends beyond the realm of finance and beyond the fable of Lady Credit to engage the fable of commodification and, by that means, the broader effects of capitalism.

IV

Even at her first appearance in the poem, Dulness is more than insubstantial. She rules in "native Anarchy, the mind" (1.16), and confers the implications of her emptiness upon the world through her agency as "Anarch" (4.655). Indeed, anarchy is this text's formal premise, referring, according to the annotation in those opening lines, to "a ruling principle not inert but turning topsy-turvy the Understanding" (1.15n), a principle thus explicitly more active than the prevalent contemporary understanding of "anarchy" as the "absence or non-recognition of authority and order" (*Oxford English Dictionary*).[24] This "ruling principle not inert" is

---

[23] Patrick Brantlinger sees in such imagery the representation of various kinds of insubstantiality—"smoke, apparitions, wind, and moonshine"—characteristic of the Augustan satirists' understanding of the "constitution of modern society." *Fictions of State: Culture and Credit in Britain, 1694–1994* (Ithaca: Cornell University Press, 1996), 60.

[24] Dullness, too, is endowed with an energy that distinguishes Pope's treatment of the idea in this poem from contemporary usage. Rogers provides a detailed account of "Pope's conscious departure" from the contemporary association of dullness with "slowness, rigidity, immobility." See "The name and nature of Dulness: proper nouns in *The Dunciad*," in *Essays on Pope* (Cambridge: Cambridge University Press, 1993), 98–128; this quote, 124.

most evident in the lists that dominate the rhetoric of the poem, and that generate the images of numerousness, mixing, indiscriminacy, disorder, and wild dancing that surround Dulness and her dunces. All these effects are linked materially to the prolific productivity of the contemporary book trade, and all allude to the central rhetorical trope of the fable of commodification, which grounds its encounter with the modern commodity in the mystification of the female body.

The prime exemplar of this fable in Pope's corpus, and in the period, is the representation of Belinda in the *Rape of the Lock* (1717), where the rhetoric of listing is concentrated in the list of imperial spoils of Belinda's toilet scene:

> Unnumber'd Treasures ope at once, and here
> The various Off'rings of the World appear;
>
> .   .   .   .
>
> This Casket *India*'s glowing Gems unlocks,
> And all *Arabia* breathes from yonder Box.
> The Tortoise here and Elephant unite,
> Transform'd to *Combs,* the speckled and the white.
> Here Files of Pins extend their shining Rows,
> Puffs, Powders, Patches, Bibles, Billet-doux.[25]

The numerousness evoked in the first couplet, the mysterious transformation from animals to objects that follows it, and the striking list of the famous last line, with its seemingly random mixing of things and values, signal the indiscriminate accumulation of the mercantile capitalist marketplace and stage that accumulation in terms of the adornment of the female body. In this fable, the woman—her character and even her body itself—is subsumed by the objects with which she is adorned in a process that is thematized as transformation and mystery. I have elsewhere traced the prevalence of the central constituents of the fable of commodification in representations of women and empire in this period, notably in the commodity catalogues that list imperial spoils for female consumption, and in the related trope of imperialist anaphora that displaces the acquisitive energies of an expansionist economy: "For you [woman] the sea resigns its pearly store, / And earth unlocks her mines of treasur'd ore."[26] The locution, "for you," is

---

[25] Alexander Pope, *The Rape of the Lock,* in *The Poems of Alexander Pope,* vol. 2, ed. Geoffrey Tillotson (London: Methuen, 1940), 1.129–138.

[26] Soam Jenyns, *The Art of Dancing,* in *Poems* (London, 1752). See Laura Brown, *Alexander Pope* (Oxford: Basil Blackwell, 1985), chaps. 1 and 2; and *Ends of Empire: Women and Ideology in Early Eighteenth-Century English Literature* (Ithaca: Cornell University Press, 1993), chaps. 4 and 6. Ellen Pollak has also defined at length the fetishization of the female figure in Pope's work; see *The Poetics of Sexual Myth: Gender and Ideology in the Verse of Swift and Pope* (Chicago: University of Chicago Press, 1985).

a poetic commonplace in which the female figure, decked out with the spoils of trade, is made to take responsibility for British imperialism. The lists and the mystery central to this fable are elaborated in the *Dunciad.*

At the beginning of the poem, Dulness's "Cave of Poverty and Poetry" generates, in a disjunct list, the whole, prolific repertory of periodical printing, representing the first and most influential phase in the modernization of the trade:

> Hence Miscellanies spring, the weekly boast
> Of Curl's chaste press, and Lintot's rubric post:
> Hence hymning Tyburn's elegaic lines,
> Hence Journals, Medleys, Merc'ries, Magazines:
> Sepulchral Lyes, our holy walls to grace,
> And New-year Odes, and all the Grub-street race.
>
> (1.39–44)

When Dulness summons "all her Race" for the games of book 2, another prominent list, this time featuring the proliferating personnel of contemporary printing, depicts the throng:

> . . . An endless band
> Pours forth, and leaves unpeopled half the land.
> A motley mixture! In long wigs, in bags,
> In silks, in crapes, in Garters, and in rags,
> From drawing rooms, from colleges, from garrets,
> On horse, on foot, in hacks, and gilded chariots.
>
> (ll. 19–24)

Other lists, which extend this effect of meaningless proliferation from the printing industry to every arena of representation, pervade the poem: the clergy is "A low-born, cell-bred, selfish, servile band" (2.356); the medieval pilgrims are "Men bearded, bald, cowl'd, uncowl'd, shod, unshod, / Peel'd, patch'd, and pyebald" (3.114–115). But larger lists mark the conclusions of books 2, 3, and 4. The second book ends with the list of those who fell asleep to the words of the dunces in the final sleeping contest: first,

> . . . Centlivre felt her voice to fail,
> Motteux himself unfinish'd left his tale,
> Boyer the State, and Law the Stage gave o'er,
> Morgan and Mandevil could prate no more;
> Norton . . .
> Hung silent down his never-blushing head;
> And all was hush'd, as folly's self lay dead.
>
> (2.410–418)

The stage farce at the end of book 3 is heralded by several lists, of "Gods, imps, and monsters" and "A fire, a jigg, a battle, and a ball" (ll. 238, 239). And book 4 ends with the apocalyptic list of the extinguishing of the lights of culture and civilization as the expansionist realm of Dulness overwhelms the nation: "'Till drown'd was Sense, and Shame, and Right, and Wrong." In this concluding passage of the poem, "one by one, . . . the sick'ning stars fade," "*Art* after *Art* goes out, and all is Night." First "*Truth*" flees to her cave, then "*Philosophy*" shrinks and disappears, then "*Physic*," "*Metaphysic*," "*Sense*," and "*Mystery*" "turn giddy, rave, and die" (ll. 625–649). And finally

> *Religion* blushing veils her sacred fires,
> And unawares *Morality* expires.
> Nor *public* Flame, nor *private*, dares to shine;
> Nor *human* Spark is left, nor Glimpse *divine*!
>
> (ll. 635–652)

Sheer random numerousness is one effect of the obsessive listing in the poem, an effect that is elaborated in its representation of multitudes, throngs, crowds, and spawn. Dulness is entertained by a "Mob of Metaphors" (1.67); she is pressed upon by "crowds on crowds" (4.135); she is attended by a "vast involuntary throng" (4.82), a mass that resembles a swarm of insects: "Not closer, orb in orb, conglob'd are seen / The buzzing Bees about their dusky Queen" (4.79–80). She presides over the "spawn" of her dunces' endeavors, the "maggots" of their poetic creations, and through her powers even language proliferates meaninglessly: "one poor word an hundred clenches makes" (1.59–63). When Cibber visits the underworld, in preparation for the historical vision of book 3, the dunces lining the banks of Lethe are described, in a grotesque extension of Dante's famous lines, as an unending crowd:

> Millions and millions on these banks he views,
> Thick as the stars of night, or morning dews,
> As thick as bees o'er vernal blossoms fly,
> As thick as eggs at Ward in Pillory.
>
> (ll. 31–34)

This image of the "thick," indiscriminate crowd is recurrent in the poem, and from it arises a trope of "thickness" or inchoate formlessness that further elaborates the effect of indiscriminacy. At the degree conferring ceremony in book 4, the virtuosi attending Dulness's throne are "thick as Locusts black'ning all the ground" (l. 397). In the same book, the crowd of Aristotelians extends "thick and more thick" around Dulness's throne, dashing "thro' thin and thick" in their academic battles (ll. 191, 197). And Dulness urges her dunces on in the diving contest of book 2 with the same words: "Here strip, my children! here at once leap in, / Here prove who best can dash thro' thick and thin" (ll. 275–276).

This representation of numerousness and meaninglessness takes the central trope of the fable of commodification to a rhetorical extreme, whose effects are further developed in the poem's elaboration of images of mixing, reversal, nonsense, and dancing. In fact, the dance is a vignette of disarticulation, condensing Dulness's repudiation of order, hierarchy, and regulation. In the apocalypse that ends book 4, when Dulness sends her children off to "MAKE ONE MIGHTY DUNCIAD OF THE LAND," she enjoins them to "Teach Kings to fiddle, and make Senates dance" (ll. 604, 598). The dance of Metaphors that Dulness observes at the beginning of book 1 overturns the order of literary culture—genres, unities, and the just imitation of nature:

> She sees a Mob of Metaphors advance,
> Pleas'd with the madness of the mazy dance:
> How Tragedy and Comedy embrace;
> How Farce and Epic get a jumbled race;
> How Time himself stands still at her command,
> Realms shift their place, and Ocean turns to land.
> Here gay Description Ægypt glads with show'rs,
> Or gives to Zembla fruits, to Barca flow'rs;
> Glitt'ring with ice here hoary hills are seen,
> There painted vallies of eternal green,
> In cold December fragrant chaplets blow,
> And hcavy harvests nod beneath the snow.
>
> (ll. 67–78)

And in turn the dance of the stage farce that concludes the historical vision of book 3, where "Hell rises, Heav'n descends, and dance on Earth," overturns natural order itself (l. 237).

In book 4, Opera, the prototype of cultural depravity, introduces the degree ceremony with a tribute to Dulness that compactly demonstrates the conjunction of these images of dancing, mixing, and disorder:

> Joy to great Chaos! let Division reign:
> . . . .
> One Trill shall harmonize joy, grief, and rage,
> Wake the dull Church, and lull the ranting Stage;

> To the same notes thy sons shall hum, or snore,
> And all thy yawning daughters cry, *encore*.
> Another Phœbus, thy own Phœbus, reigns,
> Joys in my jiggs, and dances in my chains.
>
>   (ll. 54–62)

This indiscriminate mingling and mixing is ubiquitous in the poem. The "throng" at the degree conferring ceremony of book 4 is constituted by "Whate'er of mungril no one class admits" (l. 89). Cibber describes himself in terms of class mingling, as a "Mess, toss'd up of Hockley-hole [a bear-baiting site] and White's [a gambling club]; / Where Dukes and Butchers join to wreathe my crown" (1.222–223). And the dunces' writings are everywhere characterized by incoherent mixtures and conjunctions, as when Settle, in predicting the coming of Dulness's kingdom at the end of the historical vision of book 3, describes the absurd theatrical combinations that will signal this event: "Pluto [a stage farce] with Cato [Addison's classical tragedy] thou for this shalt join, / And link the Mourning Bride [a tragedy by Congreve] to Proserpine [another farce]" (ll. 309–310). Such discordant mixtures produce the poem's repeated theme of "Nonsense," the repudiation of meaning, order, and hierarchy: "All nonsense thus, of old or modern date, / Shall in thee [Cibber] centre, from thee circulate" (3.59–60).

The lists, numbers, crowds, mongrel mixtures, and mazy dances of the *Dunciad* are built upon the established contemporary tropes of the fable of commodification, and they suggest, as we shall shortly see, all the effects of indiscriminacy, objectification, and mystification represented by that fable. But at the same time, the impression of random nonsense produced by these lists overlaps with the emptiness that we have identified with the fable of Lady Credit; her insubstantiality generates a parallel rhetoric of meaninglessness. And the heterogeneity and dancing that characterize these lists also repeat the leveling and the exuberance that we found in the fable of the city sewer. These three fables are linked by an interweaving of rhetorical effects that makes them inextricable from one another, even though we can identify their separate formal structures.

V

Each of the several fables that makes up the *Dunciad* gains depth from the conjunctions by which it is affiliated with the others. And furthermore, the combination of these fables and their grounding in Grub Street generates a distinctive trope that extends the poem's analysis of capitalism: the trope of reification, by which not only people, but concepts and institutions are transformed into objects. This trope is built upon a representation of the writers themselves as the indistinguishable and innumerable

products of the modern book trade. The names of these Grub Street figures have a special currency in the poem. Pope's opening note to Appendix 1 takes up directly the treatment of the "Persons and Names" of contemporary writers, arguing that the explicit naming that characterizes the
Dunciad is a response to the "abusive Falsehoods and Scurrilities" that appeared in the common press in response to the publication of a work
where such names were suppressed. As a result of this "Flood of Slander,"
Pope claims that the *Dunciad* "acquired such a peculiar right over their
Names as was necessary to his Design"—a right to cite them in full and to
use them as imaginative materials, as if the names now have the status of a
form of property (Appendix 1). Indeed, according to Pope's note identi-
fying the bookseller Edmund Curll in book 2, the names of the authors
are symptomatically meaningless: because Curll "caus'd them to write what
he pleas'd; they could not call their very names their own" (2.58n).[27]
We can first locate the poem's analysis of capitalism rhetorically, in
the ubiquitous list, formal centerpiece of the fable of commodification,
which becomes the site of the transformation of concepts into objects.
Listing in the *Dunciad* is not just an indiscriminate, seriatim combination
of comparable objects or attributes: "Songs, sonnets, epigrams" (2.115);
"show'rs of Sermons, Characters, Essays" (2.361); or "A Nest, a Toad, a
Fungus, or a Flow'r" (4.400). The *Dunciad*'s lists also mix incompatible
categories, going beyond the *Rape of the Lock*'s famous moral disjunction
of alliterative but incompatible objects—"Puffs, Powders, Patches, Bibles,
Billet-doux"—to incorporate the names of the Grub Street figures that
fill the poem. The noise contest of book 2 contains a sustained example
of this conjunction of Grub Street personnel with the rhetoric of listing:

> Now thousand tongues are heard in one loud din:
> The Monkey-mimics rush discordant in;
> 'Twas chatt'ring, grinning, mouthing, jabb'ring all,
> And Noise and Norton, Brangling and Breval,
> Dennis and Dissonance, and captious Art,
> And Snip-snap short, and Interruption smart,
> And Demonstration thin, and Theses thick,
> And Major, Minor, and Conclusion quick.
>
> (ll. 235–242)[28]

---

[27] Rogers reads closely the role of proper nouns in the poem; they typically "unite the
permanent and the temporary, the local and the universal, the heroic potential with the sordid actuality"; "Proper nouns," 107.

[28] This passage has attracted comments compatible with mine from many critics, among
them Maynard Mack, "Wit and Poetry and Pope: Some Observations on his Imagery," in
Pope and His Contemporaries, ed. J. L. Clifford and Louis A. Landa (Oxford: Clarendon Press,
1949), 20–40; and Rogers, "Proper nouns," 111.

Here, through the same use of alliteration that proclaims the commodi-
fied indiscriminacy of the female toilet in that famous list of the *Rape of
the Lock*, Benjamin Norton Defoe, John Breval, and John Dennis are
woven into the series of sounds in a way that alters their nature. Are they
names, or are they noises? In either case, they are no longer persons.
The incorporation of their names into this list has made them something else.[29]

This transformation of people into something else through the rhetorical troping on names is effected also through the persistent substitution
of authors' names for the books they produce. Such substitution is ram-
pant in the poem; when Cibber looks over the bookshelf containing his
own works and those of his fellow hacks, the books are represented solely
by their authors' names:

> Here lay poor Fletcher's half-eat scenes, and here
> The Frippery of crucify'd Moliere;
> There hapless Shakespear, yet of Tibbald sore,
> Wish'd he had blotted for himself before.
>
> . . . .
>
> Here swells the shelf with Ogilby the great;
> There, stamp'd with arms, Newcastle shines complete:
>
> . . . .
>
> A Gothic Library! of Greece and Rome
> Well purg'd, and worthy Settle, Banks, and Broome.
>   But, high above, more solid Learning shone,
> The Classics of an Age that heard of none;
> There Caxton slept, with Wynkyn at his side,
> One clasp'd in wood, and one in strong cow-hide;
> There, sav'd by spice, like Mummies, many a year,
> Dry Bodies of Divinity appear:
> De Lyra there a dreadful front extends,
> And here the groaning shelves Philemon bends.
>
>   (1.131–154)

This substitution of names for books results in a systematic interchangeability of animate and inanimate, person and thing, an interchangeability
that Pope highlights in a note to such a passage at the start of Cibber's
visit to the underworld in book 3, where the authors put on leather

---

[29] Rogers notes a parallel effect in a familiar couplet from book 1: "Till genial Jacob, or
a warm Third Day, / Call forth each mass, a Poem or a Play" (lines 57–58). "People are
aligned with the casual freaks of English weather"; "Proper nouns," 108.

book-bindings right before our eyes, "demand[ing] new bodies," and
"rush[ing] to the world" "in Calf's array" (ll. 29–30). The note to this line
informs the reader that "the Allegory of the souls of the Dull coming forth
in the form of Books, and being let abroad in vast numbers by Booksellers, is sufficiently intelligible" (l. 28n).

In book 2, when Dulness endows the bookseller Edmund Curll with
the magical ability to delude the town with the works of hack writers,
she says:

> Be thine, my stationer! this magic gift;
> Cook shall be Prior, and Concanen, Swift:
> So shall each hostile name become our own,
> And we too boast our Garth and Addison.
>
> (ll. 137–140)

This passage contains two transformations, one dependent on the other.
In order to make people exchangeable for one another—hacks for authentic writers—these individuals must first be subsumed in their works.
Prior and Swift are not distinct persons in this image of transformation,
but abstracted books, which can then be replaced with Cook and Concanen, an equivalent pair of nonpersons, interchangeable because they are
no longer human individuals. Elsewhere, Curll's ability to make his hacks
usurp or plagiarize major writers empties their names of human content
in exactly the same way:

> Each Songster, Riddler, ev'ry nameless name,
> All crowd, who foremost shall be damn'd to Fame.
> . . . .
> Down, down they larum, with impetuous whirl,
> The Pindars, and the Miltons of a Curl.
>
> (3.157–164)

And when Dulness imagines the genealogy of dunces in a "line immortal"
down to her chosen son, Cibber, she has a similar vision of a succession of
abstract names, people transformed into a parade of books, whose lines
and pages make up the details of the image:

> She saw old Pryn in restless Daniel shine,
> And Eusden eke out Blackmore's endless line;
> She saw slow Philips creep like Tate's poor page,
> And all the mighty Mad in Dennis rage.
>
> (1.103–105)

We can see the congruence of all these effects—listing, naming, and the symptomatic abstraction of names from persons—in Dulness's account of her works for Cibber in book 1:

> Here to her Chosen [Cibber] all her works she shews;
> Prose swell'd to verse, verse loit'ring into prose:
> How random thoughts now meaning chance to find,
> Now leave all memory of sense behind:
>
> . . . .
>
> How, with less reading than makes felons scape,
> Less human genius than God gives an ape,
> Small thanks to France, and none to Rome or Greece,
> A past, vamp'd, future, old, reviv'd, new piece,
> 'Twixt Plautus, Fletcher, Shakespear, and Corneille,
> Can make a Cibber, Tibbald, or Ozell.
>
> (1.273–286)

This passage progresses from a description of random nonsense to a series of cumulative lists, which, taken together, mix disparate items—countries, theatrical qualities, and authors. These lists build toward the final series of names, which first render persons as literary "pieces," and next explicitly represent those "pieces"—preceded by the indefinite article—not only as nonpersons but as things, created, again, through a process of magical transformation: "a Cibber." This transformation is a striking and consistent facet of the poem's use of persons. It turns the contemporary individuals, whose names and traits fill the poem, into interchangeable objects. In a vivid and rhetorical form, it represents the process of commodification, in which value is subsumed by objects, and relations between people are transformed into relations between things. In this sense, the *Dunciad*'s rhetorical use of names repeats the fable of commodification in the language of the contemporary printing industry. And the idea of transformation, with its magical appurtenances, also draws upon the fable of Lady Credit, notably upon the magical process that we observed in Lady Credit's transformation of the objects around her into gold, or her reciprocal transformation of herself from health to illness, prosperity to penury, boom to bust.

But in the *Dunciad* the process of transformation does not stop there. We have already seen how, in its conceptualization of Dulness, this poem utilizes contemporary graphic and literary conventions of personified abstraction, emblematic figures that embody a quality, perception, or concept in order to engage the universal in the work of the imagination.[30]

---

[30] On personified abstraction, see Wasserman.

Dulness's empire is populated not only by the names of the personages of Grub Street, but also by a host of personified literary genres, rhetorical devices, philosophical schools, academic disciplines, and contemporary concepts. Fortitude, Temperance, and Poetic Justice surround Dulness's throne (1.47–52); Nonsense learns to cry (1.60); Metaphors lead a dance with the figures of Tragedy, Comedy, Farce, Epic, and Time (1.67–71); History, Divinity, and Philosophy preach from a dissenter's pulpit (3.196–197); Learning flees the country (3.333); and Science, Wit, Logic, Rhetoric, Morality, Tragedy, History, and Satyr are variously bound, betrayed, or slain by Sophistry, Billingsgate, Chicane, Casuistry, and Mathesis (mathematics) (4.19–43). And in the poem's apocalypse, the personified figures of Truth, Philosophy, Physic, Metaphysic, Mystery, Religion, and Morality "turn giddy, rave, and die" (4.641–650). The *Dunciad* is a prosopopoeia factory, turning out personified abstractions at an accelerated rate, even for this emblematic era. The population of allegorical figures in this depiction of modern capitalism is almost as evidently excessive as its compendium of proper names from Grub Street.

And in fact these emblematic figures are mingled with the names of the hacks, in a way that again forcibly yokes the most generalized mode of discourse with the most concrete, and that produces a familiar transformation. As abstract ideas mix with contemporary names, each category is mutually emptied of distinctiveness. Folly meets Dr. James Monroe at Bethlehem Hospital: "Folly . . . laughs to think Monroe would take her down" (1.29–30). As we have already seen, Noise, Brangling, and Dissonance jabber in the noise contest alongside the dunces Norton, Breval, and Dennis (2.238–239). Philosophy shamefully shares the pulpit with the dissenting preacher, John Henley:

> . . . proud Philosophy repines to show,
> Dishonest sight! his breeches rent below;
> Imbrown'd with native bronze, lo! Henley stands,
> Tuning his voice, and balancing his hands.
>
> (3.197–200)

A sustained mixture of classical figures, contemporary names, and personified abstractions ends book 3, as Settle pronounces Dulness's imperialist vision of the future:

> Now Bavius [a classical poet] take the Poppy from thy brow,
> And place it here [on Cibber]! here all ye Heroes bow!
> . . . .
> See, see, our own true Phœbus wears the bays!
> Our Midas sits Lord Chancellor of Plays!

On Poets' Tombs see Benson's titles writ!
Lo! Ambrose Philips is prefer'd for Wit!
See under Ripley rise a new White-hall,
While Jones' and Boyle's united labours fall:

.   .   .   .

   Proceed, great days! 'till Learning fly the shore,
'Till Birch shall blush with noble blood no more,
'Till Thames see Eaton's sons for ever play,
'Till Westminster's whole year be holiday,
'Till Isis' Elders [Oxford professors] reel, their pupils' sport,
And Alma mater lie dissolv'd in Port [wine]!

(3.317–338)

The mingling of Benson, Philips, and Ripley, on the one hand, with Bav-
ius, Phœbus, and Midas, on the other, produces a distinctive rhetorical
dissonance, furthered by the incongruities of the following paragraph,
where all conventional connections are overturned. This first effect represents what Pat Rogers has described as a typical "merging of the mytho-
logical with the naturalistic and contemporary," another dimension of the
poem's transformation of proper names ("Proper nouns," 110).

And, finally, of course, this incongruous connection of abstract concept and concrete name forms the very premise of the poem.[31] Dulness is
matched from the start with her chosen son, Colley Cibber, an idea with a
well-known contemporary personage, and their alliance is represented
not only narratively and thematically, but through a series of intimate,
even sexual, tableaux, in which they are graphically conjoined. In book 1,
Dulness ogles Cibber with "transport" (l. 111); in book 3 she appears "in
her Temple's last recess inclos'd," with Cibber's head "repos'd" on her
lap (ll. 1–2); and book 4 begins with the same dramatic arrangement:
Dulness sits on her throne, and "soft on her lap her Laureat son reclines"
(l. 20).

What does Dulness do to Cibber, or Cibber to Dulness, by meeting in
this way? The same thing that Ambrose Philips does to Learning, Benjamin Norton does to Noise, or John Henley does to Philosophy. Since
these names are themselves only magically animated things—a Cibber, a
Norton, and a Henley—they make the poem's population of concepts
join in their objectification. In appearing in his pulpit with a personified
Philosophy, Henley makes the idea of philosophy into an empty shell, a

---

[31] Rogers sees Dulness as a focal point of the poem's play with names, things, and ideas:
he argues that Dulness "*exists* within the poem as More and Norton . . . do not. . . . [Dulness
is] now a literal goddess, now melting into pure abstraction"; "Proper nouns," 128.

word that can share the stage with the "nameless name" (3.157) of any dunce. In meeting one another in that couplet in the noise contest, Norton and Noise generate a list of equivalent words, in which any meaning is replaced by alliteration. And in consorting with Cibber, Dulness fondles a "polish'd Hardness" (1.220), a "block," a "Log," in a sexual exchange that gives a new meaning to the idea of obscenity. Book 1 ends with this idea of a "Log," in this climactic simile describing Dulness's designation of Cibber as her new king:

> She ceas'd. Then swells the Chapel-royal throat:
> "God save king Cibber!" mounts in ev'ry note.
> Familiar White's, "God save king Colley!" cries;
> "God save king Colley!" Drury-lane replies:
>
> . . . .
> And "Coll!" each Butcher roars at Hockley-hole.
>   So when Jove's block descended from on high
> (As sings thy great forefather Ogilby)
> Loud thunder to its bottom shook the bog,
> And the hoarse nation croak'd, "God save King Log!"
>   (ll. 319–330)

In a contemporary redaction of Æsop's fable, the frogs who ask Jove for a king are sent a "Log."[32] As "King Log," Cibber confers his peculiar inanimate "hardness" to Dulness herself. Indeed, all the personified ideas of this poem are potential logs, empty ciphers in a faceless crowd, phantoms in a senseless dance, "nameless names" in a random list. And Dulness is the emptiest of them all. She is not an animated concept, but the ultimate state of objectification, through which all individual identity, all human contact, and even all thoughts are transformed into things. In this sense, she is both a figure and a force of reification, embodying it and enacting it in the rhetoric of the poem. The reification of concepts—history, philosophy, science, wit, logic, rhetoric, morality, religion, tragedy, poetic justice, truth—is figured in the same way as is the commodification of people: through the listing, naming, and disjunctive mingling that levels meaningful distinction, individuality, and identity, and leaves only a "log."

Dulness, then, is the final stage of an idea that develops out of the

[32] On the political (and Jacobite) implications of Pope's allusion to John Ogilby's *Fables* in this passage, see Douglas Brooks-Davies, *Pope's Dunciad and the Queen of the Night: A Study of Emotional Jacobitism* (Manchester: Manchester University Press, 1985), 96–98; and Howard Erskine-Hill, *Poetry of Opposition and Revolution: Dryden to Wordsworth* (Oxford: Clarendon Press, 1996), 101–103.

rhetorical progression that we have traced from commodification to reification, a progression drawn from the several fables of a new world that this poem conjoins. In this sense, the *Dunciad*'s representation of reification is an analytical fantasy, an imaginative critique that places the mystery of reification in the larger context of capitalist development. J. G. A. Pocock, like the *Dunciad*, sees a systematic connection between a modernizing economy and reification in this period: "in the credit economy and polity, property had become not only mobile but speculative: what one owned was promises, and not merely the functioning but the intelligibility of society depended upon the success of a program of reification."[33] The *Dunciad* analyzes this program by drawing the lines of intelligibility from credit to commodification, from commodification to empire, and from expansion to credit, in a way that displays the complex integration of these various aspects of capitalism.

VI

Through its rhetorical sources in finance, urban expansion, and commodification, reification itself is rooted in an imaginative encounter with the figure of the woman—epitomized in Dulness but present throughout the *Dunciad*'s formal structures as it weaves its representation of capitalism from these fables of a new world. In this sense, Dulness is only the figurehead for the pervasive feminization of the *Dunciad*'s critique of capitalism. The climax of that critique, and the apocalyptic powers of Dulness, come together in the poem's approach to the mystery of reification, in its representation of transformation through the images of magic and generation. We can find a model for this mystery in one of the tropes of commodification that we extracted from the toilet scene of the *Rape of the Lock*: "The Tortoise here and Elephant unite, / Transform'd to *Combs*, the speckled and the white." The transformation of the tortoise and the elephant into combs, and their resultant indistinguishability as items of adornment for the female body, represents a form of objectification, in which a distinctive, animate creature becomes a commodity of the female toilet. The process of production is omitted here. This figure is not concerned with the means by which the raw materials of mercantile capitalism are made into the products consumed in the metropolis, but rather with the mystification of capitalism, which produces the systematic indiscriminacy that makes animate become inanimate, people become things.

[33] J. G. A. Pocock, "The Mobility of Property and the Rise of Eighteenth-Century Sociology," in *Virtue, Commerce, and History: Essays on Political Thought and History, Chiefly in the Eighteenth Century* (Cambridge: Cambridge University Press, 1985), 113.

For Dulness, too, indiscriminacy has a peculiar mystery. As we have
seen, it generates the transformation of people and ideas into things, a
process rhetorically marked by images of unnatural or shocking transposition and by references to "magic" (2.137). Significantly, "magic," "witch-
craft," and "sorcery" were terms popularly applied to the means by which
stock speculation worked upon the credulity of speculators in this period,
especially in relation to the bursting of the South Sea Bubble in 1721.[34] As
we have seen, the *Dunciad*'s lists, its indiscriminate numbering, jumbling,
mingling, and dancing, produce an inchoate animation, a promiscuous
effusion of disjunct energy. This energy issues in the "magical" creation of
new worlds "to Nature's laws unknown" (3.241). Throughout book 1, as
both Dulness and Cibber, in turn, contemplate their works, the familiar
tropes of crowds, throngs, indiscriminate numerousness, inchoate name-
lessness, and random juxtaposition give rise to a series of vivid images of
generation:

Here [Dulness] beholds the Chaos dark and deep,
Where nameless Somethings in their causes sleep,
'Till genial Jacob, or a warm Third day,
Call forth each mass, a Poem, or a Play:
How hints, like spawn, scarce quick in embryo lie,
How new-born nonsense first is taught to cry,
Maggots half-form'd in rhyme exactly meet,
And learn to crawl upon poetic feet.
Here one poor word an hundred clenches makes,
And ductile dulness new meanders takes.

(ll. 55–64)

This image of prolific and polymorphous creation is echoed in the description of Cibber's works. As he writes, "swearing and supperless" (l. 115),

[34] Terry Mulcaire describes the contemporary use of the notion of "magic" to describe
the new economic structures, citing Swift's use of "magic" to describe the imaginary nature of stock speculation. "Public Credit; or, The Feminization of Virtue in the Marketplace," *PMLA* 114 (1999): 1029–1042; this quote, 1032. Jonathan Swift's writings provide
just one example. For instance in *The Bubble* (1735), the crisis of public debt is described
thus:

Ye wise Philosophers explain
What Magick makes our money rise
When dropt into the Southern Maine,
Or do these Juglers cheat our Eyes?

Jonathan Swift, *Poetical Works*, ed. Herbert Davis (London: Oxford University Press,
1967), 198.

Round him much Embryo, much Abortion lay,
Much future Ode, and abdicated Play;
Nonsense precipitate, like running Lead,
That slip'd thro' Cracks and Zig-zags of the Head;
All that on Folly Frenzy could beget,
Fruits of dull Heat, and Sooterkins of Wit.
[Sooterkins are creatures generated by Dutch women out of the
soot of cooking stoves]

(ll. 121–126)

In fact, popular speculation on the mysteries of procreation is a minor
theme of this book. The myth of the sooterkin is matched by the fanciful
notion that bear cubs were created as their mother licked a shapeless
form into being:

[Dulness] saw, with joy, the line immortal [of dunces] run,
Each sire imprest and glaring in his son:
So watchful Bruin forms, with plastic care,
Each growing lump, and brings it to a Bear.

(ll. 99–102)

In this passage another numberless succession of indistinguishable
dunces, an assembly line of identical nonentities, becomes a magical
act of self-generation. A bear from a "lump" or a king from a "log," both
figures extend the dynamic of transformation into the realm of creation.

Such figures of spontaneous procreation are feminized tropes, extensions of the "teeming" womb of Lady Credit, and of that fable's representation of prolific generation. In Defoe's words: "[Credit] is a teeming,
fruitful *Species*, it begets it self, and generates by innumerable Mixtures"
(*Review*, 6:33, p. 130). These passages of procreation from the *Dunciad*
highlight the paradoxical sterility of this process, its perverse self-
sufficiency and its abortive or monstrous products, in a way that demonstrates its difference from the anti-usury discourse of the prior age. In this
period such self-generation reflects an imaginative encounter with the
proliferative effects of an expanding capitalist economy, especially, as the
fable of Lady Credit shows, its financial apparatus, but also and relatedly
its privileging of exchange and its consequent reification of values and relationships. All meaning follows the magical trajectory of commodification as it sets loose Dulness and her progeny to create and recreate themselves.

The generative energy expressed in these tropes of procreation is fully realized in the sustained accounts of "wild creation" of books 1 and 3.[35] In book 1, this account arises from the "mazy dance" of formal and generic disunity that we have already examined at length, when the "Mob of Metaphors" joins with "Tragedy," "Comedy," "Farce," and "Epic." This passage is characterized first by images of perverse procreativity like those of the sooterkins, the "spawn," and the "maggots" that immediately precede it: "Tragedy and Comedy embrace," and "Farce and Epic get a jumbled race." It then moves on to provide a detailed description of a "new world" outside of the natural order, a travesty of the contemporary aesthetic notion of a just imitation of nature. Here "Realms shift their place, and Ocean turns to land" (ll. 69–72), in an imperialist vision that makes explicit that central ideological inversion of the fable of torrents and oceans, where ocean is substituted for land and the *pax britannica* is represented as an "empire of the sea" in order to present a pacifist and benevolist vision of the British empire. This passage also manipulates the rhetoric of the fable of torrents and oceans in its representation of a global vista where the fantastically reimagined locales of Ægypt and Zembla are substituted for the familiar exotic sites of the trope of "expansive view," China and Peru:

> Here gay description Ægypt glads with show'rs,
> Or gives to Zembla fruits, to Barca flow'rs;
> Glitt'ring with ice here hoary hills are seen,
> There painted vallies of eternal green,
> In cold December fragrant chaplets blow,
> And heavy harvests nod beneath the snow.
>
> (ll. 73–78)

This striking scene is represented through the discourse of pastoral landscape poetry, a mode of ekphrasis directly indebted to contemporary painting, where the rhetorical gestures "here" and "there" conventionally indicate the pictorial highlights and perspectives of the view. In this way, the scene becomes a compact but fully imagined alternative *imperium*, arising from the series of images of generation with which the "mazy dance" begins. The passage concludes with an allusion to the mysterious energy that animates it:

[35] The exuberance and vitality that characterize the *Dunciad* has long been a subject of critical speculation. See for instance Emrys Jones, "Pope and Dulness," in *Pope: Recent Essays by Several Hands*, ed. Maynard Mack and James A. Winn (Hamden, Conn.: Archon Books, 1980), 612–651; and Howard Erskine-Hill, "The 'New World' of Pope's *Dunciad*," *Renaissance and Modern Studies* 6 (1962): 49–67.

> All these, and more, the cloud-compelling Queen
> Beholds thro' fogs, that magnify the scene.
> She, tinsel'd o'er in robes of varying hues,
> With self-applause her wild creation views;
> Sees momentary monsters rise and fall,
> And with her own fools-colours gilds them all.
>
> (ll. 79–84)

The "magnifying" fogs suggest a magical force, whose effects are wild, vivid, varied, and compelling, and whose transformative powers, vested in the character of Dulness, evoke the female common denominator of the fables of commodification and finance.

This sustained figure of "wild creation" is fully developed in the final vision of the stage farce, presented to Cibber by Settle, that ends the imperialist history of book 3 and that originally served, in the three-book version, as the conclusion of the whole poem. This passage brings together all of the rhetorical elements that this complex dynamic of transformation derives from the various fables of modernity that it conjoins: the trope of magic or "sorcery"; the image of the book; the indiscriminate, alliterative list of beings, ideas, and qualities; the dance; the inversion of natural order; the figures of generation; and the vision of a "new world":

> "See now, what Dulness and her sons admire!
> See what the charms, that smite the simple heart
> Not touch'd by Nature, and not reach'd by Art."
> . . . .
> [He] look'd, and saw a sable Sorc'rer rise,
> Swift to whose hand a winged volume flies:
> All sudden, Gorgons hiss, and Dragons glare,
> And ten-horn'd fiends and Giants rush to war.
> Hell rises, Heav'n descends, and dance on Earth:
> Gods, imps, and monsters, music, rage, and mirth,
> A fire, a jigg, a battle, and a ball,
> 'Till one wide conflagration swallows all.
>   Thence a new world to Nature's laws unknown,
> Breaks out refulgent, with a heav'n its own:
> Another Cynthia her new journey runs,
> And other planets circle other suns.
> The forests dance, the rivers upward rise,
> Whales sport in woods, and dolphins in the skies;
> And last, to give the whole creation grace,
> Lo! one vast Egg produces human race.
>
> (ll. 228–248)

In its local details, as Pope confirms in a note, this "new world" refers to the contemporary theater: the sorcerer is

> Dr. Faustus, the subject of a sett of Farces, which lasted in vogue two or three seasons, in which both Playhouses strove to outdo each other for some years. All the extravagancies in the sixteen lines following were introduced on the Stage, and frequented by persons of the first quality in England, to the twentieth and thirtieth time. (1729; l. 233n)

And the egg is derived from "another of these Farces [where] Harlequin is hatched upon the stage, out of a large Egg" (l. 248n). In the subsequent lines, the allusion to the contemporary stage is much more straightforward: we see the stage director manipulating the theatrical effects, controlling the lightning and thunder, the sun and the stars, the "snows of paper" and "hail of pease" (l. 262). But as this long passage begins, with a "sudden" and precipitous energy, the figures of stage farce take on a rhetorical life and agency of their own; the allusion to theatrical practice becomes the basis for a sustained representation of "wild creation" and serves as a vehicle for the exploration of the dynamic of transformation.

Whereas the fable of commodification as it appears in the *Rape of the Lock* locates that transformation in a single line describing the "combs" on Belinda's dressing table, this scene in the *Dunciad* develops and extends the trope of transformation by using it to draw together the whole rhetorical repertory that the poem has earned from its integration of the fables of a new world—Lady Credit, the city sewer, torrents and oceans, and commodification. We can trace this repertory in stages, as the passage progresses from the "dance" to the "new world," following the same pattern as that of the earlier dance of metaphors that we have just examined. In this later, climactic scene, the dance is characterized, typically, by a frenzy of energy that is specifically located in the process of reification, in a series of lists that mingle "monsters" and "music," "imps" and "mirth" in just the same way that noise meets Norton, Philosophy Henley, or Shakespeare Ozell. The "new world" that "breaks out" from this climax of indiscriminacy is "unknown": vivid, kinetic, prolific, surprising, and "other." It has "another" moon, "other planets," and "other suns," in an astronomic extension of the rhetoric of exchangeability developed through the fable of commodification, by which the numberless, nameless dunces are substituted for the particular, authentic figures of a classical past: Cibber becomes "another Phœbus" (4.61), Annius creates "other Cæsars" and "other Homers" (4.360), and "another Æschylus appears" in the expansionist account of Dulness's empire in book 3 (l. 313). In this passage, the image of "other" planets and "other" suns generalizes that effect, but also matches it with the expansionist rhetoric of the fable of torrents and oceans, which here stretches beyond its survey of the globe to include other worlds as well.

The "new world" of Dulness's empire is represented in this passage in terms of the magical transformations that we have traced to the fables of commodification and of Lady Credit, the transformations that turn the dunces into their books, people into things, and concepts into empty words. This is the new world of capitalism. It is an imperialist vision, con-cluding and epitomizing the expansionist progress of Dulness's empire that forms the centerpiece of book 3, and it draws upon and manipulates some of the central tropes of the fable of torrents and oceans. Its rivers rise "upward" in a movement that exaggerates the precipitous fluid rush-ing of that fable of global expansion, and its forests "dance" in a parody of the animation of the forests of *Windsor*, which we saw endowed with a "trembling" vitality as they stood on the shores of the feminized stream of the Loddon and with a precipitous motion as they rushed into the floods of that poem's vision of the *pax britannica*. In taking up the fable of tor-rents and oceans, so often used to celebratory ends, the *Dunciad* absorbs some of the euphoria that we have located in that fantasy of expansion. These vivid scenes of creation, despite their deflationary intent, reflect the same energy that we have seen in *Windsor*, an energy that is reinforced by the feminized vitality that the *Dunciad* derives from the fable of the city sewer, and the procreative powers that the poem adopts from the fable of Lady Credit. These passages thus register a comprehensive vision of modernity that moves through and between a variety of cultural fables in an effort to engage the relations among empire, finance, expansion, com-modification, and reification, and to project from that synthesis a visceral sense of the transformative effects of capital upon the world.

But the poem is not exhausted by these stories of "wild creation." The "new world" of capitalism that we have located in books 1 and 3 is paired, paradoxically, with a much less vital scene: the soft, dull, heavy, drowsy, dark, uncreating climax that concludes book 2 and that ends the whole poem in the expansionist apocalypse of book 4. The structure of book 2 is paradoxical in itself: the games, associated with Fleet Ditch and express-ing the vitality we have connected with the city sewer, are characterized by a violent energy like that of Dulness's "wild creation": in his race Curll "waddles" like a bird "On feet and wings, and flies, and wades, and hops; . . . with shoulders, hands, and head, / Wide as a wind-mill all his figures spread" (ll. 64–66); Curll's "impetuous" stream, "flourish[ing] o'er his head" (ll. 179–180) wins the pissing contest; the noise contest, which Dulness connects with "wond'rous pow'r" and "madness" (ll. 222, 227), produces the extended lists that include "Noise and Norton, Brangling and Breval"; and the diving contest is presented as a frenzied "dash thro' thick and thin" (l. 276) in which Arnall generates "whirlpools and storms . . . . / No crab more active in the dirty dance" (ll. 317–319). This compulsive and impetuous running, listing, diving, and dancing is concluded, however, with the sleeping contest, a "gentler exercise" (l. 366) where the "clam'rous crowd" (l. 385) is put to sleep by the "all-subduing charms" (l. 373) generated by a reading of the works of contemporary authors. These "charms" spread like ripples across the "common shore" of a Dutch cesspool, embracing a list of names that summarizes the empty, mutually exchangeable rhetoric of commodification, and locates that rhetoric in the urban landscape of the fable of the city sewer:

> Then mount the Clerks, and in one lazy tone
> Thro' the long, heavy, painful page drawl on;
> Soft creeping, words on words, the sense compose,
> At ev'ry line they stretch, they yawn, they doze.
>
> . . . .
>
> Who sate the nearest, by the words o'ercome,
> Slept first; the distant nodded to the hum.
> Then down are roll'd the books; stretch'd o'er 'em lies
> Each gentle clerk, and mutt'ring seals his eyes.
> As what a Dutchman plumps into the lakes [from a latrine],
> One circle first, and then a second makes;
> What Dulness dropt among her sons imprest
> Like motion from one circle to the rest;
> So from the mid-most the nutation spreads
> Round and more round, o'er all the sea of heads.
> At last Centlivre . . .
> Motteux . . .
> Boyer . . . and Law . . .
> Morgan and Mandevil . . .
> Norton . . .
> Hung silent . . .
> And all was hush'd, as Folly's self lay dead.
>
> (ll. 387–418)[36]

The central image of ripples that structures this list of names represents the familiar "common shore" that, as we saw in chapter 1, condenses the experience of modern urban expansion. In superimposing the ripples

---

[36] In his account of this list, Rogers notes the poem's tendency to level distinctions of gender and chronology; "Proper nouns," 114.

and the list, this passage fuses the fable of the city sewer with the fable of commodification.

The hush imposed here counters the energy that precedes it, and closely prefigures the scene of "Universal Darkness" that ends book 4, in which sleep spreads with the same trope of widening ripples and the same allusion to the common shore, and including, as we have seen, another summary list, this one of the poem's reified abstractions, which takes the place of the list of names that ends book 2:

> More she had spoke, but yawn'd——All Nature nods:
> What Mortal can resist the Yawn of Gods?
> . . . .
> Wide, and more wide, it spread o'er all the realm;
> Ev'n Palinurus nodded at the Helm:
>
> . . . .
>   O Muse! relate (for you can tell alone,
> Wits have short Memories, and Dunces none)
> Relate, who first, who last resign'd to rest;
> Whose Heads she partly, whose completely blest;
> What Charms could Faction, what Ambition lull,
> The Venal quiet, and intrance the Dull;
> 'Till drown'd was Sense, and Shame, and Right, and Wrong——
> O sing, and hush the Nations with thy song!
>
>   In vain, in vain, ——the all-composing Hour
> Resistless falls: The Muse obeys the Pow'r.
> She comes! she comes! the sable Throne behold
> Of *Night* Primœval, and of *Chaos* old!
> . . . *Fancy* . . .
> *Wit* . . .
>
> . . . .
> *Truth* . . .
> *Philosophy* . . .
> *Physic* . . .
> And *Metaphysic* . . . *Sense*
> . . . *Mystery* . . . *Mathematics* . . .
>
> . . . .
> *Religion* . . .
> And . . . *Morality* expires.
>
> . . . .
> Lo! thy dread Empire, CHAOS! is restor'd;
> Light dies before thy uncreating word:

Thy hand, great Anarch! Lets the curtain fall;
And Universal Darkness buries All.

(ll. 605–666)

The theatrical drama of book 3 is directly countered by the final falling of the curtain in this book, locating Dulness's empire at the moment of the closing off of representation, rather than within the scene of the stage farce. The "refulgent" light and "other suns" of book 3 contrast strongly with the "all-composing" darkness of book 4, where "the sick'ning stars fade" from the sky and "*Art* after *Art* goes out, and all is Night" (ll. 636, 640). The juxtaposition of these images of vitality and dulness, light and darkness, reproduces on a grand scale the poem's local oxymorons: Dulness shines in "clouded majesty" at the beginning of book 1 (l. 45) and again at the opening of book 4 where a cloud conceals her head and "In broad Effulgence all below [is] reveal'd, / ('Tis thus aspiring Dulness ever shines)" (ll. 18–19); the dunces are "precipitately dull" (2.316); and Dulness's force is "inertly strong" (4.7).

Like the oxymoron, these two global visions are intimately joined, mutual figurations of the same imaginative analysis of capitalism. Both are based on the indiscriminate listing—of names or concepts—that signals the poem's engagement with the fable of commodification; both cite the "magic," "charms," or "trance" that we have associated with the transforming powers of the fables of commodification and of Lady Credit; both evoke the complex implications of the fable of the city sewer—its vitality, its heterogeneity, its leveling effects; both adopt and manipulate the imperialist rhetoric that we have associated with the fable of torrents and oceans. And both shape from these fables reciprocal visions of modernity. Like the fable of torrents and oceans, whose hopes and fears describe this same encounter with modern history and project this same paradoxical climax, the *Dunciad* matches admiration with revulsion, exhilaration with anxiety, unbounded energy with ultimate threat, promise with despair. It sees, on the one hand, the extinction of all systems of order and meaning, all structures of relation and value; but on the other hand, an unexpected, unpredictable, vital, and explosive new world shaped by the irresistible energies of capitalism.[37]

---

[37] In a compatible reading of the poem, Nicholson emphasizes its "reification of human aspirations" and its prescient similarity to Marx's representation of modern political economy. He concludes that "*The Dunciad* . . . shadows forth uncertain futures" (194–195, 200). And Mulcaire in her summary account of the effect of Lady Credit, evokes the same paradoxical dynamic: Lady Credit reflects both "the revolutionary promises of the new market" and "its striking liabilities," the "radically unstable power of the aesthetic imagination" and its "frightening volatility" (1030, 1035).

VII

The *Dunciad* is a complex synthesis of contemporary fables of modernity, drawing together the intersecting tropes that variously constitute these fables—tropes of urban experience, exuberance, heterogeneity, dancing, vitality, imperialist expansion, global survey, fluid potency, hopes and fears, financial volatility, emptiness, phantoms, randomness, anarchy, nonsense, procreation, indiscriminacy, mixing, commodification, accumulation, economic productivity, profitability, transformation, magic, objectification, mystification, and reification. The alignment of these fables within a single literary text gives us a way of seeing the *Dunciad* as an integrative cultural event, in which the many dimensions of its discourse are accommodated to a sole imaginative project. And it exposes the analytical nature of that project, in the arrangements that specify the lines of connection among these various experiences of modernity. But the *Dunciad* also gives us a proof text for the relationships among these fables, a way of seeing a whole genre of cultural production at once, and of mapping, in a larger frame than that provided by the single cultural fable, a significant aspect of the relationship between literature and history.

The genre that these several cultural fables constitute has a very visible common theme, which the aegis of Dulness serves to emphasize. Between and among all these tropes, the figure of the woman supplies a series of imaginative transitions, superimpositions, intersections, and affiliations. The female womb underlies the representation of urban expansion as well as that of the fluctuations of modern finance; it generates images of teeming creation, ideas of unbounded heterogeneity, and figures of volatility. The mystery of female identity animates phantoms, emptiness, and anarchy; it stands as the site of mystification behind the tropes of indiscriminacy, accumulation, and commodification; it shapes the rhetoric of reification; and it merges with the powers of transformation. Woman is a catalyst, an implement, and a mediator of the modern cultural imagination; she enables these stories to occupy the same imaginative space in the *Dunciad*'s encounter with capitalism. But she is a catalyst whose role reconstitutes her own nature: in the collective imagination of the eighteenth century, capitalism is an exfoliation of the female, and the woman is associated with the deepest paradoxes, promises, and threats of modernity.

The notion of the prominence of the female figure in eighteenth-century literary culture is not new. Indeed, the role of the woman has been a sustained theme in critical studies of the period throughout the last half-century. Ian Watt's notion of "realism of presentation" singled out Richardson's representation of the female protagonist as the crucial progenitor of the realist novel, the agent of generic transformation. This position, and its feminist successors, has dominated the account of eighteenth-century fiction. Extensive work on the ideology of domesticity and the cult of sensibility has focused attention on female conduct and the ideological significance of a female "private sphere." Feminist critics have pointed out the prominence of women in eighteenth-century satiric writing. Others have seen the representation of women as central to imperialist ideology or to a culture of consumption. And from the perspective of politics, J. G. A. Pocock has speculated on the feminization of the idea of "economic man" in this period:

> [He] was seen on the whole as a feminised, even an effeminate
> being, still wrestling with his own passions and hysterias and with
> interior and exterior forces let loose by his fantasies and appetites,
> and symbolised by such archetypically female goddesses of disorder
> as Fortune, Luxury, and most recently Credit herself. . . . There-
> fore, in the eighteenth-century debate over the new relations of
> polity to economy, production and exchange are regularly equated
> with the ascendancy of the passions and the female principle. (114)

The *Dunciad*, in its own formal heterogeneity and through its own cultural syntheses, helps to articulate the various perspectives on this question of the role of the woman in this period. The political, medical, economic, financial, social, and literary dimensions of her prominence, taken together, suggest that she is not a casual, occasional, or discrete facilitator, but a much larger player in the cultural activities of the age. She expresses a powerful collective contemporary experience of history. As we shall see in the chapters that follow, another figure of difference, the non-European "native," plays a similar animating role in eighteenth-century print culture, attracting and focusing various dimensions of the experience of modernity in ways that alternately distance and embrace alterity.

PART III : ALTERITY

Joshua Reynolds, *Omai* (1775). From the Castle Howard Collection, by permission of the Castle Howard Estate.

CHAPTER 5

Spectacles of Cultural Contact: The Fable of the Native Prince

O N February 1, 1749, an African "prince" and his companion, recently ransomed from slavery in Barbados, attended a performance of Thomas Southerne's tragedy *Oroonoko* at the Covent Garden Theater in London. Their response to the play, a public spectacle that rivaled the drama itself, was recorded in *The Gentleman's Magazine* for February 2:

> They were received with a loud clap of applause, which they acknowledged with a very genteel bow, and took their seats in a box. The seeing persons of their own colour on the stage, apparently in the same distress from which they had been so lately delivered, the tender interview between *Imoinda* and *Oroonoko*, who was betrayed by the treachery of a captain, his account of his sufferings, and the repeated abuse of his placability and confidence, strongly affected them with that generous grief which pure nature always feels, and art had not yet taught them to suppress; the young prince was so far overcome, that he was obliged to retire at the end of the fourth act. His companion remained, but wept the whole time; a circumstance which affected the audience yet more than the play, and doubled the tears which were shed for *Oroonoko* and *Imoinda*.[1]

Four years later, another weeping aristocrat claimed center stage in the developing cultural drama of masculine sensibility. Samuel Richardson's

---

[1] *The Gentleman's Magazine*, 19 (1749): 90.

Sir Charles Grandison, in a series of scenes of affect and precipitous re-
tirement that mark his encounters with his pathetically deranged Italian
Catholic lover, Clementina, demonstrates the same "generous grief" at
the account of suffering, and the same participation in the mirroring
process that "doubles" the tears recorded at these paradigmatic moments.
In one of the last of such scenes, in an encounter in the garden after the
lovers have determined that their religious differences prevent their mar-
rying, Sir Charles announces his plan to leave Italy and Clementina for-
ever. Sir Charles hesitantly names the day of his intended departure:

> ——SUNDAY EVENING, if you please, I will——I could not speak out
> the sentence.
> She burst into tears; reclined her face on my shoulder——her
> bosom heaved——and she sobbed out——Oh, Chevalier! [her
> name for Sir Charles] ——*Must, must*——But *be* it——*Be* it so!——
> And God Almighty strengthen the minds of both!
> The Marchioness, who was coming towards us, saw at distance
> the emotion of her beloved daughter, and fearing she was fainting,
> hastened to her, and clasping her arms about her——My child, my
> Clementina, said she——Why these streaming eyes? . . .
> I arose, and walked into a cross alley from them. I was greatly
> affected! . . . Why have I a heart so susceptible; yet such demands
> upon it for fortitude?[2]

The audience for these central scenes in *Sir Charles Grandison* signifies cultural difference: it is a group of devoted and eloquent Roman Catholics,
the extended family of the noble Clementina, who understand a marriage
between Clementina and the Protestant Grandison to entail the loss of
Clementina's immortal soul. Religious difference of precisely this sort was
a major and ubiquitous factor in the formation of British national identity
in the eighteenth century, functioning both to define a unified Protestant
nation against the internal alterity of Catholicism and to distinguish the
English from the "heathen" populations of the globe. Linda Colley describes what she calls the "Protestant construction of British identity":

> Protestantism . . . gave the majority of men and women a sense of
> their place in history and a sense of worth. It allowed them to feel
> pride in such advantages as they genuinely did enjoy, and helped
> them endure when hardship and danger threatened. It gave them

[2] Samuel Richardson, *Sir Charles Grandison*, ed. Jocelyn Harris (Oxford: Oxford University Press, 1972), 2:632.

identity . . . to the question: Who were the British, and did they even exist? Protestantism could supply a potent and effective answer, perhaps the only satisfactory answer possible. . . . And as long as a sense of mission and providential destiny could be kept alive, by means of maintaining prosperity at home, by means of recurrent wars with the Catholic states of Europe, and by means of a frenetic and for a long time highly successful pursuit of empire, the Union flourished, sustained not just by convenience and profit but by belief as well. Protestantism was the foundation that made the invention of Great Britain possible.[3]

Nevertheless, the Catholic spectators of this love affair, witnessing Sir Charles's tears of sympathy at Clementina's suffering, participate in a powerful process of identification in which their hero's sensibility serves as a model for their own, and for their construction from his demeanor of a moral paradigm for the novel and the age. In the words of the Bishop of Nocera, brother to Clementina, as he embraces Sir Charles: "O Grandison! You are a Prince of the Almighty's creation" (236), or, as the younger brother Jeronymo repeatedly calls him, in the formulaic catch-phrase of the cult of sensibility, the "best of men" (231).

The Englishman and the African, each a noble exemplar, might seem an incongruous pair. Sir Charles Grandison represents the cultural values of Europe's most successful expansionist nation; the Prince of Annamaboe, the group most in the thrall of European expansionism through the institution of slavery. Sir Charles is the canonical literary figure of the cult of sensibility; the Prince of Annamaboe, an imaginative redaction of a historical personage, representing a prominent popular negotiation with cultural difference. But between the two we can trace a distinctive formal connection. The Prince of Annamaboe and Sir Charles Grandison are partners in the same imaginative project. This fragment of the Prince of Annamaboe's story participates in an influential cultural fable, that of the native prince, a fable that takes on the problem of cultural difference and transforms it into identification. The currency of this fable runs from the period of the heroic tragedy of the Restoration to the climax of the British antislavery debates at the end of the eighteenth century. Like Richardson's novel, the fable of the native prince engages in an imaginative projection of male character, a projection that condenses a century-long exploration of the process of identification and affect. Such an affective

---

[3] Linda Colley, *Britons: Forging the Nation 1701–1837* (New Haven: Yale University Press, 1992), chap. 1. Citing Colley, Roxann Wheeler describes religion as a "proto-racial ideology"; *The Complexion of Race: Categories of Difference in Eighteenth-Century British Culture* (Philadelphia: University of Pennsylvania Press, 2000), 17.

exchange—in which the reader or observer takes the place of the object of suffering and through this act of sympathy transfers onto him or herself the demeanor of that object—constitutes a major new cultural mode, which has been associated variously with the universalist structures of bourgeois ideology, the intellectual developments from Lockean theories of sensation, the aesthetic implications of literary realism, the innovations in the evolving science of physiology, or even the influence of a female audience in the theater and among the reading public. All these explanations of what we have learned to call the cult of sensibility give partial perspectives on the extended cultural movement characterized formally by the process of affective identification. But the richness and complexity of this movement can also be understood in terms of the contemporary response to the encounter with cultural difference, and, in the case of the fable of the native prince, to the metropolitan contact with non-European peoples.

The "native prince" is an individual from a traditional, unurbanized, non-European culture, who enters the purview of European experience by visiting the British metropolis and thereby producing a visible and public occasion of cultural contact. Non-European, nonurban peoples—especially of Africa, the new world, and Polynesia—begin in this period to acquire the designation of "native," a term that in the course of English imperial expansion becomes detached from a specific geographical place of origin and associated with "a non-European and imperfectly civilized or savage race"(*Oxford English Dictionary*) as traditional cultures are increasingly contrasted with urbanized ones. The native visitor to London is also decisively a "prince" in contemporary English parlance: the natives who attract the attention of the London population in the eighteenth century are consistently understood in terms of European categories of elite status.[4] Significantly, the native prince is a composite figure, including African, native American, and sometimes Polynesian identities. Repeatedly and symptomatically, these separate traditional cultures are confused or exchanged with one another in this period, even within the space of a single text.[5] Specific cultural details are not as relevant to the fable of the native prince as is the overarching imaginative accommoda-

[4] The major early work on this phenomenon was conducted by Wylie Sypher, to whom we are all indebted, in "The African Prince in London," *Journal of the History of Ideas* 2 (1941): 237–247; and *Guinea's Captive Kings: British Anti-Slavery Literature of the Eighteenth Century* (New York: Octagon Books, 1969). Srinivas Aravamudan provides a thumbnail sketch of what he calls the "cliché of the royal black captive." See *Tropicopolitans: Colonialism and Agency, 1688–1804* (Durham: Duke University Press, 1999), 250–252.

[5] The evolving story of Yarico and Inkle provides a prominent example of this indiscriminacy; usually an Indian woman, Yarico can also be African, as in the version of the story told in *The London Magazine* (1734): 257–258.

tion of alterity. Finally, the native prince is also programmatically male. Though female characters served as a common resource for the production of affect—notably in the she-tragedy of the last decades of the seventeenth century—and though female natives (especially Imoinda and Yarico) populate the literature of contact in this period, the sensibility attached to an elite, public, male figure posed a different problem and produced a different imaginative response from that evoked by the vulnerable, domestic female protagonist. Weeping female figures might surround the native prince, but this fable focuses on a masculine cultural ideal.

The fable of the native prince tells a story that constructs that ideal in a distinctive way, which this chapter seeks to explicate. Just as, in the cultural fable of torrents and oceans, the ocean is more than a local trope, in the fable of the native prince the topos of the native prince calls up a complex formal process the general contours of which we can find repeated throughout the course of this period. The ocean is the protagonist of the fable of torrents and oceans, but that fable is not evoked in every reference to ocean in the eighteenth century, and the simple documentation of such references would not account for the formal dynamic of hope and fear, the process of evolving fate, and the climax in a transcendent destiny that we have seen in that fable. In the same way, the trope of the native prince is not coterminous with the fable that often forms around that topos. Not every reference to a native prince entails the imaginative employment of that character in the cultural fable that will be our focus here. The frequency of such references indicates the general cultural currency of this topos in the period, as we shall see. But the fable of the native prince is not containable as a local trope. It is a dynamic formal structure that fashions that cultural currency into a meaningful shape.

This formal structure decisively separates the fable of the native prince from the numerous other approaches to the representation of native peoples, slavery, and the exotic that proliferate in the course of the eighteenth century. For example, throughout its tenure in English print culture, the fable of the native prince is incoherently or ambiguously implicated in the representation of the problem of slavery; but though this fable can be used as a tool in the antislavery debate, it is not constituted in the cultural imagination in terms of a political position. Similarly, the native prince himself can serve the local reformist arguments on the topic of the regulation of plantation labor and discipline; but though it sometimes appears in such contexts, his fable is not limited to those didactic effects. Often, especially in the second half of the eighteenth century, the trope of the native prince shares the idyllic images and social themes of the evolving philosophical and political concept of the noble savage; but his fable depends on a manipulation of difference and identification, which give it an extension well beyond those self-contained themes of innate nobility. And although the native prince might occasionally take up, in his visit to the metropolis, the reformist or satiric discourse of the foreign traveler— in the mode of Montesquieu's *Persian Letters* (1721) or Oliver Goldsmith's *Citizen of the World* (1762)—the fable of the native prince treats cultural difference not as a means of gaining perspective on Europe, but as a paradigm of identification in itself. That is, the fable of the native prince is often an enabling factor in various contemporary representations of difference, but it is not itself contained by them.

In the late seventeenth and early eighteenth century, the fable of the native prince evokes the motifs and discourse of the heroic drama, but it is not reducible even in its early forms to the subgenre of heroic tragedy. And by the second half of the eighteenth century, this fable shares the tone and themes of the cult of sensibility, and its construction of a model for male demeanor parallels other contemporary images of affective male protagonists. In this respect the anecdote of the Prince of Annamaboe intersects with Sir Charles Grandison's canonical narrative of male virtue. But the fable of the native prince has a more systematic formal structure than the broader cultural movement of sensibility, and a more specific significance than the constitution of the character of the male paragon. Neither sensibility nor Sir Charles fully accounts for the fable of the native prince. On the other hand, as we shall see, both Sir Charles and the cult of sensibility—at least as it implicates the representation of ideal male demeanor—owe some part of the intricacy and intensity of their structures of affect to the complex manipulation of the process of identification and difference so visibly rehearsed in this contemporary fable.

I

In eighteenth-century London, the spectacle of the native prince—at the playhouse, touring the public monuments, passing in the street, and immediately retailed in newspapers, playbills, and historical accounts—was a vivid aspect of both popular and elite metropolitan experience. With the major growth in foreign trade and imperialist expansion came the suddenly visible phenomenon of the native visitor—African, native American, or Polynesian. Natives had been brought to England in earlier periods—Eskimos by Martin Frobisher in the sixteenth century, native Americans by Walter Raleigh and George Weymouth in the seventeenth.[6] But in the

[6] Michael Alexander, *Omai: "Noble Savage"* (London: Collins and Harvill Press, 1977), 68. Benjamin Bissell, *The American Indian in English Literature of the Eighteenth Century* (New Haven: Yale University Press, 1925), 55–57.

eighteenth century native visitors were more frequent, more widely visible, and much more influential than their earlier predecessors. Unlike European dignitaries, whose state visits were well institutionalized by at least the Elizabethan era, and also unlike the fifteen or twenty thousand Africans, who were mainly domestic servants or, later in the century, urban poor,[7] these "noble" natives generated a complex cultural controversy and figured forth a new contemplation of cultural difference.[8]

The Prince of Annamaboe, who with his companion modeled the pure, affective response to Southerne's *Oroonoko* for its midcentury audience, was, according to modern historians, William Ansah Sessarakoo, the heir of a Fante chief, John Corrente, from the region of the Gold Coast, who sent this son with a companion to England to be educated.[9] In Barbados, however, the prince and his friend were sold into slavery and only ransomed by a group of merchants backed by the English government, when his father, himself an influential local slave trader, refused further commerce with the British. He and his companion were then brought to London in 1749, where they were placed under the protection of the Earl of Halifax, "richly dressed, in the *European* manner," instructed in Christianity, baptized, received at court, and entertained in elite social circles until they were returned safely to Africa in December of 1750.[10] This prince is the subject of a novel, *The Royal African: Or, Memoirs of the Young Prince of Annamaboe* (1745),[11] William Dodd's epistolary poems between the prince and his purported lover "Zara," and periodical accounts in *The London Magazine* and *The Gentleman's Magazine*, both including versions of

[7] On the question of this population estimate, see Anthony J. Barker, *The African Link: British Attitudes to the Negro in the Era of the Atlantic Slave Trade, 1550–1807* (London: Frank Cass, 1978), 35. On the broader social context, see Gretchen Holbrook Gerzina, *Black London: Life Before Emancipation* (New Brunswick: Rutgers University Press, 1995). Barker cautions that "the visits of such free and sometimes privileged Negroes probably did little to break down the association between colour and lowly status. . . . In the seventeenth and eighteenth centuries there were far more Negroes in servitude in Britain than enjoying the patronage of nobility or of institutions connected with Africa" (29).

[8] Peter Hulme uses the context of native visitors as the backdrop for his discussion of Inkle and Yarico in *Colonial Encounters: Europe and the Native Caribbean, 1492–1797* (London: Methuen, 1986), 228–233.

[9] On the Prince of Annamaboe, see Sypher, "African Prince," 239–243; and Barker, 27–28. The descriptions that follow of the visits to London of royal Africans in the eighteenth century are indebted to Sypher's important research.

[10] *The Gentleman's Magazine* 19 (1749): 89–90.

[11] An anonymous work. See Sypher, "African Prince," 239–240 n.5. And for a brief account of this text (with its correct title and date) and the Prince's reception in London, as well as an excerpt from the narrative, see Aphra Behn, *Oroonoko: or, the Royal Slave*, ed. Catherine Gallagher (Boston: Bedford/St. Martin's Press, 2000), 278–302.

that moving story of the appearance of the Africans at the performance of *Oroonoko*.[12]

The contemporary responses to this visit raise several themes, which recur persistently in the parallel anecdotes describing other native visitors to London, earlier and later in the century. Natives like the prince and his companion are repeatedly brought to the theater, where, as we have seen in the *Gentleman's Magazine*'s report of the Prince of Annamaboe's attendance at *Oroonoko*, their appearance constitutes as much of a spectacle as the play, and where they initiate a movement of reciprocal affectivity in which the contemplation of their response itself becomes a significant part of the cultural event. They thus generate a literary discourse of affect, most directly in the form of the epistolary romance of separated lovers made fashionable by recent redactions of the Eloisa and Abelard correspondence.[13] And like actors in a performance of cultural difference, native visitors are costumed for their London appearance; they are stripped of their own clothing and dressed in carefully designed attire meant to signify their nobility, both of status and of nature. In the context of her evaluation of "categories of race," Roxann Wheeler has suggested that dress should be seen as one crucial "category of difference" in this period, "key to the constitution of religious, class, national, and personal identity . . . differentiating groups of people from one another" (17). The native prince's European costume is a visible manifestation of this fable's intervention in the contemporary encounter with cultural difference.

The most widely attested native visitors in the first part of the eighteenth century were the four Iroquois sachem from the Confederacy of the Five Nations, who came to London for two weeks in the spring of 1710 during the War of the Spanish Succession with France, in a diplomatic mission organized by American colonial leaders to consolidate the Iroquois' allegiance to England and to urge a united British and Iroquois invasion of Canada.[14] Their embassy was carefully and publicly orchestrated by their American and British sponsors. They were supplied with invented royal titles: Etow Oh Koam, an Algonquian Mahican, was to be

[12] Periodical accounts appear in *The Gentleman's Magazine* 19 (1749): 89–90; 21 (1751): 331; 25 (1755): 184; and *The London Magazine* 18 (1749): 94.

[13] Dodd's love poems are indebted to Pope's *Eloisa to Abelard* (1717) and the influential seventeenth-century translation of the *Lettres portugaises* (1668), *Five Love Letters from a Nun to a Cavalier* (1678).

[14] The visit of the Iroquois is documented at length in Richmond P. Bond's *Queen Anne's American Kings* (Oxford: Clarendon Press, 1952), on which my brief account is based. I am also indebted to Joseph Roach's description of the visit in *Cities of the Dead: Circum-Atlantic Performance* (New York: Columbia University Press, 1996), chap. 4. The essential compilation of the documentary materials is provided in John G. Garratt, *The Four Indian Kings/Les Quatre Rois Indiens* (Canada: Public Archives, 1985).

called King of the River Nation; Sa Ga Yeath Qua Pieth Tow, a Mohawk, was named King of the Maquas; Ho Nee Yeath Taw No Row, another Mohawk, was King of the Generethgarich; and the fourth, a Mohawk named Tee Yee Neen Ho Ga Row, the most prominent of the visitors, acquired the royal title Emperour of the Six Nations.[15] Their dress too was arranged for public effect. After their welcoming progress through the streets of London in the finery of their native wardrobe, they were reattired for their stay. According to a contemporary observer:

> On the Arrival of these Kings, the Queen was advised to make the
> most of shewing them; and the Dressers at the Play-house were con-
> sulted about the clothing of these Monarchs, and it was determined
> that part of their Dress should be a Royal Mantle. The Court was
> then in Mourning, and they were clothed with black Breeches,
> Waistcoat, Stockings, and Shoes, after the *English* Fashion, and a
> Scarlet in grain Cloth Mantle, edg'd with Gold, overall. They had
> Audience of the Queen with more than ordinary Solemnity.[16]

The "Kings" were tracked through the city by curious crowds. Some assembled spontaneously when the visitors came into sight, but some Londoners followed them from place to place through much of their day, as the opening of Joseph Addison's *Spectator* essay on the Indians suggests: "When the four *Indian* Kings were in this Country about a Twelve-month ago, I often mix'd with the Rabble and followed them a whole Day together."[17] They were entertained with a myriad of London sights and events, including numerous festive social functions, a military review, an audience with the Commissioners for Trade and Plantations, an interview with the Society for the Propagation of the Gospel in Foreign Parts, a visit to Bethlehem Hospital, a call at the Work-House for the poor, a bear baiting, and at least one and, most likely, a series of plays. During their visit, they were featured on several playbills, apparently on the assumption that the mere claim that a play was presented for their entertainment would draw a large audience of Londoners for whom the spectacle was not the repertory production at hand, but the visible appearance in their metropolitan midst of these representatives of cultural difference.

We have contemporary evidence of the kings' attendance at William Davenant's operatic *Macbeth*—advertised "For the Entertainment of the

---

[15] Roach, 119; Bond, 39–40. On the spelling of the names, see Garratt, 7 n. 10.

[16] John Oldmixon in *The British Empire in America* (London, 1741), 1:247. Quoted in Roach, 164.

[17] Joseph Addison, *Spectator*, no. 50 (27 April 1711), ed. Donald F. Bond (Oxford: Clarendon Press, 1965), 1: 211.

Four INDIAN KINGS lately arriv'd in this Kingdom"[18]—where their appearance, like that of the African princes at *Oroonoko*, evidently upstaged the play. They were followed by a crowd to the theater, where they occupied a front box. But the gallery audience, swollen by viewers who had come "in order to survey the swarthy monarchs," demanded a better view of the kings. John Genest, in his retrospective history of the eighteenth-century stage, describes the scene:

> The curtain was drawn, but in vain did the players attempt to perform—the Mob, who had possession of the upper gallery, declared that they came to see the kings, "and since we have paid our money, the kings we will have"—whereupon [actor-manager Robert] Wilks came forth, and assured them the Kings were in the front box—to this the Mob replied, they could not see them, and desired they might be placed in a more conspicuous point of view—"otherwise there shall be no play"—Wilks assured them he had nothing so much at heart as their happiness, and accordingly got four chairs, and placed the Kings on the stage, to the no small satisfaction of the Mob.[19]

Joseph Roach notes that in this period royalty and other dignitaries were often placed on the stage for the contemplation of the audience, as the Iroquois were on this occasion (164). There they would serve as a kind of spectacle in their own right, but also as an index of the true, noble response to the performance, in just the way that the African prince's response to *Oroonoko* was a model for the pure, unalloyed and thus necessarily generous reaction to that drama.

The visit of the Indian Kings was featured prominently in the print culture of this period. Their modern historian, Richmond P. Bond, records their impact on the "Art and Letters" of the day:

> they appeared in newspaper accounts and periodical comments, diplomatic dispatches, official notations, letters and diaries; and they found their way into such varied publications as epilogue, ballad, occasional poem, prose tract, annal, and essay, composed on demand of purse or self by Anonymous of Grub and Mr. Hack of Fleet Street as well as by Steele and Addison. (90)

[18] *The London Stage 1660–1800*, part 2: *1700–1729*, ed. Emmett L. Avery (Carbondale: University of Southern Illinois Press, 1965), 220 (April 24, 1710).

[19] John Genest, *Some Account of the English Stage, from the Restoration in 1660 to 1830* (Bath, 1832), 2:451. Quoted in Bond, 4, and Garratt, 8. Joseph Roach also describes the reception of the kings at this performance, 163–164.

Not to mention their appearance in works by Elkanah Settle, Alexander Pope, and Daniel Defoe. Thus, the kings had a pervasive and lasting effect on the city, an effect that significantly anticipates the theme of sympathy and affect that was later to highlight the visit of the Prince of Annamaboe.

At the conclusion of the Indians' stay, one essayist summarizes the general approval with which they were received: "Men of good Presence, and those who have convers'd with them, say, That they have an exquisite Sense, and a quick Apprehension."[20] This impression of their "exquisite Sense" apparently led to an apocryphal story of native sensibility. The kings were said to have spontaneously offered a tract of land in the Mohawk valley (Schoharie) as a new homeland for the Rhineland refugees, who had fled to England from war and religious persecution in Germany in the months just preceding the Iroquois's visit. The Indians, it was said, were moved by the suffering and destitution they witnessed in the German refugee encampments at Camberwell and on Blackheath where the Rhinelanders were placed before they were relocated to Ireland, Carolina, and New York.[21] Like the tears shed by the Prince of Annamaboe and his companion during the performance of *Oroonoko*, the kings' purported sympathy for the persecuted Germans makes the native visitors into royal exempla of a contemporary affective ideal.

Various other native American visitors attracted urban attention in the course of the century. One of the Iroquois kings, Tee Yee Neen Ho Ga Row, returned to England in 1740 when he had an audience with George II (Bond, 40). Another delegation of native Americans, Cherokees from Carolina, came to London in 1730, taking up the same lodgings in Kingstreet, Covent Garden, as the four Iroquois had two decades earlier (Bond, 96). In 1734 a group of Creek Indians, led by their "king" Tomo Chachi, who was accompanied by the "queen and prince"—his wife and nephew—among others, were "entertained in the most agreeable manner possible" and widely observed by an excited populace. Tomo Chachi was painted by William Verelst in an attitude of commanding gravity. The question of the Indians' dress, for their audience with the king, was the subject of a comment in the *Gentleman's Magazine.*

> The War Captain, and other Attendants of *Tomo Chachi*, were very importunate to appear at Court in the Manner they go in their own Country, which is only with a proper Covering round their Waste, the rest of their Body being naked, but were dissuaded from it by Mr. *Ogelthorpe.* But their Faces were variously painted after their

[20] *The Present State of Europe* (April 1710) 21:160. Cited in Bond, 16.
[21] Bond, 11. Bond shows that in fact these refugees had been dispersed before the kings' visit.

Country manner, some half black, others triangular, and others
with bearded Arrows instead of Whiskers. *Tomo Chachi* and *Senuaki*
his Wife, were dress'd in Scarlet trimm'd with Gold.[22]

And Ostenaco of the Cherokees visited England with two other Cherokee
sachems in 1762 (Bond, 89). In *The Shows of London*, Richard D. Altick describes the accumulation of cultural events surrounding this visit:

> During their London stay, from mid-June to mid-August, one
> of them was painted by Reynolds, Oliver Goldsmith waited three
> hours for the privilege of an interview with them, magazines pub-
> lished their copperplate portraits, a ribald song "on the Cherokee
> Chiefs, Inscribed to the Ladies of Great Britain" went on sale at six-
> pence, and, it was rumored, puppet showmen transformed Punch
> into the likeness of a Cherokee.[23]

The Cherokees' urban appointments were publicized for profit, since
they swelled the attendance at every site and event they visited. When they
were entertained at Vauxhall Gardens, their visit attracted ten thousand
people, a phenomenon that elicited a critique in the *London Chronicle*:

> What . . . can apologize for people running in such shoals to all
> public places, at the hazard of health, life, or disappointment, to
> see the savage chiefs that are come among us? These poor crea-
> tures make no more than theatrical figures, and can be seen with
> no satisfaction from the pressure of a throng; why then are people
> mad in their avidity to behold them?[24]

This observer's question points to one of the cultural cruxes of the century.
   The stage bills and periodical literature of the time give us glimpses of
other visits of native "royalty." *The Emperour of the Moon*, in a 1702 stage bill,
is advertised as performed "for the Entertainment of an African Prince
lately arrived here, being Nephew to the King of Bauday."[25] "Prince
Adomo Tomo," actually an interpreter employed by an English slave
trader, was sold as a slave and then redeemed by his employer and taken

---

[22] *The Gentleman's Magazine* 4 (1734): 571, 449. On Tomo Chachi's visit, see Helen
Todd, *Tomochichi: Indian Friend of the Georgia Colony* (Atlanta: Cherokee Publishing Company,
1977), chap. 5.

[23] Richard D. Altick, *The Shows of London* (Cambridge: Harvard University Press, 1978),
47.

[24] *London Chronicle*, cited in Altick, 46.

[25] *The London Stage*, 26 (16 September 1702).

to England on an abortive and dubious diplomatic mission. During the time of his visit to London in 1731 and 1732, this "Prince" was "an immediate social success. . . . [H]e was taken into the patronage of . . . the Duke of Chandos, and later in May was baptised at the Duke's seat at Edgworth, in Lancashire. For several months thereafter he was lionized in London society, several plays being performed in his honour." He was eventually returned to Africa under the sponsorship of the Duke of Montagu.[26] In 1733 and 1734, Job Ben Solomon, a theocratic "prince" abducted from his homeland in Senegal and sold in Maryland, also came under the protection of the Duke of Montagu. He was brought to England, freed, and entertained in Hertfordshire and London, where he was received by the aristocracy and the royal family and sent home laden with gifts.[27] And in 1759 *The Gentleman's Magazine* describes a ransomed African prince, who "appeared publickly at the Theatre Royal in *Drury Lane*" during his stay in London on his way back to his native country.[28] In the last decade of the century, Prince Naimbanna, sent by his father from his homeland in the area of Sierra Leone to be educated in London, attracted the attention of the periodical press for the strength of his "attachments to the principles of the Protestant faith," and became the subject of an issue of Hannah More's moralistic *Cheap Repository Tracts*.[29] And in this same period another native "prince," the son of King Peter of Mesurado, was redeemed from slavery and sent to school in England (Barker, 28).

[26] Robin Law, "King Agaja of Dahomey, the Slave Trade, and the Question of West African Plantations: The Embassy of Bulfinch Lambe and Adomo Tomo to England, 1726–32," *Journal of Imperial and Commonwealth History* 19 (1991): 137–163; this quote, 146. Barker describes the "wildly improbable" assignments of royal status to various Africans in London at this time (26–27).

[27] Sypher summarizes this visit ("African Prince," 238–239) and provides its contemporary sources: Thomas Bluett, *Some Memoirs of the Life of Job, the Son of Solomon, the High Priest of Boonda . . .* (London, 1738); Francis Moore, *Travels into the Inland Parts of Africa . . . with a particular Account of Job Ben Solomon . . .* (London, 1738); and [no author], "The Remarkable Captivity and Deliverance of Job Ben Solomon, a Mohammedan Priest of Bûnda, near the Gambia, in the Year 1732," in *A New General Collection of Voyages and Travels . . .* (London, 1745), 2: 234–240.

[28] *Gentleman's Magazine* 29 (1759): 240.

[29] *Gentleman's Magazine* 63 (supplement): 1215–1216. Altick describes other purported "princes," in the possession of contemporary entrepreneurs, who were shown for a fee—privately or publicly—to an eager London audience. At the end of the seventeenth century, Prince Giolo, known as the "Painted Prince" because of his elaborate tatooing, was brought with his mother from Mindanao by William Dampier, sold and made available for inspection at private homes or in the Blue Boar's Head, Fleet Street. And in the early years of the eighteenth century, an "Indian King," betrayed into West Indian slavery and redeemed by a London merchant, was on view for twopence at the Golden Lion in Smithfield. Such displays suggest the appetite of the metropolitan audience for sights of native princes, but these paid exhibitions have a different valence from that of the native visitors under aristocratic or

In the last quarter of the century another prominent visitor captured the imagination of the city. This period saw the completion of the last wave of European global exploration, in which the Pacific became the locus for a series of epic navigations by Samuel Wallis, Louis-Antoine de Bougainville, and James Cook, and the islands of Polynesia attained for some Europeans the status of an Arcadia that seemed designed to substantiate Rousseau's notion of the state of nature. The Tahitian Mai, popularly known as Omai, unlike some of the native princes and kings who preceded him to London, was not a member of the *aree*—the native elite—in his Polynesian archipelago, but he was granted the unofficial status of natural nobility through those assumptions of the spontaneous sensibility of primitive man that set the tone for his reception in England. In fact, a theatrical pantomime performed ten years after Omai's visit explicitly dubbed him "Prince Omai" in the recitative describing his trip to England.[30]

Omai was brought to London by Captain Tobias Furneaux, Cook's second in command, in July of 1774, only seven years after the first "discovery" of Tahiti by Samuel Wallis. He stayed for two years, primarily in London, at first as the guest of his sponsors, John Montagu, Earl of Sandwich, and the botanist Joseph Banks, and subsequently as the recipient of public funds from the Admiralty, until he was returned to Tahiti in 1776.[31] Omai was an instant celebrity, whose influence extended well beyond the limited duration of his stay in England. Received directly into elite London social circles, he was granted an early audience with George III, attended the opening of Parliament, visited with Frances Burney and her family, sat for portraits by Joshua Reynolds and other eminent artists, met with members of the Royal Society, and served as a point of debate on "savage man" for Samuel Johnson and James Boswell. He was entertained at the theater and the opera, and by numerous dinners, dances, and assemblies; he was taken on several provincial visits, notably to the Earl of Sandwich's estate in Hinching-

---

royal sponsorship upon whom I focus in this chapter. See Altick, 46; for these sights, Altick cites Henry Morley, *Memoirs of Bartholomew Fair* (London, 1880; reprint, Detroit: Singing Tree Press, 1968), 248–249, 254–255.

[30] On Omai's departure for England, high priest Otoo ensures that "Britains [will be convinced] / That in Omai she receives a Prince." John O'Keeffe, *Omai: or A Trip Round the World* (1785), "Recitative Otoo." I am grateful to Michelle Elleray for calling my attention to this work.

[31] My account of Omai's visit is indebted to E. H. McCormick, *Omai: Pacific Envoy* (Auckland: Auckland University Press, 1977); Michael Alexander, *Omai: "Noble Savage"* (London: Collins and Harvill Press, 1977); and Neil Rennie, *Far-Fetched Facts: The Literature of Travel and the Idea of the South Seas* (Oxford: Clarendon Press, 1995), chap. 5.

brooke, where he was taught to celebrate Christmas; he made a tour to Yorkshire; and he learned to shoot, to play chess and backgammon, and even to skate on what he called the "stone-water" of the frozen Serpentine River in Hyde Park, during the coldest London winter in decades (McCormick, 162–163).

Like the other famous native visitors, Omai was immediately provided with a European wardrobe, and his dress became a subject for frequent comment by contemporary observers. On his voyage from the Pacific, even before he reached England, he made a tour of Cape Town in an "elegant velvet suit" (Alexander, 66) provided for him by his sponsors. Newly arrived in London, he was dressed for his audience with the King in "a reddish-brown velvet coat, white silk waistcoat and grey satin knee breeches" (Alexander, 73). But he was dressed again in many styles during his stay in England. He appeared in a visit to Cambridge in a "military uniform, with his hair dressed and tied behind" (Alexander, 82). At the Burney's house he arrived in "a suit of Manchester velvet, Lined with white satten, a *Bag*, lace Ruffles, & a very handsome sword which the King had given to him."[32] And for his portrait by Reynolds he was dressed in a European fantasy of Polynesian costume—elaborately wrapped about with a tapa cloth that Banks had brought from Tahiti, with a tapa turban on his head (Alexander, 103).

Especially in his first year, Omai was constantly before the public eye, in his appearances about the city and its environs, as well as through the numerous accounts in the London newspapers and magazines. During his visit, at the time of his departure, and later, especially on the occasions of the publications of accounts of Cook's subsequent voyages, he inspired a host of literary responses, including the successful pantomime *Omai: or A Trip Round the World* (1785) by John O'Keeffe with scenery and costumes by Philippe Jacques de Loutherbourg, and a series of satires, verse epistles, heroic poems, and sermons, as well as numerous cameo literary appearances, like the well-known lines in William Cowper's *Task* (1785) that address Omai directly:

> But far beyond the rest, and with most cause
> Thee, gentle savage! whom no love of thee
> Or thine, but curiosity perhaps,
> Or else vain glory, prompted us to draw
> Forth from thy native bow'rs, to show thee here

[32] Frances Burney, *The Early Journals and Letters of Fanny Burney*, ed. Lars E. Troide (Oxford: Clarendon Press, 1990), 69. Subsequent references to Burney's letters are to this edition; page numbers are given within the text.

> With what superior skill we can abuse
> The gifts of providence, and squander life.[33]

The contrast here between the "gentle savage" and the metropolitan Europeans is a central dimension of Omai's reception.

Omai's cultural uses were many, but his public impact was permeated by contemporary assumptions about his natural sensibility. His modern historian, E. H. McCormick, summarizes the situation:

> Circumstances could scarcely have been more favourable for
> Omai's reception. The educated public were familiar with
> Rousseau's views that man in his "natural" state was superior to
> "civilised" man, that the ills of modern society were due to the
> denial and suppression of primitive simplicity. In the recent past,
> moreover, they had been both instructed and entertained by varied
> accounts of the Pacific. These ranged from Bougainville's lyrical
> descriptions of New Cythera to a sensational narrative of the
> *Endeavour* expedition and verse satires on Banks's supposed amours
> with the "Queen" of Tahiti. Above all, readers in their thousands
> had perused and pondered over John Hawkesworth's *Voyages*, from
> the *Dolphin*'s to the *Endeavour*'s—a prose epic of British enterprise
> in the South Seas. In Omai they saw not merely a denizen of this
> remote region, the representative of a new race, but the embodi-
> ment of that Rousseauist abstraction, "natural" man.[34]

Omai was often described, in general observations of his character or demeanor, as "naturally genteel and prepossessing" (Alexander, 81, 101; McCormick, 117). As Banks himself observed: "so much natural politeness I never saw in any Man" (Alexander, 83). One theme in these descriptions of Omai's natural "humanity" (McCormick, 117) is his favorable comparison with his European acquaintance: according to Mrs Thrale, "When Omai played at chess and backgammon with Baretti, everybody admired at the savage's good breeding and at the European's impatient spirit" (Alexander, 110; McCormick, 169).

Frances Burney's diaries and letters express this same understanding of Omai's character. Burney's account of her visit with Omai, about whom she had been "very curious" (41), is framed by the occasion of her brother and sister's encounter with him in the theater, at a performance

---

[33] William Cowper, *The Task*, in *The Poems of William Cowper*, ed. John D. Baird and Charles Ryskamp, vol. 2: *1782–1785* (Oxford: Clarendon Press, 1995), lines 632–638.

[34] John Tarlton and E. H. McCormick, *The Two Worlds of Omai* (Auckland: Auckland City Art Gallery, 1977), 12.

of Southerne's sentimental tragedy of *Isabella* (59). Against this backdrop, Omai's visit to the Burneys is arranged. Subsequently, when he comes to dinner, Burney finds Omai "a perfectly rational & intelligent man, with an understanding far superior to the common race of *us cultivated gentry*" (62). She accords him the honorary nobility which was typical of his London reception: "his manners are so extremely graceful, & he is so polite, attentive, & easy, that you would have thought he came from some foreign Court" (60). He substantiates his generosity in his demonstration of a polite and natural sympathy for the author, who was at the time suffering from a cold (60). In her account of a later visit, Burney notes that Omai is "so open & Frank Hearted that he looks *every* one in the Face as his Friend & well wisher" (194). She reflects upon the superiority of Omai, the native, to a well-known contemporary aristocrat, educated but "after it all a meer *pedantic Booby*" (63). In contrast, Omai

> appears in a *new world* like a man [who] had all his life studied *the Graces*, & attended with [unre]mitting application & diligence to form his manners, [to] render his appearance & behaviour *politely easy*, & *thoroughly well bred*: I think this shews how much more *Nature* can do without *art*, than *art* with all her refinement, unassisted by *Nature.*" (63)

Other anecdotes provide similar testimony to Omai's sensibility. One observer describes an occasion reminiscent of the sentimental journey of Laurence Sterne's Yorick: "Walking along the Strand we approached an old man begging. Without hesitation Mr Omai bestowed some charity upon him, saying as he did so, 'Must give poor old man, old man not able to work'" (Alexander, 84). And contemporary witnesses remarked upon Omai's tearful behavior at a funeral: he found it "so painful a scene he could not see it finished, but, handkerchief before his face, got up and fled" (Alexander, 84; McCormick, 117).

These testimonies, and others, provide some indication of the impact of historical "native princes" on the experience of urban life in eighteenth-century England. Native visitors were an established and at times widely celebrated facet of contemporary culture. Among the various accounts of their presence, a trope of native sensibility and natural gentility unites many of these reports, a trope that begins to give these native princes a common character, even in the diverse and brief contemporary records of their appearance. Omai's flight from the funeral, like the Prince of Annamaboe's from the performance of *Oroonoko*, shows a spontaneous sensibility to suffering, an overflowing of fellow feeling that figures these emblems of cultural difference—Polynesian or African—as paragons of a

distinctive mode of contemporary male demeanor. The constitution of this
paradigm is often structured as a chiasmus, where—as in Mrs. Thrale's
comparison of Omai with Baretti, or Frances Burney's of Omai and the
"*Booby*" Philip Stanhope—the terms of difference and identity, native and
European, are suddenly transposed, and the native takes the place of the
noble European, while the European becomes the "savage." As we shall see,
the fable of the native prince uses this transposition as a central facet of its
structure, in which the movement of sentimental identification is rehearsed
under the most strenuous conditions—those of cultural difference.

II

The moving tragedy of Oroonoko that the Prince of Annamaboe witnessed on the London stage in the first half of the eighteenth century was
Thomas Southerne's dramatization of Aphra Behn's novella *Oroonoko: or,
the Royal Slave. A True History* (1688), depicting what was to become the
prototypical native prince of the age. Both David Brion Davis and Wylie
Sypher have traced the development of the "Oroonoko legend" from
Behn's work to the antislavery movement of the late eighteenth century,
including *Oroonoko*'s several dramatic adaptations and the many literary
royal slaves enacting similar themes.[35] In the backdrop of recent critical
reflections on Behn's novella and Southerne's play is the question of the
status of *Oroonoko* in relation to the British antislavery debate of the 1780s,
a full century after *Oroonoko*'s original publication.[36] Behn's work itself

[35] Sypher, *Guinea's Captive Kings*, chap. 3. David Brion Davis, *The Problem of Slavery in Western Culture* (Ithaca: Cornell University Press, 1966). Southerne's *Oroonoko* (1695) was adapted
by John Hawkesworth in 1759, Francis Gentleman in 1760, and John Ferriar in 1788.

[36] The play and novella have attracted sustained attention in the last decade from critics
concerned with issues of race, gender, and colonialism. Some examples include: Laura
Brown, "The Romance of Empire: *Oroonoko* and the Trade in Slaves," in *The New Eighteenth
Century: Theory, Politics, English Literature*, ed. Felicity Nussbaum and Brown (New York:
Methuen, 1987), 41–61; Margaret W. Ferguson, "Juggling the Categories of Race, Class and
Gender: Aphra Behn's *Oroonoko*," *Women's Studies* 19 (1991): 159–181; Moira Ferguson,
"*Oroonoko*: Birth of a Paradigm," in *Subject to Others: British Women Writers and Colonial Slavery,
1670–1834* (New York: Routledge, 1992), 27–49; Charlotte Sussman, "The Other Problem
with Women: Reproduction and Slave Culture in Behn's *Oroonoko*," in *Rereading Aphra Behn:
History, Theory, and Criticism*, ed. Heidi Hutner (Charlottesville: University Press of Virginia,
1993), 102–120; and Suvir Kaul, "Reading Literary Symptoms: Colonial Pathologies and the
Oroonoko Fictions of Behn, Southerne, and Hawkesworth," in *The South Pacific in the Eighteenth
Century: Narratives and Myths*, ed. Jonathan Lamb, special issue of *Eighteenth-Century Life* 18
(1994): 80–96. Aravamudan takes on this body of criticism, which he calls "oroonokoism,"
and incorporates it into a reading of Behn's and Southerne's works that sees both *Oroonoko*
and modern "oroonokoism" as a celebration of a domesticated, virtual African, a collabora-
tion with the violence of colonialism (chap. 1).

cannot be said to represent an antislavery position—only the royal slave generates sympathy, and slavery resulting from honorable battle carries no opprobrium. It might seem surprising, then, that the royal slave that springs from Behn's novella subsequently becomes a staple of antislavery literature. But the local political and social complexities of the antislavery debate can be separated from the formal position that Oroonoko takes in the developing fable of the native prince.[37] Indeed, the very elitism of the Oroonoko story—which limits its credibility as an antislavery work—is the main facet of the formal process of identification that defines the fable of the native prince.

In Behn's novella, Oroonoko represents a European aristocratic ideal, associated with the Stuart monarchs and the Roman heroes and distinguished from the common sort who surround him—either the common slaves, who fail him in his attempted rebellion, or the European colonists, who have no right regard for monarchy and who ultimately put him to death. These elite qualities are evident in his appearance, as well as his manners and sentiments. The following description of Oroonoko sets the terms for the physical depiction of the native prince in the course of the following century:

> the most Illustrious Courts cou'd not have produc'd a braver Man. . . .
> He had heard of, and admir'd the *Romans*; he had heard of the late
> Civil Wars in *England,* and the deplorable Death of our great
> Monarch; and wou'd discourse of it with all the Sense, and Abhor-
> rence of the Injustice imaginable. He had an extream good and
> graceful Mien, and all the Civility of a well-bred great Man. He had
> nothing of Barbarity in his Nature, but in all Points address'd him-
> self, as if his Education had been in some *European* Court. . . . He was
> pretty tall, but of a Shape the most exact that can be fancy'd: The
> most famous Statuary cou'd not form the Figure of a Man more
> admirably turn'd from Head to Foot. . . . The whole Proportion and
> Air of his Face was so noble, and exactly form'd, that, bating his
> colour, there cou'd be nothing in Nature more beautiful, agreeable
> and handsome.[38]

---

[37] Wheeler shows that attitudes toward slavery and representations of racial difference cannot be matched up against one another in any simple or straightforward way in this period (253–260). For another account of the diffuseness and variety of the antislavery theme in the eighteenth century, specifically in relation to the sentimental novel, see Markman Ellis, *The Politics of Sensibility: Race, Gender and Commerce in the Sentimental Novel* (Cambridge: Cambridge University Press, 1996), 55.

[38] Aphra Behn, *Oroonoko*, ed. Joanna Lipking (New York: Norton, 1997), 13. Subsequent references to *Oroonoko* are to this edition; page numbers are given within the text.

This normalizing of the African body through the familiar terms of European statuary performs the same function as the Europeanized clothing emphasized in the accounts of native visitors to London in the decades following the publication of Behn's novella: to accommodate the physical figure of the native to a European eye. And indeed, though his setting and the specific manner of his death reflect the distinctive experiences of the new world as they were represented especially in travel narrative, Oroonoko's characterization and action closely follow the precedent of the aristocratic protagonist that dominated the heroic drama of the Restoration.[39] He has the "large Soul" of these dramatic redactions of heroic romance, and like them, lionlike, he pants after "renown'd Action" (42). And he also exemplifies the corollary magnanimity that adheres to this elite hero, exhibiting an exemplary sensibility that ties him to the female characters of the novella. He "never heard the Name of *Love* without a Sigh, nor any mention of it without the Curiosity of examining further into that tale, which of all Discourses was most agreeable to him"; he is "charm'd" by the narrator's stories of "the lives of the Romans, and great Men," for this reason preferring "the Company of us Women much above the Men" (38, 41). Though he is not yet initiated into the cycle of suffering and pity that comes to mark the later versions of the fable of the native prince, Oroonoko here displays that distinctive sympathetic responsiveness that grounds the noble sensibility projected by this fable throughout the eighteenth century.

Oroonoko's paradigmatic nobility, established through this reference to the tradition of the heroic drama, is contrasted with the barbarity of the nonheroic, colonial figures of the novella, who are represented as a rabble "of such notorious Villains as *Newgate* never transported . . . who understood neither the Laws of *God* or *Man*; and had no sort of Principles to make 'em worthy the Name of Men" (59). This transposition becomes a hallmark of the fable of the native prince: like the dynamic between Omai and Baretti in Burney's account of the chess game, the Europeans are the barbarians, while the slave Oroonoko becomes the paradigm of European nobility. In Behn's version of the fable, this transposition is effected through the incorporation of heroic discourse into the developing notion of the superiority of natural man.

But the novella also figures a European world for which Oroonoko is a more direct ideal. Behn's heroic protagonist engages "our Western World" on its own terms, entering directly into the social circle of the colonial elite, "discoursing" of contemporary English politics, "receiving . . . visits" at Parham House, and confiding with Trefry on the topic of

---

[39] See Brown, "Romance of Empire."

love (37, 13, 38). In these passages, Oroonoko is the celebrated paragon
of a world whose values he condenses and displays, a world that receives
him as its idol. In fact, Oroonoko's arrival in Surinam creates a public
spectacle among the colonists, which resembles the excited reception of
the Indian kings and Omai in London or, a century later, the eager social
round taken up by Anna Maria Mackenzie's fictional native prince, Adolphus: "if the King himself (God bless him) had come a-shore, there cou'd
not have been greater expectations by all the whole Plantation, and those
neighbouring ones, than we on ours at that time; and he was receiv'd
more like a Governor, than a Slave" (37). This immediate and unprob-
lematic adoption of the native prince as a European and metropolitan
celebrity is a frequent dimension of the fable of the native prince. But
here that image is not fully compatible with the representation of the contrast between Oroonoko and the barbaric European colonists: Behn's
Oroonoko is both the celebrated paradigm of European elite identification and the noble native opposite of European barbarity. This tension is
symptomatic of the structure of this fable as it manipulates and moves between cultural difference and European ideals.

Southerne's dramatic *Oroonoko* (1695), not surprisingly, draws even
more exclusively on the aristocratic protagonist of the heroic play in its
representation of the royal slave. Like Behn's Oroonoko, Southerne's
play combines the lofty language and invincible actions of the heroic protagonist with both the suffering and the sympathy that characterize this
redaction of the heroic romance. Thus Southerne structures his play,
even more closely than Behn does her novella, upon the love and honor
dilemma that Oroonoko faces, in which his allegiance to Imoinda must
be brought into line with his honorable struggle for the freedom requisite
to monarchy. Southerne, like Behn, gives his protagonist a magnanimous
sensibility to match his heroic prowess. Telling his "sad tale" of love to
Blanford, who expresses pity, Oroonoko exclaims,

> Do, pity me.
> Pity's akin to love, and every thought
> Of that soft kind is welcome to my soul.
> I would be pitied here.[40]

In this passage, Southerne picks up Behn's suggestion that Oroonoko
"never heard the Name of *Love* without a Sigh." After his "sad tale" is

[40] Thomas Southerne, *Oroonoko*, ed. Maximillian E. Novak and David Stuart Rodes (Lincoln: University of Nebraska Press, 1976), 2.2.57–60. Subsequent references are to this edition; act, scene, and line numbers are given within the text.

done, Oroonoko assures Blanford: "I'll trouble you no farther. Now and then/ A sigh will have its way; that shall be all" (2.2.114–115). These sighs are signs both of suffering and of sympathy, and they make the hero himself a paradigm for the sympathetic identification that his story generates in the audience. The confluence of these two effects reaches a climax at the end of the play. When Oroonoko resolves to kill Imoinda in order to save her from slavery, his tears indicate not only his suffering, but his sensibility to the affective power of his and Imoinda's own tale. He enacts the response his story is designed to evoke:

> My heart runs over; if my gushing eyes
> Betray a weakness which they never knew,
> Believe thou, only thou could'st cause these tears.
>
> (5.5.129–131)

For both Behn's and Southerne's Oroonoko, as for the aristocratic protagonists of the heroic drama upon whom he is modeled, nobility of affect is a direct extension of heroic exemplarity. The protagonist of these works is distinguished not only for his military prowess and acts of daring but for the magnanimity of his generous response to the sufferings of others. Dryden's Anthony, for instance, in *All for Love* (1677), is a "god" not only in battle but "in soft pity to th' oppressed."[41] Eugene Waith has shown that the sympathetic tears generated by noble magnanimity—a central attribute in the rigid and hierarchical aristocratic code—serve to elicit affect from an elitist literary mode, in a way that provides a surprising link between the heroic and the sentimental, the aristocratic and the bourgeois.[42] In this way, the noble hero, overwhelmed with the tears evoked by his own story, supplies a new model of masculine demeanor in which elite admiration is ineluctably transformed into sentimental identification. And by this means, an elitist aspect of the tradition of heroic romance retains a cultural function throughout the eighteenth century, even in a bourgeois literary mode. Sir Charles Grandison exemplifies this idealization of a specific kind of elite model, as does the protagonist of the fable of the native prince.

This constitution of identification out of distance is a singular effect of the heroic tragedy, a form that emphasizes the artificial and the remote,

[41] John Dryden, *All for Love*, ed. David M. Vieth (Lincoln: University of Nebraska Press, 1972), 2.151.

[42] Eugene Waith, "Tears of Magnanimity in Otway and Racine," in Waith and Judd D. Hubert, *French and English Drama of the Seventeenth Century* (Los Angeles: William Andrews Clark Memorial Library, 1972), 1–22. See also Altick for a perspective on this "exotic type of hero" (46).

constructing from these qualities a self-consciously inaccessible ideal, fully congruent with the rigid and symmetrical rules of its plot and the baroque artificiality of its mode of performance. This class distance is extended further by the cultural distance that distinguishes this literary material: the heroic drama of the Restoration is a genre of cultural alterity, characterized by a focus on exotic characters and remote worlds.[43] Moorish Spain, North Africa, India, China, Turkey, Mexico, Peru, North America—these are the typical settings of the original serious drama from William Davenant's *Siege of Rhodes* (1656, 1661) and *The Cruelty of the Spaniards in Peru* (1658) to Dryden's *Indian Queen* (with Robert Howard, 1664), *Indian Emperour* (1665), and *Aurengzebe* (1675), Elkanah Settle's *Empress of Morocco* (1673) and *Conquest of China* (1676), Behn's *Abdelazer* (1676) and *Widow Ranter* (1689), Mary Pix's *Ibrahim* (1696), and Delarivier Manley's *Royal Mischief* (1696), among others. In this context, the appearance on the stage of an African slave is no anomaly; the native prince emerges from a form that is premised upon the representation of elite, exotic characters. In fact, Richard Altick places these elite dramatic characters in the context of the popular reception of the native prince's metropolitan appearances: for "the cultivated Londoner [the native prince] . . . was a Noble Savage, an exotic type of hero, the concept of whom had been imported from France after the Restoration and who was now appearing, as an Aztec or a Peruvian, in the plays of Davenant, Howard, and Dryden and the romances of Aphra Behn" (46).

The staging of cultural difference in this drama has been understood in many ways: as an allegory of contemporary politics, as a negative commentary on non-English European imperialist ventures, as an evasion of English history following the political crises of the seventeenth century, as a displaced representation of anxieties about the political turmoil of the Interregnum and the Restoration, as a projection of a positive English imperial future, or as an idealization of other, oriental, modes of absolutist power. Not one of these views, or even all of them, fully account for this genre's unique and powerful obsession with alterity. But the generative connection of the heroic play with the fable of the native prince can suggest a way of understanding the effect of this representation of difference for the cultural imagination of the age. Thus those noble Indian, Moorish, Chinese, Turkish, Aztec, and Incan heroes, so lavishly dressed in the costumes supplied by the contemporary European fantasy of exoticism,[44] open a space in the contemporary imagination for the representation of

[43] On exotic subjects and cultural difference in the heroic drama, see Bridget Orr, *Empire on the English Stage 1660–1714* (Cambridge: Cambridge University Press, 2001).

[44] On the feathered costumes favored in the theatrical representation of these peoples, see Roach, chap. 4.

the prominent contemporary theme of cultural difference on a global scale. The experience of alterity in the city streets of London, or, for Behn and some others, in the European outposts of the colonial periphery, finds its closest contemporary rendering in the heroic play. In this sense, this coterie aristocratic drama supplies a formal precedent for the fable of the native prince by constituting an elite non-European character type with the potentially powerful affective quality of heroic magnanimity, a quality essential to the process of identification that defines this fable. A strange accommodation, but one that shadows the fable of the native prince throughout its long unfolding.

In Behn's and Southerne's *Oroonoko*, then, this fable acquires many of the constituents that are to define it for the course of the coming century. As the fable of the native prince develops, it absorbs the aristocratic tropes that *Oroonoko* draws from the heroic play: the native prince is consistently an elite character—a prince, a king, or a figure of natural nobility; he is defined by his adherence to standards of honor and by his expression of the magnanimity incumbent upon his elite status; he is often engaged in an affecting romantic relationship that exploits the heroic problematic of love and honor, magnanimity and suffering; and he exhibits the affect that his plight is gauged to evoke in a process characteristic of the self-reflexive structure of literary sensibility. As we have seen, *Oroonoko* also provides a precedent for the ready and seamless integration of the protagonist of this fable into "our Western World," where he becomes an instant model of European demeanor; for the visual accommodation of the native figure—through the representation of his physical appearance or of his dress—to conventions of European beauty and rank; and for the transposition of savage and civilized, in which the familiar European figure occupies the place of barbarity, while the exotic, the foreign, the non-European, or the slave becomes the model of ideal European demeanor. By all these means, the fable of the native prince, as it emerges from Southerne's and Behn's *Oroonoko*, signifies difference as exemplarity.

III

In its poetic redactions, the fable of the native prince generates the affect that promotes this exemplarity primarily through the representation of its protagonist as a bereaved, unrequited, or ill-fated lover. *The Ballad of the Indian King*, a popular composition inspired by the visit of the four Iroquois sachems in 1710, focuses on just this aspect of the native prince's story. One of the most popular ballads of the century, it is extant in at least fifteen broadside and chapbook versions, printed mainly in London, but also by several provincial printers.[45] The ballad opens with a familiar contextualization, which emphasizes the striking situation of the native prince in the modern metropolitan setting, and immediately accommodates him to that setting just as Oroonoko is readily welcomed into "our Western World":

> Listen to a true Relation,
> Of four *Indian* kings of late;
> Who came to this Christian nation,
> To report their sorrows great:
> Which by French they have sustained,
> To the overthrow of trade;
>
> . . . .
>
> Many lords and ladies grieved,
> At these *Indian* kings report.
>
> . . . .
>
> They were farther still befriended
> Of the noble standers by,
> With a glance of *Britain*'s glory,
> Buildings, troops, and twenty Things,
> But now comes a melting story,
> Love seiz'd one of these great kings.[46]

The love story emerges immediately from the thumbnail synopsis of "*Britain*'s glory," which serves both to establish the Indian kings' alterity—the natives must be awed by these "buildings, troops, and . . . things"—and also to suggest their integration into this world—they must be readily assimilable to "our Western World" if they can so quickly enter the discourse of romance and be "seiz'd" by "Love" according to the most conventional romantic trope. Again, we can see in this ballad the fable's typically instant link of alterity and identity.

In some versions, the ballad is divided into two parts, whose titles emphasize the romantic premise of the tale: "How a beautiful Lady conquered one of the Indian Kings" and "The Lady's Answer to the Indian King's Request." The story is characteristically simple: the youngest king falls in love with a "fair lady" while walking in St. James' Park. The ballad emphasizes his affecting situation:

[45] The best source for a textual account of the numerous broadside and chapbook publications of the ballad, including reproductions of these materials, is Garratt, 36–75.

[46] Garratt, B7, 52. Subsequent references to the ballad are to this version, reproduced by Garratt.

Whilst he did his grief discover,
  Often sighing to the rest,
Like a broken hearted lover,
  Oft he smote his wounded breast.

The lady at first rejects him, "tho' [he is] an *Indian* king"—with the emphasis on "king." But she determines to accept him if he agrees to "become a Christian"—here, with the emphasis on "Christian." The lady's focus on the noble status of the native prince enacts that conjunction of elitism and alterity that we have seen to be characteristic of this fable. Early versions end at this point; but some copies from the second half of the century add a passage in which the Indian king converts to Christianity and weds the lady, with Queen Anne looking on in approval. These versions, especially, emphasize the effect of identification central to the ballad and highlight the significance of religion in the contemporary understanding of alterity. Through the conventions of romance, the king's sufferings are made to generate a sympathetic identification, which is directly authorized in the appearance of the Queen, whose presence confers a public exemplarity upon this story of the romantic accommodation of cultural difference.

The same effort of imaginative transformation distinguishes the fable as it appears in the Zara poems (1749) by William Dodd, another romantic response to a native visitor to the metropolis, this time that of the Prince of Annamaboe and his companion. Entitled "The African Prince, Now in England, To Zara, At his Father's Court" and "Zara, At the court of Anamaboe. To the African Prince, When in England," these two poems construct a pathetic tale of the separation of the Prince from his lover in Africa. They assume, without lengthy explication, the familiar context of the topos of the native prince—that the Prince on his way to England was "lost" to slavery, but then freed by the English king and brought by "propitious gales" to London.[47] The first poem inserts the native prince into the same familiar conventions of romance that characterize *The Ballad of the Indian King*, yoking alterity and sympathy to the same effect. It begins by situating the Prince in relation to the conventional love and honor structures of the heroic drama, counterposing heroic duty, which requires him to embark for England, against his love for Zara:

Yet conscious Virtue, in the silent hour,
Rewards the hero with a noble dower.

[47] William Dodd, "The African Prince, Now in England, To Zara At his Father's Court" and "Zara, At the Court of Anamaboe. To the African Prince, When in England," in *Bell's Classical Arrangement of Fugitive Poetry* (London: John Bell, 1788), 7:120. Subsequent references to the two Zara poems are to this volume; page numbers are given within the text.

For this alone I dar'd the roaring sea,
Yet more, for this I dar'd to part with Thee.
But while my bosom feels the nobler flame,
Still unreprov'd, it owns thy gentler claim.
Though virtue's awful form my soul approves,
'Tis thine, thine only, Zara, that it loves.

(117)

In providing the African Prince with this fictional romance, these poems focus on the familiar tropes of weeping, sighing, and parting that mark Oroonoko's separation from Imoinda and that consistently function, in this literary tradition, to signal the accession of sympathetic identification:

We met to sigh, to weep our last adieu.

. . . .

That palm was witness to the tears we shed,
When that fond hope, and all those joys were fled.
Thy trembling lips, with trembling lips, I prest,
And held thee panting to my panting breast.
Our sorrow, grown too mighty to sustain,
Now snatch'd us, fainting, from the sense of pain.
Together sinking in the trance divine,
I caught thy fleeting soul, and gave thee mine!
O! blest oblivion of tormenting care!
O! why recall'd to life and to despair!

(118)

So central is this trope of parting to the imaginative rendering of the African Prince, that it is immediately replicated in a similar separation scene between the Prince and his father, who also suppresses "struggling sighs" and "dumb anguish" (119) at the Prince's departure. This naturalization of the native prince through the affective tropes of heroic romance is juxtaposed, as in *The Ballad of the Indian King*, with the striking image of the "Western World" against which the Prince's accommodation is measured, an account climaxed by the emblematic scene of his attendance at the performance of *Oroonoko*:

I long to tell thee what, amaz'd, I see,
What habits, buildings, trades, and polity!
How art and nature vie to entertain
In public shows, and mix delight with pain.

O! Zara, here, a story like my own,
With mimic skill, in borrow'd names, was shown;
An Indian chief, like me, by fraud betray'd,
And partner in his woes an Indian maid.
I can't recall the scenes, 'tis pain too great,
And, if recall'd, should shudder to relate.

(122–123)

This passage subsumes "Africans" in "Indians" with an indiscriminacy typical of the period. Though the "habits, buildings, trades, and polity" of "our Western World" evoked here might at first suggest a space of cultural distance, that distance is instantly traversed by affect: the Prince's response to the play confirms the sensibility with which the poem has already endowed him, in a circular imaginative effort that reiterates his embodiment of precisely that aesthetic "delight [and] pain" that defines the metropolitan world. Is the native prince an "amaz'd" outsider, or the paradigm of the "Western" cultural ideal of masculine sensibility? This poem demonstrates the process by which the fable of the native prince makes those poles of alterity and identity merge.

Tragic martyrdom, the other affective strategy of the fable of the native prince powerfully modeled in Oroonoko's story, is a prominent dimension of the redactions of this fable in the second half of the eighteenth century, around the time of the British antislavery debates. In both poetry and drama, this period saw a revival of interest in the themes of Mexico and Peru that were introduced a century earlier, in the Restoration heroic drama of Davenant and Dryden, which, as we have seen, shaped the central tropes of the native prince's story. These new versions of the tragic fate of the Aztec and Incan princes coincide with and often imitate the major contemporary continental redactions of the subject, notably Jean François Marmontel's philosophical verse epic *Les Incas* (Paris, 1777; English translation, 1777) and August Friedrich Ferdinand Kotzebue's drama *Die Spanier in Peru, oder Rolla's Tod* (Leipzig, 1795).[48] English dramatic versions of the story are represented in Thomas Morton's *Columbus; or, A World Discovered* (1792), Henry Brooke's *Montezuma* (1778)—a sentimental rewriting of Dryden's *Indian Emperour*, and Richard Sheridan's *Pizarro* (1799)—a very popular play that remained a frequent repertory choice through the first half of the next century. These works demonstrate the cultural currency of one of this fable's most prominent features.

In the poetry of the second half of the century, Incas and Aztecs were

[48] As an indication of the popularity of this topic at the time, Bissell lists seven English translations and adaptations of Kotzebue's play before the turn of the century, 154 n. 73.

powerful magnets of affect. Joseph Wharton's *Dying Indian* (1758), whose speaker is evidently a final victim of the fall of the Incan empire, seems designed to avoid conventional sentimental tropes in his violent and vengeful discourse. This Indian does not at first attract the sort of sympathy that characterizes the fable of the native prince. But even this defiant, angry prince, who speaks to his son at the moment of his death, describes the loss of his "much-loved" wife and urges his heir to

> . . . . kindly stab her
> With thine own hands, nor suffer her to linger,
> Like christian cowards, in a life of pain.[49]

The familiar conjunction of tragic love and heroic martyrdom marks even this poem and suggests the power of the fable to infect even unconventional expressions of the topos of the native prince. Other poems of the period echo much more directly those features that came to define the character of the native prince in the fable's earliest manifestations in the heroic drama—the images of suffering and nobility. Helen Maria Williams's six-canto epic, *Peru* (1784), provides a sentimental account of the Spanish conquest, full of images of Indians suffering unbearable torture. And in Edward Jerningham's epic poem, *The Fall of Mexico* (1775), the central scene of Indian martyrdom—the torture of Guatimozino at the hands of the Spaniards—gives the hero the same affecting role as Dryden's Montezuma or Southerne's Oroonoko:

> He said—and to his rigid doom resign'd
> Along the flaming couch his form reclin'd:
> The partner of his fate submissive bends,
> And o'er the tort'ring bed his frame extends;
> Yet then unequal to the conq'ring pain,
> He spoke his suff'rings in lamenting strain:
> "O, royal master, give me to disclose
> "Where in the mine the golden treasure glows—
> "I shrink, I faint, inferiour to my part,
> "And this frail frame betrays my daring heart."
> Amidst the raging flames that round him blaz'd,
> The royal chief his martyr'd figure rais'd,
> Cast on the youth a calm-reproaching eye,

---

[49] Joseph Wharton, *The Dying Indian*, in *Eighteenth-Century English Literature*, ed. Geoffrey Tillotson, Paul Fussell Jr., and Marshall Waingrow (New York: Harcourt, Brace and World, 1969), 929–930, lines 19, 23–25.

And spoke—oh eloquent, sublime reply!
Oh heav'n! oh earth! attend "Do I REPOSE
ALL ON THE SILKEN FOLIAGE OF THE ROSE?"
He ceas'd—and deep within his soul retir'd,
To honour firm, triumphant he expir'd.[50]

In the first Zara poem, the exotic native prince becomes an exemplar of English sensibility through the mediation of the aesthetic, when "art and nature," a projection of the modern European "polity," render his suffering in dramatic form. For Guatimozino, even more explicitly, exotic suffering is given an aesthetic status, which renders it not only familiar, but even canonical: the "royal chief" in his defiant martyrdom is represented as a prototype of the sublime. Here the fable of the native prince effects the same transposition of distance and identity that we noted in its earlier forms and results in the same projection of alterity as exemplarity. But this projection is represented in the new aesthetic language of sublimity.

Our fable has distinctive features and a characteristic structure, but its cultural currency cuts across genres, literary traditions, and aesthetic modes, which it incorporates to its own ends. In the long eighteenth century, it is implicated with the dramatic conventions of Restoration heroic drama, the public discourse of popular balladry, the themes of heroic romance, and the rhetorical elevation of the sublime. While it participates in all these discourses, and draws its local manifestations from them, it transcends them in the sense that it holds to an imaginative experience with a specific shape, the transformation of difference into identification.

IV

In the prose fiction of the eighteenth century, the fable of the native prince finds a more diffuse and extended venue than in the poetry. We can see this fable blended with various other discursive modes, including economic argument, antislavery discourse, and the philosophical idea of the noble savage now strongly shaped by the influence of the popular reception of Rousseau. But the distinctive process by which alterity is signified as identity persists, even through the end of the century. Defoe's *Captain Singleton* (1720) takes up this fable in the character of the Black

---

[50] Edward Jerningham, *The Fall of Mexico, a Poem* (London, 1775), lines 775–792. The image of the rose—derived from the Spanish historians—is often used in the accounts of the fall of Mexico. See Bissell, 16.

Prince, whom the adventurer/pirate protagonist Captain Bob encounters at the outset of his journey across Africa. The Black Prince's physical appearance is a telegraphic version of the public accommodation of the native prince to the European eye, a physical normalizing that we saw in Oroonoko's resemblance to "famous Statuary" or the accounts of the Indian kings' and Omai's European dress: he is a "tall, well-shap'd, handsom Fellow, to whom the rest seem'd to pay great Respect, and who, as we understood afterwards, was the Son of one of their Kings."[51]

Captain Bob perceives that the Black Prince possesses an "honourable" character (62) and decides to use him as a slave driver. Thus, this native prince manages the other captured Africans in their attendance on the travelers as they cross the continent. The Black Prince's nobility explicitly differentiates him from the other natives whom he governs and whom Captain Bob encounters; these are "a fierce, barbarous, treacherous People" (73), more like animals than like Europeans, and utterly alien in their inability to grasp the significance of exchange value. Captain Bob exclaims upon "the Folly of the poor People," who trade "Fifteen or Sixteen Pounds" worth of provisions for a bit of silver carved like a bird, which was "not worth Six-pence to us" (28), and who have so little judgment—or, in Defoe's terms, humanity—as to value brass even more highly, and gold below both silver and iron (107). The Black Prince, on the other hand, fully shares the Europeans' economic value system. He is instrumental in finding the gold that Captain Bob and his company eventually collect, and, more important, he quickly learns to manage it, an indication, in Defoe's narrative, of the native prince's proximity to the norm of European civilization, his recognizability as a human being.

Though Defoe's Black Prince does not appear in the European metropolis, his connection with the European-centered phenomenon of exchange value places him well within the purview of "our Western World" in the formal paradigm typical of this fable. Indeed, this Prince's accommodation is ultimately perfect. In the end, "The *Negro Prince* we made perfectly free, clothed him out of our common Stock, and gave him a Pound and a half of Gold for himself, which he knew very well how to manage, and here we all parted after the most friendly Manner possible" (137). In this version of the fable, the native prince's alterity is accommodated through economic rather than affective means. The Black Prince has no romantic connection and undergoes little suffering, but the assertion of his honor and his elite status—as the "Son of one of their Kings"—trans-

---

[51] Daniel Defoe, *Captain Singleton*, ed. Shiv K. Kumar (Oxford: Oxford University Press, 1969), 57. Subsequent references are to this edition; page numbers are given within the text.

forms difference into "friendly" intimacy and enables him, as the next logical step, to embody the capitalist ideal that grounds this text's definition of humanity. In this case, though, the elitism of the fable of the native prince makes a bad match with the bourgeois values of trade and exchange that dominate Defoe's world. The Black Prince can only be an exemplary capitalist who earns his value by his ability to engage in trade because he is an aristocrat who, in contradiction, acquires his value through the mere fact of his social status. This implicit tension—between aristocrat and capitalist—is a testimony to the relative autonomy of the fable of the native prince, which brings its connection with the elitist forms of the heroic tradition along, even into a narrative dominated by the protocapitalist themes of contemporary economic discourse.

Defoe's economic accommodation of the native prince to a European ideal is a distinctive one. More conventionally, the character of the native prince is shaped by the structures of heroic honor and magnanimity, and their sentimental successors in prose narrative. In *The History of the Life and Adventures of Mr. Anderson* (1754) by Edward Kimber, for instance, the hero meets a friendly American Indian named Calcathony, who possesses a "greatness of soul which he displayed either in prosperity or adversity."[52] Under pressure from the French to turn against the English, Calcathony says that he will "sooner submit to all you can inflict, than purchase life at the price of losing my honour."[53] This heroically honorable or naturally noble native constitutes one strain in the fictional accounts of native Americans in the eighteenth century, alongside other representations of the excessive cruelty and savagery of the American Indians especially prominent in the growing contemporary subgenre of captivity narratives. But in the cultural imagination the native prince remains an ideal figure, even despite these, often historically attested, accounts of Indian barbarity. The persistence of his fable suggests its imaginative power in the period.

John Shebbeare's *Lydia; or Filial Piety* (1755) contains a more sustained development of the fable of the native prince. Here the native prince introduces and frames a story of female misfortune and reward that is set in the context of an extended narrative satire on English society. The American Indian paragon, Cannassatego, opens the novel and in his emblematic character sets the standard of virtue against which the many scenes of corruption and folly that follow are measured. This native prince is described in the familiar heroic mode of *Oroonoko*, with its classical allusions and its explicit visual accommodation of the non-

---

[52] Edward Kimber, *The History of the Life and Adventures of Mr. Anderson* (London, 1754), 110. Quoted in Bissell, 87–88.

[53] *Mr. Anderson*, 113. Quoted in Bissell, 88.

European model to a European standard of beauty: but that mode is overwritten by an implicitly republican version of the discourse of the noble savage:

> No human Form was ever seen more graceful, than that of *Cannas-satego*, . . . his Stature six Foot, the most perfect Height in Human Nature; on his large Neck his Head stood erect and bold, his Face was animated with Features that spoke Sensibility of Soul, high and open was his Forehead, from his Eyes flashed forth the Beams of Courage and Compassion, as each Passion at different Moments animated his Bosom, within which his Heart beat with honest Throbbing for his Country's Service; . . . The Air, Attitude and Expression of the beauteous Statue of *Apollo*, . . . were seen animated in this *American* . . . ; and tho' the fair Complexion of the *European* Natives was not to be found in this Warrior, yet his Shape and Countenance hindered you from perceiving the Deficiency.[54]

Cannassatego is a denizen of the arcadian world of the noble savage. He lives in a country where "the primæval laws of Nature still hold their native Sway over human Hearts; the Views of Heaven have not yet been violated by the pernicious and impious Schemes of corrupted Men; . . . each sympathetic Power darting from the Soul, is received and fostered by that which is congenial to it" (1:17–18).

Cannassatego's sensibility—his "tears" for the "fallen Condition of his native Land" (1:7, 11) under the destructive and dishonest sway of the Europeans—inspires his trip to London to test the honesty and virtue of the "King and People" of England (1:9). This account of his expedition alludes explicitly to the contemporary metropolitan fascination with native visitors, and specifically to the famous visit of the four Indian kings: Cannassatego "knew perfectly from Tradition, that, before his Time, *Indian* Chiefs had pass'd the Ocean to the *British* Kingdom, and returned" (1:9). Like the Prince of Annamaboe in the Zara poems, Cannassatego must part with his beloved Yarico in an affecting scene of separation before taking ship, and in the context of that separation he engages in the familiar debate between love and honor that marks the fable of the native prince in its redactions from *Oroonoko* to the Prince of Annamaboe:

> "What is this Honour which is so incompatible with Love? Must I be deprived of all my Soul holds dear, in Obedience to a rash Pro-

---

[54] John Shebbeare, *Lydia; or Filial Piety* (London, 1755; reprint, New York: Garland, 1974), 1: 3–4. Subsequent references are to this edition; volume and page numbers are given within the text.

posal, springing from Vanity, and useless to my Country? It must
not be."—Then, pausing he would say, "Shall it be said, that *Cannassatego*, enthralled by Love and Woman, renounced his Country's
good, and broke his Resolutions?" (1:28)

Like other native princes in the prose narrative tradition, Cannassatego
intervenes on board ship to rescue a victim of barbaric wickedness. The
virtuous titular character, Lydia, first appears in this shipboard episode,
when Cannassatego saves her from rape by the lying and cowardly Captain Bounce. This scene introduces a rare distinction between the native
American and the African hero. Cannassatego's sentimental shipboard intervention calls up the sufferings of the middle passage for late eighteenth-
century readers, since this scene repeats the trope in which the African
prince steps in to prevent the mistreatment of a slave. Anna Maria
Mackenzie's African protagonist, Adolphus, as we shall see, twice halts the
shipboard whippings of fellow Africans of lowlier rank. In *Lydia* the Indian hero takes on the same role of sentimental intervention, but he
comes to the aid not of a fellow slave, but of a victimized woman.

This scene links the sentimental female protagonist and the native
prince, in an alliance that serves as a frame for the diffuse action of this
novel, and that indicates the imaginative proximity of the sympathetic female paragon and the exemplary native. The fable of the native prince in
its earlier versions, as we have seen, often contains a female victim whose
sufferings serve to augment the affective force of the native's situation:
Imoinda and Zara play this role for the protagonists of their works. But in
the prose fiction of the second half of the century, this significant alliance
is strengthened and extended. The suffering and exemplary female takes
a more prominent place, becoming an indispensable corollary character
in the representation of that process of identification that makes the native prince a model of European sensibility. These female characters lend
to the fable of the native prince the affective energy of the long literary
tradition of the suffering woman, developed most prominently in this period in the paragon female protagonist of prose fiction.

After their arrival in London, Lydia's story guides the main course of
the narrative, though her alliance with the noble Cannassatego forms its
recurrent theme and ultimate frame. A flat imitation of Clarissa, but with
the fortunate fate of Pamela, Lydia confronts a familiar litany of urban
misfortunes—sexual threat, betrayal into a house of prostitution, erro-
neous arrest and imprisonment—in the course of which she displays constant virtue and "filial piety," in the form of devotion to her ailing mother,
and at the end of which she is happily united with a lover from shipboard,
now elevated to the status of an earl. After her marriage to Lord Liberal,

she meets the native prince again, in his wanderings about London, and is empowered through her new wealth and title to aid him. The benevolent aristocratic couple hears Cannassatego's account of his activities since he came to the metropolis, which constitute a repetition of the theme of English corruption that dominates the narrative. Cannasatego is used here as an instrument of satire, just as he serves earlier as an agent in the contemporary discourse of the noble savage. But though the fable of the native prince as it appears in this novel takes up those significant contemporary themes, it retains the distinctive structure of alterity and identification that characterizes its appearance throughout the century.

Cannassatego's arrival in the metropolis affords the native prince the opportunity for a familiar change of clothes—he is "now dressed in the European Manner" (2:76; 3:263). And he recounts to the Liberals the consequences of his visit to the "Great Man," the English prime minister, whom he promised to confront in order to confirm the Onondagan peace treaties and describe the mistreatment of the Indians by the British colonists. Predictably, the "Great Man's" behavior and response demonstrate only self-interest and absence of principle, and he refuses to meet again with Cannassatego. This mistreatment reduces the native prince to a state of despair from which the honesty and generosity of Lydia and her husband, who "have *Indian* souls, unconscious of deceit; [and who] cherish nobler Sentiments than *Britons* know" (3:261), enable him to recover.

Cannassatego's stay in London under the protection of the Liberals occasions an exchange of affecting love letters, on the model of the Zara poems, with the distant Yarico (4:10–15). And the virtuous Indian further serves as the center of a series of set-piece contrasts between natural virtue and civilized barbarity as he encounters a parade of corrupt metropolitan characters. Like the barbarism of the colonists who torture Oroonoko, or the rude impatience of Baretti in his chess game with Omai, these exchanges serve to transpose the places of the European and the native. And like these other native princes, Cannassatego is not just a noble savage; he is a European exemplar, a status that is confirmed in his last interview with the novel's female protagonist. When Lydia and her aristocratic husband send the native prince home to America laden with gifts for Yarico, his departure occasions a final sentimental scene that serves as an ultimate model for the process of identification by which Cannassatego is made to embody an ideal of European sensibility:

> the parting Moment was piercing to his Bosom; he had determined
> to make a long Speech of Thanks for all the friendship which he
> had received from this happy Pair; when beginning, "If Heaven
> restore me to the Arms of her I love, my Vows—" Then bursting

into Tears, his Voice suspended, he eagerly embraced the Earl, and cried, "Imagine what I would express, from what I suffer in parting from you tho' to return to all I love." Then saluting the Countess [Lydia], "My Friend, my next in Love to *Yarico*, adieu; may ye be for ever happy." Saying this, he left the House choaked with Tears, the Earl and Countess weeping abundantly as he walked away. At length, "Go, generous Man, and meet in Joy thy lovely *Yarico*," escaped from the Lady's Lips. (4:16)

Here, Lydia plays the same role as does the Prince of Annamaboe at the performance of *Oroonoko* with which we began this chapter. Weeping at the scene of native sensibility, the female paragon protagonist—herself a powerful cultural paradigm of affective identification—imitates Cannassatego's own response, and thus enables the eighteenth- century English audience to take the place of the native prince and to define through his tears its own ideal image of itself.

In Henry Mackenzie's *Julia de Roubigné* (1777), Savillon, the male protagonist, demonstrates his sensibility and his affinity with the titular female paragon, Julia, through an alliance with the native prince of his narrative. Mackenzie's novel reflects its author's engagement with a significant event in the contemporary juridical disputes about the status of slaves in England and Scotland—the case of Joseph Knight, tried in Scotland and resolved in 1777 in favor of the ex-slave's freedom under Scottish law (Ellis, 117). Though *Julia de Roubigné* might seem to subordinate the antislavery sentiments of its author to the sentimental and tragic romance that constitutes its main plot, this text exemplifies the prototypical role of the fable of the native prince in defining the nature and formal dynamic of sensibility in this period. Even as a minor character, this novel's native prince is a central affective touchstone.[55]

The inset story of Savillon's reformation of the treatment of the slaves on his Caribbean plantation through the offices of the noble Yambu supplies an affective context for the central tragedy of the ill-fated love between Savillon and Julia. Julia, married by mistake to another man in Savillon's absence, is finally poisoned by her husband when he realizes her preference for Savillon. The constitution of these exemplary, separated and eventually martyred sentimental characters is the novel's central effort. Yambu's exchange with Savillon epitomizes this text's attempt to produce, through sentimental identification, an emblematic model of masculine demeanor.

[55] My sense of the implication of sensibility with issues of slavery and race and my readings of Sterne, Mackenzie, and Scott are indebted, in this chapter and in chapter 6, to Markman Ellis's work on "the politics of sensibility," especially chaps. 2 and 3.

Yambu possesses an heroic fortitude that immediately marks his nobility:

> One slave, in particular, had for some time attracted my notice,
> from that gloomy fortitude with which he bore the hardships of his
> situation. . . . On being further informed, that several of his fellow-
> slaves had come from the same part of the Guinea coast with him, I
> sent for one of them who could speak tolerable French, and ques-
> tioned him about Yambu. He told me, that, in their own country,
> Yambu was master of them all; that they had been taken prisoners,
> when fighting in his cause, by another prince, who, in one battle,
> was more fortunate than theirs; that he had sold them to some
> white men, who came in a great ship to their coast; that they were
> afterwards brought hither, where other white men purchased them
> from the first, and set them to work where I saw them; but that
> when they died, and went beyond the Great Mountains, Yambu
> should be their prince.[56]

Savillon's subsequent interview with Yambu is a test of the noble sensibility of the native prince:

> he seemed to regard me with an eye of perfect indifference. One
> who had enquired no further, would have concluded him pos-
> sessed of that stupid insensibility, which Europeans often mention
> as an apology for their cruelties. . . . "Can this man have been a
> prince in Africa?" said I to myself.—I reflected for a moment.—
> "Yet what should he now do, if he has?—Just what I see him do. I
> have seen a deposed sovereign at Paris; but in Europe, kings are
> artificial beings, like their subjects.—Silence is the only throne
> which adversity has left to princes." (207–208)

When Savillon puts into place on the plantation a new system, in which
the slaves only work voluntarily, he wins Yambu's trust, and a final proof
of his natural nobility:

> "from this moment [Savillon promises to Yambu] you are mine no
> more!" . . . "You would not," said I, "make your people work by the
> whip, as you see the overseers do?"—"Oh! no, no whip!"[Yambu
> replies]—"Yet they must work, else we shall have no sugars to buy
> them meat and clothing with."—(He put his hand to his brow, as if

[56] Henry Mackenzie, *Julia de Roubigné* (Edinburgh: James Ballantyne and Company, 1808), 205–207. Subsequent references are to this edition; page numbers are given within the text.

I had started a difficulty he was unable to overcome.)—"Then you
shall have the command of them, and they shall work chuse work
[work by choice] for Yambu."—He looked askance, as if he
doubted the truth of what I said; I called the negro with whom I
had the first conversation about him, and, pointing to Yambu,
"Your master," said I, "is now free, and may leave you when he
pleases!"—"Yambu no leave you," said he to the negro warmly.—
"But he may accompany Yambu if he chuses."—Yambu shook his
head. . . . "Then if you think it better you shall both stay; Yambu
shall be my friend, and help me to raise sugars for the good of us
all: you shall have no overseer but Yambu, and shall work no more
than he bids you."—The negro fell at my feet and kissed them;
Yambu stood silent, and I saw a tear on his cheek.—"This man has
been a prince in Africa!" said I to myself. (209–211)

In this version of the fable, the ultimate proof of the elite status of the
native prince is withheld until the final, dramatic moment of sentimental
performance. The native must demonstrate his nobility to a European
witness, who stages a drama of sensibility for his own affective contemplation—and that of the reader.[57] When Savillon finally sees the "tear on
[Yambu's] cheek," he affirms not only Yambu's status, but his own claim
to sympathy for the slaves on his plantation, his own value as a man of feeling. Savillon does not flee the scene, as the Prince of Annamaboe does
when he witnesses his own suffering in the drama of Oroonoko, but he
plays the same role, both witnessing and mirroring the sentiment that
confirms the nobility of the native prince, a nobility that makes Yambu a
paradigm for Savillon himself, the native slave a model for the European
slaveholder.

At the end of the century, in Anna Maria Mackenzie's sentimental epistolary novel *Slavery, or the Times* (1793), the fable of the native prince, now
fully fitted out in the discourse of sensibility, draws together many of the
strains that have marked its cultural currency since Behn's *Oroonoko.* Adolphus, the young African prince, heir to the throne of "Tonouwah," is sent
by his royal father, Zimza, to be educated in London, where he is conducted by the wise and sentimental Mr. Hamilton, and soon joined by another friend and tutor, the Reverend Mr. Hawkins. Adolphus quickly becomes the center of a complex marriage plot, in which his false libertine
friend Berisford seeks to separate him from the woman he loves, his sentimental soul-mate, the exemplary Mary Ann St. Leger, Hawkins's niece.
Mary Ann supplies the place of the suffering and endangered female. Ap-

[57] Ellis describes the sentimentalist trope of "bodily display" in this passage (123).

parently orphaned and unprotected, she is pursued by Berisford, who covets her fortune and schemes to discredit Adolphus with his generous and sympathetic advisors. Mary Ann is under the control of the villainous Abrams, who has falsified her lost father's will in order to gain control over her and her fortune. The native prince and the heiress are finally united after Adolphus commits a series of indiscretions arising from his generous and innocent nature, contemplates suicide as a result of these errors, travels to the Caribbean with a new benefactor, and there discovers not only Mary Ann's long lost father, General St. Leger, but also his own royal sire Zimza, who had been betrayed and sold into slavery some months before.

In this full exfoliation of the fable of the native prince, the typical traits of that character are shared out between Zimza and Adolphus, father and son. Like Oroonoko and the Prince of Annamaboe, Zimza is a royal slave, stolen from his native land. His very appearance, dressed like Omai at Cambridge in "complete military uniform" (250), evokes that ideal of heroism yoked with sensibility which defined the exotic protagonist of the heroic drama. These qualities are evident in General St. Leger's description of Zimza after his liberation from slavery:

> with what *noble humility*, if I may couple the terms, does he express the highest obligation to me for my former indulgence and present services. I think you once, in a transient view of him, expressed much admiration of his form and figure; but, could you behold him in a complete military uniform, you wou'd be ready to prefer him to the finest European nature ever created. The thoughtful majesty that beams in his eyes, the exact harmony of his features, and the grandeur of his soul, which informs every action, inspire one with a sort of veneration none but Zimza could create, and none but Adolphus is likely to equal.[58]

Adolphus's stature, too, is attributed to the distinctions connected with his class. In fact, that royal status enables Adolphus to accommodate himself readily to English society, while his lower-class servants, Sambo and his wife Omra, whom Adolphus has redeemed from slavery, beg to return to Africa. Adolphus's appearance creates a social sensation, much like that generated by the Indian kings, Omai, or Oroonoko in "our Western World": "The arrival of an African prince was a circumstance which, when our doors were open to company, drew together all who, from interest or

---

[58] Anna Mackenzie, *Slavery: Or The Times* (Dublin, 1793), 250. Subsequent references are to this edition; page numbers are given within the text.

acquaintance, could claim admission" (61). But in the same town, Sambo and Omra are received with "ungenerous observations [on] their persons, dress, and manners" (58). Adolphus supports their petition to be sent home, but explains that he does not share their alienation, because "Adolphus is a *prince*, [and] Sambo and Omra are but his father's subjects. How should *they* then think as *I* do? I know they are my fellow-creatures; but do not, good sir, do not suppose they are my equals, in strength of mind, self-denial, or descent" (59). This comparison explicates the elitism that we have seen to be essential to the character of the native prince throughout his career: princes are readily incorporated into the experience of the English metropolis, as the natural gentility of their "dress and manners"—here and throughout the factual and fictional accounts of their visits—demonstrates. Elite status is central to the peculiar formal process of this cultural fable, in which the native prince enters the heart of a cultural paradigm and shapes the identity of the "GOOD MAN."

Zimza himself defines this paradigm for Adolphus in a speech that directly translates class status into the cultural ideal of the man of feeling through the model of the native prince. Having lost his throne as a result of his betrayal into slavery, Zimza explains:

> though deprived of every brilliant recommendation, though the outward glare of wealth distinguishes not my appearance, yet is Zimza's soul, that superior principle which actuates the human frame, still the same.——And may that spirit of independence and probity, which, I trust, no earthly mortification can ever subdue, descend unsullied to his son.——To him I shall not cease occasionally to enforce the practice of every moral, every Christian virtue.——Yes, Adolphus, I would see thee more than a brave, more than a generous, more than a polite,——I would see thee a GOOD MAN. (271–272)

And Adolphus is the ideal man of feeling from the outset of the novel. The opening scenes are devoted to the representation of his sympathetic responses, and especially to a series of paradigmatic rescues, inspired by his sensibility. On shipboard in a scene closely parallel to Cannassatego's rescue of Lydia, "while the tears rushed into his eyes" (12), he intervenes as Sambo is whipped, and he subsequently prevails upon Mr. Hamilton to buy both Sambo's and Omra's freedom. At the death of their newborn child, he gave "way to the operation of his nobler passions. He sat down upon the bed and broke into tears: for some minutes, they flowed unchecked" (22). He intervenes again, with "flowing tears" which prove the "natural goodness of his heart" (26–27), on behalf of the cabin boy when he is whipped for negligence. After his arrival in London, he saves his false friend, Berisford, from drowning. And at the end of the novel, he rescues his own father from shipboard whipping and certain death.

Adolphus's native innocence gives him these natural sympathies. We learn that "his heart knows no guile. His passions wear no mask. His intercourse with our world has not soiled the purity of a mind which reflects, with added brilliancy, the virtues set before it" (78). Thus his indiscretions, which serve to complicate the plot and delay his marriage to Mary Ann St. Leger, are all readily attributed to his sensibility. Zimza explains "You have been to blame, Adolphus; but your best virtues have been your betrayers" (259). In his account of Adolphus's behavior to General St. Leger, Zimza demonstrates his own sensibility in the act of explicating his son's, in a replication typical of the structure of this novel:

> Zimza turns to me his fine eyes, sparkling through a tear.—
> " . . . . those who have looked into a human heart, unbiassed by
> cold restraining caution, alive to every benevolent sensation,
> and ready to draw sudden and undistinguishing conclusions
> from momentary impressions, will be free to confess; the youth
> has but acted in consequence of his title to the above character."
> (250–251)

Unlike *Oroonoko*, *Slavery* was written against the backdrop of the established antislavery movement of the last two decades of the century and thus can and often has been read as an antislavery work.[59] Zimza recites a set antislavery speech, including the familiar evocation of Christian principles, common humanity, and "European tyranny" (281); a humane slave owner, on the model of Henry Mackenzie's Savillon, demonstrates to Adolphus the greater productivity to be gained from the kind treatment of his slaves. But these conventional gestures toward the antislavery and reformist politics of the period are offset by the elitist premise of the fable of the native prince, an elitism that we have seen to be essential to that fable's distinctive structure. Slavery has a different significance for "the noble Zimza" than for common slaves, even when they are drawn as sympathetically as Sambo and Omra. So essential is the role of elite status in this story that Zimza, "this injured king," like Oroonoko, simply cannot be seen to survive the fall in rank entailed by slavery:

> the noble Zimza will never submit to a state of slavery.——The fel-
> low who purchased him gives a shocking account of his rage, sor-
> row, and fruitless resistance, when constrained to remain on board

[59] Moira Ferguson, however, calls it a racist and anti-Semitic caricature. See *Subject to Others: British Women Writers and Colonial Slavery, 1670–1834* (New York: Routledge, 1992), 221.

[the ship in which he had been betrayed] . . . .——He would not
eat, speak, nor move, after his spirits were exhausted by his efforts
to resist the attempts they made to put on his irons. . . . And, from
that time, he could scarcely be said to breathe, nor would he have
taken the smallest refreshment. (209)

Indeed, at the conclusion of this report of Zimza's enslavement, a desper-
ate escape attempt apparently ends in his death, because he is "too noble
to bear even the contemplation" of subjection (210). This nobility, as we
have seen, underlies the process of accommodation that defines the fable
of the native prince from the time of the heroic drama. It gives him his
ability to model a new paradigm of masculine character, to reflect, in the
mirror of the cultural imagination, the demeanor of the "GOOD MAN." We
have seen this reflection before; Adolphus describes a familiar scene:

> On the seventeenth of March we went to the theatre. Of all the ele-
> gant amusements congenial to youth this, in my estimation, takes
> the lead. And, in this instance, my inclinations met Mr. Hamilton's
> hearty concurrence. Oronoko was performed by command. My
> tears were the plaudits of a feeling heart. (121)

The image of the "GOOD MAN"'s tears at the sight of himself sold into slavery enacts the distinctive mutuality of this fable. Like the Prince of Annamaboe, the virtuous Lydia, and the sentimental slave owner Savillon,
Adolphus identifies with the affecting performance of difference, thereby
modeling the very process that structures his story. His resulting tears enable an English audience to see itself in the visage of the native, and to
construct from that visage a moral paradigm for its day.

                                    V

The fable of the native prince has a peculiar longevity. It survives a series
of literary subgenres, philosophical formulae, and political positions, in
the representation of which it often plays a supporting and sometimes a
central role. Its persistence suggests the significance of the imaginative effort it undertakes and the currency of the cultural problem it addresses.
In a century of accelerated global contact that includes Europe in an exchange with many of the peoples of a world fully opened to Western imperial and colonial exploitation, the fable of the native prince absorbs
and interprets the striking experience of cultural difference. As we have
seen, the native prince approaches the issue of alterity by presenting
difference as aristocratic status, the powerful imaginative resource of

Restoration heroic drama.[60] The native in this fable is invariably a prince. Though the aristocratic hero of the heroic plays is distinguished by his class status, as a nobleman he projects a cultural ideal, and despite his rank, his magnanimity gives him access to the affecting virtue of sensibility. In other words, he can be both a noble paragon and a locus of affective identification, and this unique conjunction gives him his special role in the structure of the fable of the native prince—as a paragon of sensibility. In this elite guise, the native acts as a prominent contemporary vehicle for the formal exploration of the complex process of identification. But of course this nobility does not confer historical status or power to the many peoples of the globe whose difference from the peoples of Europe stands behind the fable of the native prince, and it adds a complex dimension to our understanding of eighteenth-century bourgeois thought, highlighting an attraction to social hierarchy that might seem to belie a universalist ideology. In his account of the idea of the noble savage, Hayden White finds a social contradiction in the attention to nobility on the part of bourgeois or radical Enlightenment thinkers. In White's formulation, nobility is manipulated so that it functions to lay claim to a bourgeois assertion of status: "in fact, the claim to nobility was meant to extend neither to the natives of the New World nor to the lowest classes of Europe, but only to the bourgeoisie."[61]

What remains of that native, then? The fable of the native prince is certainly not to be understood as a story of cultural contact or an encounter with alterity on its own terms. It might even be judged as a repudiation of difference in the service of the ideology of the *pax britannica*, which sees all the world as England, or of the new colonialism, which replaces the cruel, Catholic regime of Spain with the humane, Protestant or deist one of Britain. Unlike the fables of a new world that combine in the *Dunciad*, the fable of the native prince does not analyze the modern crisis from which it draws its materials. And unlike the fable of the city sewer, it does not project a future from the vital energies of the modern metropolis. But though in this fable the native prince dwindles as a figure of difference, as

[60] In a chapter on the eighteenth-century novel, Wheeler describes the importance of rank: the understanding of human difference in the novel "allowed for a selective acceptance of high-rank individuals despite their dark color or cultural origin because racial ideology had not yet shifted in all realms to make appearance more important than behavior" (174). My argument locates the significance of rank at an earlier time and in another genre, but the issue of physical appearance that Wheeler documents intersects with the fable of the native prince.

[61] For White, this is the result of a fetishistic (or ideological) acceptance of a pair of dialectically opposed views of the "savage"—the "wild man" and the "noble savage." Hayden White, *Tropics of Discourse: Essays in Cultural Criticism* (Baltimore: Johns Hopkins University Press, 1978), chap. 8; this quote, 194.

a man of feeling he looms largely over the imaginative life of the century. The complex structure of his story helps to shape the self-reflexive process of identification that dominates the print culture of the eighteenth century through the many manifestations of the cult of sensibility. Amidst all the various strains of this diffuse movement, and among all its multiple sources—in the history of science, philosophy, and medicine, in the social and intellectual theories of the noble savage, in the humane teachings of the Latitudinarian divines, in the rise of bourgeois identity, or in the development of theories of aesthetics and sympathetic imagination—the native prince contributes a distinctive formal structure and a peculiar affective intensity. The complex movement of his story of the accommodation of difference provides a model for the exchange of sympathy that defines the cult of sensibility. And the imaginative stretch of his accommodation—from alterity to identity—displays that exchange in its most strenuous form.

The story of Sir Charles Grandison can be understood as an exhaustive formal experiment in the construction of imaginative identification with a male protagonist, a noble paragon whose own sufferings—projections of his sympathy for the tears of others—makes him a mirror in which an ideal masculine demeanor is modeled. The spectacle of difference is a central parameter of this experiment, intensifying the effect of identification. *Sir Charles Grandison*, as we have seen, depends upon the religious difference that for contemporary readers defined the British nation, the difference within Western European culture between Protestant and Catholic. Sir Charles's distance from Clementina and her Catholic family is essential to the imaginative and cultural power of the exercise of identification that his demeanor exacts. The fable of the native prince is an extreme test of that imaginative project, generating the same sympathetic identification out of the experience of global difference. Though they may never have been seen in their own attire, or understood on their own terms, those native visitors did not pass through London without effect. Imagined as men of feeling, the Prince of Annamaboe and his many historical and fictional counterparts played a distinctive role in the long cultural experiment condensed in those exemplary tears of Sir Charles Grandison.

CHAPTER 6

The Orangutang, the Lap Dog,
and the Parrot:
The Fable of the Nonhuman Being

I N the fourth canto of Alexander Pope's *Rape of the Lock* (1717), Belinda, the poem's fashionable female protagonist, laments the loss of her "fav'rite Curl," snipped off by the Baron as they drink coffee after a game of Ombre. Belinda is incited to vengeance by her friend the "fierce *Thalestris*," who calls up a striking collection of beings in her evocation of the indignity that will result from the Baron's triumphant exhibit of his prize:

> Gods! shall the Ravisher display your Hair,
> While the Fops envy, and the Ladies stare!
>
> . . . .
>
> Sooner let Earth, Air, Sea to Chaos fall,
> Men, Monkies, Lap-Dogs, Parrots, perish all![1]

We can readily grasp the reductive assumptions of Belinda's world in the compact satiric sequence of this last line, in the incongruous alignment of "men" with the subsequent nonhuman beings—pets and exotic species— with which humankind is yoked. Countering the incongruity of these items is the alliteration that gives them a euphonic coherence. The consonants "m" and "p," respectively, hold together the first and second pairs—"Men" and "Monkies" on the one hand, and "Lap-Dogs" and "Parrots" on the other, and that "p" serves to attach the second pair to the

---

[1] Alexander Pope, *The Rape of the Lock*, in *Poems of Alexander Pope*, vol. 2, ed. Geoffrey Tillotson (London: Methuen, 1940), 4.148, 103–104, 119–120. Subsequent references are to this edition; line numbers are given within the text.

William Hogarth, *Guglielmus Hogarth* (1749). Self-portrait with his pug, Trump. By permission of the Division of Rare and Manuscript Collections, Cornell University Library.

"perish" of the line's apocalyptic conclusion, so that the series has a close-knit verbal continuity that stands in striking and deflationary contrast to the satiric discontinuity of its association of incomparable beings. Unlike Belinda, the reader confidently distinguishes men from monkeys, lap dogs, or parrots, whose perishing must be weighed in a different scale from that of humankind.

Or must it? This line expresses the failure of Belinda's society to grasp the distinctions that confer meaning and seriousness upon human endeavor. But it also deliberately condenses a prominent contemporary problematic that calls those very distinctions into question. "Monkies, Lap-Dogs, [and] Parrots" make up a striking nonhuman cohort, regularly linked in the contemporary imagination: the *Spectator* (1712), in an almost identical phrase, attacks the frivolity of the upper-class female by describing her affection for "Parrots, monkeys and Lap Dogs."[2] And, as Pope's poem shows us, this familiar group of animals occupies a complex position in relation to "Men." Together, this cohort of beings is the center of an anxious, heated, even virulent debate on the topic of alterity, a debate in which the idea of "Men" is systematically problematized by its juxtaposition with a different category of being, and through which, consequently, one dimension of the European encounter with the non-European is imaginatively absorbed and debated. "Monkies, Lap-Dogs, [and] Parrots" are the collective protagonist of a cultural fable that explores the nature of being in relation to humanity. This exploration entails a sustained intimacy with alterity, an intimacy that provides a counterpoint to the repudiation of difference that we observed in the representation of the native prince in chapter 5.[3] In this respect, these two cultural fables—that of the native prince and that of the nonhuman being—might be seen as paired poles of an early and formative modern reflection upon cultural encounter.[4]

[2] Joseph Addison, *Spectator*, no. 343 (3 April 1712), ed. Donald F. Bond (Oxford: Clarendon Press, 1965), 3:273. Subsequent references are to this edition; volume and page numbers are given within the text.

[3] Srinivas Aravamudan also develops an argument that evokes both the native prince and the pet in an account of the colonialist approach to alterity. But his view connects these figures where I would hold them apart; he argues that in the character of Oroonoko the images of "pet" and African slave collaborate in a joint fantasy of subordination: "the royal slave as pet." See *Tropicopolitans: Colonialism and Agency, 1688–1804* (Durham: Duke University Press, 1999), 33–49; this quote, 49.

[4] I have profited in this chapter from recent unpublished work on "Romantic Anti-Anthropomorphisms" by Adela Pinch, whose reading of the intimacy of human and animal focuses on Romantic poetry.

I

Animals intruded upon European consciousness in distinctive and novel ways in the course of the eighteenth century. To use Harriet Ritvo's words, "a fundamental shift in the relationship between humans and their fellow creatures" has been located in this period by various historians from various perspectives.[5] This shift was highly visible and broadly evident in the daily lives of individuals from the countryside to the city, and from the middling to the upper classes. In rural areas, the major innovations in agricultural practices that marked this period of transformation were accompanied by widespread experimentation in animal husbandry, including stock breeding and the development of breed specialization in horses, cattle, and sheep, with the concomitant rise of influential national and local agricultural societies (Ritvo, *Animal Estate*, 47–48). Ritvo suggests that such innovations, in which "people systematically appropriated power they had previously attributed to animals, and animals became significant primarily as the objects of human manipulation," reflected and institutionalized assumptions of domination and hierarchy comparable, later in the nineteenth century, to larger rhetorics of power and authority (*Animal Estate*, 2–3, 5–6). But these changes augmented and dovetailed with various other new practices—in biology, anatomy, and pet breeding—that suggest that this widespread transition in the perception of the relationship of animals and humans also involved substantial confusion and ambiguity.

In the life sciences, new paradigms in biology, zoology, and natural history raised controversial questions about the nature of the physiological and developmental links among animals, or between animals and men. In these contexts, the theologically sanctioned distinctiveness of man, as a being created by God in his own image and thus separated absolutely from the beasts, was challenged by an increasingly persuasive and prominent strain of thought that discovered various forms of proximity, connection, or intersection between animals and humans.[6] One central constituent of these scientific developments was the invention of modern biological classification, a consequence of the empiricist projects of seventeenth- and eighteenth-century science. This period saw the creation of several rival taxonomic systems—by Ray, Buffon, and Linnaeus—which "reflected a new human assertiveness with regard to the natural world" (Ritvo, *Animal*

[5] Harriet Ritvo, *The Animal Estate: The English and Other Creatures in the Victorian Age* (Harvard: Cambridge University Press, 1987), 2.

[6] My account of the relation between animals and humans is indebted throughout to Keith Thomas, *Man and the Natural World: A History of the Modern Sensibility* (New York: Pantheon, 1983).

Estate, 13), but which simultaneously raised fundamental questions about the status of the human itself.

Many of these questions found a focal point in the eighteenth-century debate about the status of monkeys and apes, members of the Primate Order who were not systematically distinguished from one another until the nineteenth century.[7] According to Keith Thomas, the discovery of the great apes held major implications for European definitions of humanity (129). But this "discovery" was in part a matter of cultural readiness. H. W. Janson observes that reports of anthropoid apes "were received with almost complete equanimity" before the eighteenth century. Marco Polo brought back descriptions of orangutangs from South Asia, and several other early sources enabled sixteenth-century zoologists to form an image of the great ape. But, as Janson says, "despite their ever widening horizon of factual information [zoologists of the earlier period] continued to deal with their material in a frame of mind akin to that of the philologist, emphasizing problems of nomenclature and the authority of the written word rather than comparative anatomy and physiology."[8] The exploration of the relationship between apes and humans was first taken up by the early anatomists of the mid-seventeenth century, who were much more attentive to the problems posed by the great apes, problems which they pursued through an analysis of the structural differences and similarities between apes and humans.

The first major moment in the shift of the understanding of the anthropoid ape came in 1641 with the publication in Amsterdam of Nicolaas Tulp's *Observationum medicarum libri tres,* which included a representation of "Homo Sylvestris—Orang-outang," a picture of the body of the first anthropoid ape known to have reached Europe.[9] Dr. Tulp's rendering was followed by Edward Tyson's *Orang-Outang, sive Homo Sylvestris: or, the Anatomy of a Pygmie* (1699), which Janson describes as "the formal entry of the anthropoid ape into the consciousness of Western civilisation" (336). Tyson, a Fellow of the Royal Society and the age's preeminent figure in the fast developing science of comparative anatomy, performed a dissection of a juvenile chimpanzee—at this time typically designated as an orangutang—which he compared in full physiological detail with a man. Tyson's work was the first to document the connection between human and animal through the link of the anthropoid ape, and

[7] For a sketch of the early naturalists' treatment of the anthropoid ape, see Londa Schiebinger, *Nature's Body: Gender in the Making of Modern Science* (Boston: Beacon Press, 1993), chap. 3.

[8] H. W. Janson, *Apes and Ape Lore in the Middle Ages and the Renaissance* (London: The Warburg Institute, 1952), 327, 334–335.

[9] On this event, see Janson, 334.

his treatise served as the grounding statement in a century-long physiological, biological, and philosophical discussion of the relation between
apes and humans.

In the context of his anatomical comparison, Tyson maintained that the
orangutang, "coming nearest to Mankind; seems the Nexus of the Animal
and Rational," and he ended his anatomy with an essay on the "*Pygmies*, the
Cynocephali, the *Satyrs*, and *Sphinges* of the Ancients," arguing that the close
resemblance of orangutangs and men demonstrated by his dissection explains the mythical animals of ancient reports, which must have been actual creatures rather than fantasy—apes so man-like that they were readily
mistaken for men.[10] Janson describes the influence of Tyson's work:

> the impact of the *Orang-Outang* could be felt almost immediately;
> it not only attracted wide attention among natural scientists but
> stirred the imagination of poets and philosophers, arousing them
> to flights of speculation about the nature of this novel creature,
> which they viewed as more human than simian. Tyson himself,
> while emphasizing its extraordinary resemblance to man, had
> clearly treated the *orang-outang* as an animal, but the very fact that
> he called it a *Homo Sylvestris* and a *Pygmie* suggested to the non-
> technical reader that it was essentially human. (336)

The terms and examples of Tyson's study informed the contemplations
of the connection between apes and humans that extended throughout
the century. An essay in the *Lay-Monk* from 1713, for example, argues that
apes are as much like humans as are Hottentots. This text extrapolates
from the physiological similarities evident in Tyson's dissection to other
resemblances—including the potential for language, the comparability of
intellect, and ultimately even the possession of a "feeling heart":

> The most perfect of this Order of Beings, the *Orang Outang*, as he is
> call'd by the Natives of *Angola*, that is, the Wild Man, or Man of the
> Woods, has the Honour of bearing the nearest Resemblance to
> Human Nature, tho' all that Species have some Agreement with us
> in our Features, . . . yet this has the greatest Likeness, not only in
> his Countenance, but in the Structure of his Body, his Ability to

[10] Edward Tyson, *Orang-Outang, sive Homo Sylvestris: or, the Anatomy of a Pygmie* (1699), facsimile ed., introd. Ashley Montagu (London: Dawsons of Pall Mall, 1966), "Epistle Dedica-
tory." In the introduction to this edition, Ashley Montagu points out that Tyson's work "had
a powerful influence upon all subsequent thought on man's place in nature" reaching to
Darwin's *Descent of Man* (2). Subsequent references to Tyson's treatise are to this edition;
page numbers are given within the text.

walk upright, as well as on all fours; his Organs of Speech, his ready Apprehension, and his gentle and tender Passions, which are not found in any of the Ape Kind, and in various other Respects.[11]

The notion that Africa was populated by herds of these "men of the woods," who lacked only civilization to attain all the defining characteristics of the human, was widely available and frequently debated in the course of the eighteenth century. Though some writers—notably Buffon—argued for an absolute distinction between humans and beasts, there was a growing tendency to blur that boundary, or to shift its location on the new hierarchies of zoological classification, and, relatedly, to accord human status to the ape. Contemporary discussions of the role of civilization and the nature of language lent strength to this tendency. Rousseau's influential definition of the state of nature, and especially his inclusion of language as an effect of civilization, accorded well with such accounts of the "men of the woods." And the Scottish philosopher James Burnet, Lord Monboddo, argued at length in *Of the Origin and Progress of Language* (1774) that the orangutangs of Angola were primitive men who had not yet developed language.

The intersection of human and animal was felt widely and variously in the intellectual movements of the eighteenth century. Influential social ideas about progress and improvement—extensions of philosophical optimism—drew concrete credibility from the suggestion that animals might be able to better themselves: that apes could learn to speak, and other animals could attain parallel advantages. Discussions of the Platonistic "chain of being" also accommodated and supported the proximity of man and beast. The principle of continuity—which saw differences in the hierarchy of beings that populated the chain as minute gradations rather than clear distinctions—found an apt match with contemporary speculation about the status of animals. Bolingbroke, for instance, saw "many degrees of comparison between the human intelligence and that of various animals. . . . [such that] intellectual faculties and corporeal senses, of the same and of different kinds, [seem to be] communicated in some proportion or other to the whole race of animals."[12] And Soame Jenyns in this context argued for a kind of "blending" or "shading":

---

[11] Richard Blackmore and John Hughes, *The Lay-Monk* (25 November 1713). Cited in Maximillian E. Novak, "The Wild Man Comes to Tea," in *The Wild Man Within: An Image in Western Thought from the Renaissance to Romanticism*, ed. Robert Dudley and Novak (Pittsburgh: University of Pittsburgh Press, 1972), 190. On this material, see A. O. Lovejoy, *The Great Chain of Being: A Study of the History of an Idea* (Cambridge: Harvard University Press, 1953), 234–235.

[12] Henry St. John, Lord Bolingbroke, *Fragments, or Minutes of Essays* in *Works* (1809), 8:168–169; cited in Lovejoy, 196 n. 29.

The various qualitites with which these various beings are endued, we perceive without difficulty, but the boundaries of those qualities which form this chain of subordination, are so mixed, that where one ends, and the next begins, we are unable to discover. . . . The manner by which the consummate wisdom of the divine artificer has formed this gradation, so extensive in the whole, and so imperceptible in the parts, is this:—He constantly unites the highest degree of the qualities of each inferior order to the lowest degree of the same qualities belonging to the order next above it; by which means, like the colours of a skilful painter, they are so blended together, and shaded off into each other, that no line of distinction is anywhere to be seen.[13]

A. O. Lovejoy finds it "curious" that this implication of the great chain of being was so "tardily drawn" in the course of the long history of the idea: that the "blending" of human and animal only arose as an explicit consideration in the early eighteenth century, even though that idea was a relevant corollary to the chain of being from classical times. Lovejoy observes that "blending"—the sense of the "consanguinity of man and the animals next to him in the scale"—once it arises in the eighteenth century, anticipates the general establishment—in the nineteenth century—of theories of biological evolutionism or the transformation of species. This anticipation is evidence, for Lovejoy, of the almost self-contained and self-perpetuating influence of intellectual history on contemporary thought (195–198). But the broader cultural context that we have observed suggests that Lovejoy is registering a precedent—within the intellectual history of the chain of being—for the "shading" of human and animal that is widely evident elsewhere in the cultural history of the period, a "shading" that represents the powerful contemporary imaginative engagement with the alterity of the animal kingdom, and which extends through various strata of contemporary popular and intellectual experience. The idea of "blending," like the issue of the relevance of the great apes, became available in intellectual discourse at the same time that the modern encounter with alterity gained cultural prominence.

The interest in the "consanguinity" of human and beast was supported by the contemporary discoveries of "wild boys"—much publicized specimens of humans purportedly raised by beasts or reverted to a bestial state—who served as living evidence of the role of civilization and the characteristics of the state of nature. The story of Pedro Serrano, taken up

---

[13] Soame Jenyns, "On the Chain of Universal Being," in *Disquisitions on Several Subjects* in *Works* (1790), 1:179–185; cited in Lovejoy, 197 n.33.

from Garcilaso de la Vega's accounts of the new world, told of a European who had reverted to a wild state and consequently grown a coat of hair.[14] Bern Connor, in a contemporary history of Poland, describes various men raised in the wild, one of whom when tamed had no recollection of his wild state.[15] But, as Maximillian Novak has shown, Peter, the "wild boy," was the figure most vividly present to and influential upon the contemporary English imagination. Peter was brought from Germany to London in 1726 where he was the subject of experiment, baptism, and debate: "his arrival produced a number of pamphlets, a sermon, a book-length satire by Daniel Defoe, and at least one poem" (185).

The instability of the boundary between the human and the nonhuman being pervaded the everyday experience of the metropolitan residents of Europe in the long eighteenth century. Popular urban audiences were the recipients and witnesses of myriad anecdotes and spectacles that supported these notions about animals.[16] Samuel Pepys observed an ape—probably either a chimpanzee or a gorilla—that seemed to him "so much like a man in most things, that . . . I cannot believe but that it is a monster got of a man and a she-baboone. I do believe it already understands much english: and I am of the mind it might be tought to speak or make signs."[17] Indeed, an orangutang, owned by Sir Ashton Lever, was widely believed to have been taught a few words.[18]

During this century and the next, as Richard Altick has shown, Londoners were entertained by a host of shows featuring animals displayed to produce a connection with the human. One account from the early part of the century describes a

> Man Teger, lately brought from the *East Indies*, a most strange and wonderful Creature, the like never seen before in *England*, it being of Seven several Colours, from the Head downwards resembling a Man, its fore parts clear, and his hinder parts all Hairy; having a long Head of Hair, and Teeth 2 or 3 Inches long; taking a Glass of

---

[14] I am indebted to Novak's description of "wild boys" for this account. For Serrano's story, see Novak, 188.

[15] Bern Connor, *The History of Poland* (London, 1698), 1: 342–343; cited in Novak, 190.

[16] I am indebted in this section to Richard D. Altick's essential compilation of accounts of animals on display in London in *The Shows of London* (Cambridge: Harvard University Press, 1978), chap. 3.

[17] *The Diary of Samuel Pepys*, ed. Robert Latham and William Matthews (Berkeley: University of California Press, 1970), 2.160 (22–24 August 1661).

[18] James Burnett, Lord Monboddo, *Antient Metaphysics*, vol. 3 (London, 1784; reprint, New York: Garland, 1977), 40.

Ale in his hand like a Christian, Drinks it, also plays at Quarter Staff.[19]

Altick surmises that the "man teger" was a West African baboon (38 n. 18). Another show "at the White Horse Inn in Fleet Street, any time of the Day or Evening," featured a "little Black Hairy Pigmey [probably a monkey], bred in the Desarts of Arabia, [with] a Natural Ruff of Hair about his Face, two Foot high, walks upright, drinks a Glass of Ale or Wine, and does several other things to admiration" (Ashton, 1:269–270). Yet another "Noble Creature which much resembles a Wild *Hairy Man*" performed rope dances at Epsom and Bath as well as London (Ashton, 1:274). The *Spectator* prints a description of this being that emphasizes his "blending" with the human: "He is by birth a Monkey; but swings upon a Rope, takes a pipe of Tobacco, and drinks a glass of Ale, like any reasonable Creature" (no. 28, 1:119). Another "monster" from "Mount Tibet" was said to "approach the Human Species nearer than any hitherto exhibited, and is supposed to be the long lost link between the Human and Brute Creation." This creature possessed "great beauty and sagacity," as well as "affability, friendship and good nature."[20] Especially appealing to the ladies was a female ape known widely as "Madame Chimpanzee" and displayed in London in 1738. She was said to be modest, affectionate, and distinguished by her table manners. According to Thomas Boreman she:

was very pretty Company at the Tea-table, behav'd with Modesty and good Manners, and give great Satisfaction to the Ladies who were pleased to honour her with their Visits, . . . it would fetch its Chair, and sit in it naturally, like a Human Creature, whilst it drank Tea: It would take the Dish in its Hand, and if the Liquor was two hot, wou'd pour the Tea into the Saucer to cool it.[21]

Apes were displayed in this way through the nineteenth century, and that later period affords many vivid examples of this phenomenon. According to Ritvo, they were

invariably . . . exhibited in ways that emphasized their likeness to people. They ate with table utensils, sipped tea from cups, and slept

---

[19] John Ashton, *Social Life in the Reign of Queen Anne* (London: Chatto and Windus, 1882), 1:271–272.

[20] Altick, 83, 83 n. 20; citing the *Morning Herald and Advertiser*, 1793.

[21] Thomas Boreman, *A Description of Some Curious and Uncommon Creatures* (London, 1739), 24; cited in Schiebinger, 101.

under blankets. One orangutan displayed in London's Exeter Change Menagerie amused itself by carefully turning the pages of an illustrated book. At the Regent's Park Zoo a chimpanzee named Jenny regularly appeared in a flannel nightgown and robe. Apes often boasted Christian names, which heightened the suggestiveness of clothes, forks, and books. Tommy, a chimp who lived at the Regent's Park Zoo in 1835 and 1836, was pronounced by one admirer to be greatly superior in "shrewdness and sagacity . . . [to the] human infant, and . . . for that matter, many grown individuals." A chimpanzee acquired by the Earl Fitzwilliam in 1849 was reported to walk "perfectly erect" and handle "everything like a human being"; its food was "choice, and wine a favorite beverage." (*Animal Estate*, 31–33)

This movement of proximity to the human was not limited to apes or monkeys, however. "Learned" animals of other species displayed a human-like intelligence to avid eighteenth-century audiences. The "learned" horse was a familiar example; one horse shown at Exeter Change in 1760 and 1772 was so accomplished that, like the "man of the woods," it "only want[ed] speech."[22] The "learned pig" that appeared in London in 1785 was "well versed in all Languages, perfect Arethmatician & Composer of Musick";[23] "he reads, writes, and casts accounts by means of typographical cards, in the same manner that a printer composes and by the same method . . . sets down any capital or surname; solves questions in the four rules of Arithmetic," and even tells time.[24] So suggestive was this spectacle that one contemporary witness commented:

> I have . . . been for a long time accustomed to consider animals as mere machines, actuated by the unerring hand of Providence, to do those things which are necessary for the preservation of themselves and their offspring; but the sight of the Learned Pig, which has lately been shown in London, has deranged these ideas and I know not what to think.[25]

[22] Altick, 40, 40 n. 37; citing Clippings Enthoven Collection, Theatre Museum, London, Exeter Change file.

[23] Altick, 40, 40 n. 43; citing Robert Southey, *Letters from England*, ed. Jack Simmons (London: Cresset Press, 1951), 340.

[24] Altick, 40, 40 n. 44; citing Daniel Lysons, *Collectanea; or, A Collection of Advertisements from the Newspapers . . . [1661–1840]*, 5 scrapbooks at the British Library, 1889.e.5., 2:86–90.

[25] Sarah Trimmer, *Fabulous Histories designed for the Instruction of Children* (3d ed., 1788), 71; cited in Thomas, 92.

In this period, to "know not what to think" on the subject of animals was to open up the possibility that they could be compared with humans in "reason, intelligence, language and almost every other human quality" (Thomas, 129).

Other animals came into even more intimate connection with the human denizens of eighteenth-century England. This period saw the full flowering of a modern phenomenon "undoubtedly unique in human history," the keeping of pets. Aristocrats kept selected animals for display in the sixteenth century and earlier, and upper-class women in the eighteenth century, as we have already seen, were frequently satirized for their affection for monkeys, parrots, and lap dogs, as well as squirrels and ferrets. But the socially widespread assumption of household intimacy with a companion animal is an eighteenth-century invention. Thomas argues that pet keeping supplies the cultural context against which the modern tendency "to break down the rigid boundaries between animals and men" can be understood (119, 122). The breeding of ornamental fish, especially goldfish, an aristocratic pastime in the early part of the period, became widespread in the course of the eighteenth century. And the keeping and breeding of cage birds—especially canaries and pigeons—came to be a popular obsession. J. H. Plumb summarizes the development of bird-keeping in the period:

> Canaries had been on sale in London from the sixteenth century, but the growth in the trade was not very rapid until after 1700. In the early eighteenth century families were encouraged to buy nesting boxes to try and breed their own outstanding songsters. The variety of birds for sale constantly expanded, and novelties were eagerly sought. Parrots and cockatoos, the pets of the aristocracy of the sixteenth and seventeenth centuries, now adorned the parlours of shopkeepers and artisans. So popular were unusual birds that the owners of pleasure gardens around London and the provincial towns set up aviaries in order to attract customers.

Plumb cites, for example, a contemporary advertisement for "Choice Parakeets, Talking Parrots, the finest Cockatoo that was ever seen in England, choice Canary Birds . . ."[26]

[26] J. H. Plumb, "The Acceptance of Modernity," in *The Birth of a Consumer Society: The Commercialization of Eighteenth-Century England,* ed. Neil McKendrick, John Brewer, and Plumb (Bloomington: Indiana University Press, 1982), 321–322. On the history and spread of parrot keeping, see also Edward J. Boosey, *Parrots, Cockatoos and Macaws* (Silver Springs, Md.: Denlinger's, 1956), chap. 1.

But most evident, even ubiquitous, in the eighteenth century was the canine house pet. The foundations for the canine obsession were laid before this period: toy spaniels were kept by upper class women in the sixteenth century, and pugs in the seventeenth. But it was in the eighteenth century that the canine house pet rose to the status of companion and acquired general recognition for intelligence, affection, and loyalty. Thomas shows that

> by 1700 all the symptoms of obsessive pet-keeping were in evidence. Pets were often fed better than the servants. They were adorned with rings, ribbons, feathers and bells; and they became an increasingly regular feature of painted family groups, usually as a symbol of fidelity, domesticity and completeness, though sometimes (as in the case of dogs) as an emblem of mischievous irreverence. (117)

For instance, in the self-portrait *Guglielmus Hogarth* (1740) designed to serve as the frontispiece to his complete prints, William Hogarth included a pug, whose face seems to be studied as closely as his own. This dog is probably "Trump," Hogarth's companion animal and a successor of the earlier "Pugg," kept by Hogarth in the 1730s and appearing in several of the conversation paintings of that decade. Pugg and Trump were artistic signatures for Hogarth, often interpreted iconographically as a sign of the artist's independence, pugnaciousness, or doggedness. But the cultural context of pet keeping suggests that they were also something more, figures of a complex and significant connection between the human and the nonhuman that iconography cannot fully explicate.[27]

As modern historians have shown, pet keeping is a hallmark of modernity, a bourgeois phenomenon sponsored by the middle class and linked at once to urbanization, commercialization, and alienation—"a development of genuine social, psychological, and indeed commercial importance" (Thomas, 119). Kathleen Kete in her study of nineteenth-century Parisian pet keeping, suggests that animals occupy the place of feeling and meaning for the modern bourgeoisie.[28] And Thomas shows that pets came to constitute a lucrative new source of speculation and profit in this

[27] See Ronald Paulson, *Hogarth*, vol. 2: *High Art and Low 1732–1750* (New Brunswick: Rutgers University Press, 1992), 260–264, and vol. 1: *The 'Modern Moral Subject' 1697–1732* (New Brunswick: Rutgers University Press, 1991), 222–224. On the repeated appearance of the pug, Paulson "wonders why, so early in his career, Hogarth insists on including . . . an aspect of himself . . . in so many pictures" (1: 223).

[28] Kathleen Kete, *The Beast in the Boudoir: Petkeeping in Nineteenth-Century Paris* (Berkeley: University of California Press, 1994).

period, leading directly to the institutionalization of dog fancy in the formation of the dog show and the Kennel Club in the nineteenth century (107). But the obsession with pets also contributed, like the display of the "learned pig" or the discovery of the "man of the woods," to a problematization of the distinctiveness of the human. According to Thomas, pet keeping "encouraged the middle classes to form optimistic conclusions about animal intelligence; it gave rise to innumerable anecdotes about animal sagacity; it stimulated the notion that animals could have character and individual personality; and it created the psychological foundation for the view that some animals at least were entitled to moral consideration" (119). Thomas sees in the phenomenon of pet keeping an epistemological confusion and a moral contradiction typical of the paradox of modernity, in which an unprecedented proximity to the animal kingdom on the part of humankind was ironically matched by an equally unprecedented "ruthless exploitation of other forms of animate life," an exploitation upon which the very "material foundations of human society" depended (302).

The fable of monkeys, parrots, and lap dogs represents the imaginative redaction of this complex contemporary encounter with the nonhuman. Its protagonist is a specific nonhuman being, one of a cohort marked in the contemporary imagination for its approach to the human: a monkey, a cage bird, or a canine pet, as Pope's couplet compactly indicates. This proximity to the human is the center of a systematic, sustained inquiry or negotiation. Unlike the native prince, the protagonist of this fable is not recuperated as a European ideal; the fable of the nonhuman being depicts a creature whose vivid and physical difference from his European and human author and audience is the central constituent of his story. The defining dynamic of this fable, then, is an imaginative approach to a radical alterity. Such an approach is specific to the eighteenth-century experience of difference, and distinguishes this cultural event from earlier representations of the relation between human and nonhuman beings.

In Shakespeare's *Tempest* (1611), for instance, Caliban's character blends human and beast in a manner the presages the central theme of the eighteenth-century fable, but with a different structure and focus. After the shipwreck, Trinculo encounters Caliban for the first time on the island, playing dead to avoid the pursuit of Prospero's spirits. At first glance, Trinculo mistakes him for a nonhuman being—a fish:

> What have we here, a man or a fish? Dead or alive?—A fish, he
> smells like a fish; a very ancient and fish-like smell; a kind of not-of-
> the-newest poor-john. A strange fish! Were I in England now, as

once I was, and had but this fish painted, not a holiday-fool there
but would give a piece of silver. There would this monster make a
man. Any strange beast there makes a man. When they will not give
a doit to relieve a lame beggar, they will lay out ten to see a dead
Indian. Legged like a man, and his fins like arms! Warm, o'my
troth! I do now let loose my opinion, hold it no longer. This is no
fish, but an islander that hath lately suffered by a thunderbolt.[29]

Here the boundary between human and animal is represented from the
perspective of the human rather than the animal: Caliban is the vehicle of
a comparison in which the fish is the tenor, and he quickly regains his full
humanity as an "islander." Trinculo abandons the figure of the nonhuman shortly after he generates it, with a decisive formulation—"this is no
fish"—that asserts a distinction between human and animal with a confidence not to be found in the eighteenth-century fable. Shakespeare's
image is a slippery and partial version of the fully contradictory figure that
appears in eighteenth-century print culture.

But this passage makes explicit the analogy that becomes pervasive in
later versions of the fable: that of the nonhuman and the non-European
human being. Caliban's brief blending with the fish directly evokes the
contemporary display of non-European bodies—"dead or alive"—in contexts that identified them with "monsters" brought back from the voyages
of discovery, "beasts" belonging to those regions beyond European civilization that in the Elizabethan period had begun to represent the allure
of a world newly opened to European exploitation. In her account of the
development of early modern taxonomy, Ritvo describes precisely this
cultural mode:

> The taxonomic relationship between Europeans and other human
> populations was mapped concretely as well as in words. Exhibitions
> inevitably emphasized the gap between observer and observed.
> Museums frequently displayed the remains of non-European
> human beings in ways that underlined their difference from Euro-
> peans or that suggested their greater affinity with other animals.
> Thus in 1766 a travelling [sic] collection of "curiosities" grouped a
> "Negro Child" with a "Monstrous Cat with 8 legs," a "Chicken's
> Foot with 6 Toes," a sloth, and an armadillo.[30]

[29] William Shakespeare, *The Tempest*, 2.2.23–34, in *The Norton Shakespeare*, ed. Stephen
Greenblatt et al. (New York: W. W. Norton, 1997). Subsequent references are to this edition;
act, scene, and line number are given within the text.
[30] Ritvo, *The Platypus and the Mermaid and Other Figments of the Classifying Imagination*
(Cambridge: Harvard University Press, 1997), 125.

No fishes in this list, though the "mermaid" was a famous object of such attention in London exhibitions in the seventeenth and eighteenth centuries,[31] and Locke himself cited "what is confidently reported of mermaids or sea-men" as an example of nature's infinite variety.[32] The eighteenth-century fable of the nonhuman being, as we shall see, extends this cultural engagement with non-European human beings in a way that gives the contradictions and exploitations of our fable a particular historical significance.

II

As we have seen, apes staged the question of the relation between human and animal most directly in eighteenth-century experience, and most explicitly in the print culture of the period. Prominent in the discursive representation of the ape was the trope of interspecies miscegenation, in which the male ape, usually the orangutang, is said to carry off the female African, often described as a "Hottentot," in order to enjoy her in his "woody retreat." This anecdote, emerging from a motif initially located in seventeenth-century travel literature, becomes established in eighteenth-century prose narrative and provides us with a powerful and provocative example of the fable of the nonhuman being.

H. W. Janson shows that what he calls the "rape-ape" theme is a new motif in the early modern period, with no significant classical or medieval versions.[33] He finds traces of this motif in a few sixteenth-century graphic representations of lascivious male apes but locates its first literary appearance in John Donne's *Progresse of the Soule* (1601). Donne's poem is a complex rendering of metempsychosis, gathering and negotiating various biblical, Cabalistic, and humanist strains of thought in order to represent the migration of the "deathlesse soule."[34] In the course of its incarnations, the

---

[31] Ritvo, *Platypus*, 180. See also Altick, 302–303.

[32] John Locke, *An Essay concerning Human Understanding*, ed. Peter H. Nidditch (Oxford: Clarendon Press, 1975), bk. 3, chap. 6, §12. See also Lovejoy, who notes in this context that the belief in mermen "supported as it seemed to be both by the principle of plenitude and the supposed testimony of many witnesses, could claim a certain respectability down to the late eighteenth century" from the first major natural history, Gesner's *Historia animalium* (1551–1587) (368). Subsequent references to Locke's *Essay* are to this edition; book, chapter, and paragraph numbers are given within the text.

[33] This account of the sources of the "rape-ape" theme is indebted to Janson's important work; see chap. 9. Winthrop D. Jordan also canvasses this theme, relying in part on Janson. See *White over Black: American Attitudes Toward the Negro, 1550–1812* (Chapel Hill: University of North Carolina Press, 1968), 28–32, 228–234.

[34] John Donne, *The Progresse of the Soule* in *Metempsychosis*, in *The Complete Poetry of John Donne*, ed. John T. Shawcross (New York: New York University Press, 1968), line 1. Subsequent references are to this edition; line numbers are given within the text.

soul enters the body of an ape and in that form falls in love with Siphatecia, the fifth daughter of Adam. Donne's poem raises the question of the
ape's relation to the human in a way that prefigures the eighteenth-
century debate:

> His organs now so like theirs [humans] hee doth finde,
> That why he cannot laugh, and speake his minde,
> He wonders.
>
> (ll. 454–456)

Janson speculates that this "startlingly 'modern' thought"—that imagines
apes as humans without speech—could be Donne's anticipation of the
major themes of the eighteenth century debate, through early information
about the great apes that he might have obtained from travel writings before the first anatomical evaluations of actual apes. Donne's poem fore-
shadows the eighteenth-century negotiation of the relation between human
and nonhuman, but its Cabalistic concerns and its formal rendering of the
love affair distance it from the eighteenth-century anecdote. Donne's ape
courts Siphatecia, gazing on her, wooing her, making her merry, and finally, "up lifts subtly with his russet pawe / Her kidskinne apron without
feare or awe / Of nature" (ll. 478–480). And she responds in a like manner:

> First she was silly'and knew not what he ment.
> That vertue, by his touches, chaft and spent,
> Succeeds an itchie warmth, that melts her quite;
> She knew not first, nowe cares not what he doth,
> And willing halfe and more, more than halfe loth,
> She neither puls nor pushes, but outright
> Now cries, and now repents.
>
> (ll. 481–487)

Their congress is interrupted by her brother, who throws a "great
stone . . . After the Ape, who, thus prevented, flew" (ll. 488–490). The
subtlety, the reciprocity, and the gradual approach of human and nonhuman in Donne's story are replaced, in the eighteenth-century fable, with a
symptomatic suddenness, haste, and violence.

Janson finds the most influential versions of the story in seventeenth-
century travel narrative: "Presented as a true experience in some remote
corner of the world, the story gained a new flavour of authenticity, until it
was eventually accepted as one of the established facts of natural history"
(275). He locates the "archetype" of this theme in a tale in Francesco
Maria Guazzo's *Compendium Maleficarum* (Milan, 1608), which we shall

see recounted by Tyson below. And he describes several subsequent versions of the story in the French tradition to which he traces the scene of the ape lovers in Voltaire's *Candide* (1759) (275–276). In eighteenth-century England, the sexual encounter of ape and human is a staple trope in the fable of the nonhuman being, offering a fertile instance in which a radical alterity is countered by a sudden intimacy, a formal dynamic that is emphasized and developed in the many contemporary redactions of this anecdote.[35]

The most influential version of the miscegenation anecdote was that recited by Edward Tyson in the *Anatomy of a Pygmie* (1699). At the point in the anatomy of his examination of the chimpanzee's reproductive organs, Tyson evokes the "infinite Stories" of these animals, which are very "salacious":

> That the whole *Ape*-kind is extreamly given to *Venery*, appears by infinite Stories related of them. And not only so, but different from other *Brutes*, they covet not their *own Species*, but to an Excess are inclined and sollicitous to those of a *different*, and are more *amorous* of fair *Women*. Besides what I have already mentioned, *Gabriel Clauderus* tells us of an *Ape*, which grew so amorous of one of the *Maids* of *Honour*, who was a celebrated Beauty, that no Chains, nor Confinement, nor Beating, could keep him within Bounds; so that the *Lady* was forced to petition to have him banished the Court. But that Story of *Castanenda* in his *Annals of Portugal* (if true) is very remarkable; of a Woman who had two Children by an *Ape*. I shall give it in *Latin*, as 'tis related by *Licetus*; and 'tis quoted too by *Anton. Deusingius* and others.

The Latin text describes the story, reproduced from the *Compendium Maleficarum*, of the abduction of a woman, left on a desert island, by an ape, the leader of a tribe of such nonhuman beings, who keeps her as a wife and to whom she bears two children. Rescued from the ape, the

---

[35] In addition to the texts by Tyson, Long, and Swift cited below, other references to the story are to be found in George Louis Leclerc Buffon, *Buffon's Natural History* (London, 1797), 9: 289–290; Thomas Herbert, *A Relation of Some Yeares Travaile . . . Into Afrique and the Greater Asia* (London, 1634), 17–20 (cited in Jordan, 31 n. 64); Thomas Phillips, *A Journal of a Voyage Made . . . from England to Cape Monseradoe, in Africa*, in John and Awsham Churchill, comps., *A Collection of Voyages and Travels* (London, 1704–32), 4: 211 (cited in Jordan, 31 n. 64); William Smith, *A New Voyage to Guinea . . .* (London, 1744), 52 (cited in Jordan, 31 n. 64); Lionel Wafer, *A New Voyage and Description of the Isthmus of America* (1699), ed. George Parker Winship (New York: Burt Franklin, 1970), 113 n; Charles White, *An Account of the Regular Gradation in Man* (London, 1799), 34 (cited in Harriet Ritvo, "Barring the Cross: Miscegenation and Purity in Eighteenth- and Nineteenth-Century Britain," in *Human, All Too Human*, ed. Diana Fuss [New York: Routledge, 1996], 37–58, 43).

woman is taken away by ship, and the ape throws the children, and then himself, into the sea (43).[36] Tyson's representations of the anecdote of miscegenation, like almost all subsequent ones, claim to recite an earlier testimony. As this story is retold in the eighteenth century, its form comes to dwell on the sudden and violent—the beating of the ape-courtier and the death of the hybrid infants—but to counterpose those effects with a sense of the inevitability or even the anatomical necessity of this connection, so that the anecdote represents a leap of affinity, in which a posited alterity is reversed by a surprising connection. This leap is the hallmark of the fable of the nonhuman being.

In the case of the miscegenation anecdote, this leap can generate an anxious reaction that is used to separate, not the ape from the human—the core of the experience of the fable of the nonhuman being—but the non-European human from the European human. Thus Edward Long in his *History of Jamaica* (1774) concludes from his recitation of the miscegenation story that the mixing of apes and Hottentots proves the African to be of a different species from the European:

> it is also averred, that [orangutangs] sometimes endeavour to surprize and carry off Negroe women into their woody retreats, in order to enjoy them. . . that they conceive a Passion for the Negroe women, and hence must be supposed to covet their embraces from a natural impulse of desire, such as inclines one animal towards another of the same species, or which has a conformity in the organs of generation. . . [this is proof that] the oran-outang and some races of black men are very nearly allied.[37]

This passage, in a form typical of the miscegenation story, imagines the encounter with radical alterity as both a "surprize" and a "natural impulse," and it structures the anecdote around those contrasting poles. In this version of the story, though, an "alliance" is emphasized between the orangutang and "some races of black men," an alliance that implies a division between the non-European and the European, and results in an assertion of European identity that is meant to enforce that division among the readers of this text. Arguments, like Long's, claiming the inferiority of certain non-European human beings to Europeans or "whites," arose in

[36] This tale extends the story of interspecies miscegenation into the trope of separation, which is taken up later in various imaginary accounts of cultural contact, notably, for instance, that of Yarico and Inkle. In fact, the representation of interspecies miscegenation is one of the most direct rhetorical contexts for the Yarico and Inkle story, prefiguring the scene of courtship in the cave and the shipboard separation, as well as the murder of the child.

[37] Edward Long, *The History of Jamaica* . . . (London, 1774), 1:360, 364, 370.

the latter part of the eighteenth century in support of a newly popular theory of polygenism. This notion of biologically separate human species countered the more orthodox monogenism that maintained both the distinction between human and nonhuman beings, and the assumption of human superiority and uniqueness. The "blending" of human and nonhuman challenged these assumptions of human superiority in a way that destabilized contemporary thinking about alterity—among humans and between humans and animals.[38]

The complex and reciprocal relationship between the attack on human superiority and the development of racialist thinking finds a canonical expression in the most widely read version of the miscegenation story, the bathing scene in the fourth voyage of Jonathan Swift's *Gulliver's Travels* (1726). In the Yahoos of the fourth voyage, Swift combined the traits of both apes and Africans, in the latter case the "Hottentots," commonly thought to be the most primitive race of humans.[39] In this scene, the female Yahoo's sexual interest in Gulliver proves his connection with the Yahoos:

> Being one day abroad with my protector the sorrel nag, and the weather exceeding hot, I entreated him to let me bathe in a river that was near. He consented, and I immediately stripped myself stark naked, and went down softly into the stream. It happened that a young female yahoo, standing behind a bank, saw the whole proceeding, and inflamed by desire . . . came running with all speed, and leaped into the water within five yards of the place

[38] Anthony J. Barker has shown Long's extensive debt to Samuel Estwick's idea of racial gradation, in which Negroes are seen as a different species from Europeans, taken from the second edition of Estwick's *Considerations on the Negro Cause* (1772). See Barker, *The African Link: British Attitudes to the Negro in the Era of the Atlantic Slave Trade, 1550–1807* (London: Frank Cass, 1978), 47–48. Roxann Wheeler provides a reading of Long's *History* that indicates the complexity of its construction of a racialist hierarchy, a construction that nevertheless moves toward the development of hierarchy based on physical differences. Wheeler's study of race places Long at a pivotal point in the development of a modern, essentialist idea of racism, which she sees as arising gradually out of the "general lack of coherence of discourses of human difference" that characterize the earlier eighteenth century. *The Complexion of Race: Categories of Difference in Eighteenth-Century British Culture* (Philadelphia: University of Pennsylvania Press, 2000), 232. And Ritvo has highlighted the overdetermined significance of hybrid creatures and animal miscegenation in this century and the next, showing that "discussions of animal miscegenation inevitably connected general zoological matters with more narrowly human concerns. . . . In a period of global empire . . . the zoological . . . discussion of these matters . . . may have derived much of its structure, as well as its heated tone, from its easy compromise of the taxonomic barrier that ostensibly separated animals from people" ("Barring the Cross," 52).

[39] On the Yahoos' relation to apes, see Janson, 339; on their relation to Hottentots, see Laura Brown, *Ends of Empire: Women and Ideology in Early Eighteenth-Century English Literature* (Ithaca: Cornell University Press, 1993), chap. 6.

where I bathed. I was never in my life so terribly frighted . . . She embraced me after a most fulsome manner; I roared as loud as I could and the nag came galloping towards me, whereupon she quitted her grasp, with the utmost reluctancy, and leaped upon the opposite bank, where she stood gazing and howling all the time I was putting on my clothes. . . . now I could no longer deny that I was a real yahoo in every limb and feature, since the females had a natural propensity to me as one of their own species.[40]

This passage stages the approach to alterity in the same form that we have detailed in the other appearances of the anecdote. In fact, it elaborates and emphasizes those distinctive formal traits. Expressions of suddenness, haste, and loud alarm—"running," "leaping," "roaring," "galloping," and "howling"—disrupt a contrastingly quiet and peaceful moment in the text as Gulliver goes "down softly into the stream." That abrupt and rapid movement is matched with a subsequent assertion of inevitability, the familiar allusion to a "natural propensity" towards "one of their own species." The leap of affinity here is marked by a statement of identification—"I could no longer deny that I was a real yahoo"—which makes explicit the movement of proximity that provides the underlying dynamic of the fable of the nonhuman being, and at the same time asserts a specific human identity.

The question of course in the fourth voyage of *Gulliver's Travels* is whether the Yahoo is a human or a nonhuman being, precisely the problematic that underlies contemporary thinking both about the human and about cultural difference. Thus, in *Gulliver's Travels*, the dynamic of proximity typical of the fable of the nonhuman being doubles upon itself. This passage proliferates the leap of affinity, twisting the miscegenation anecdote in a way that highlights and deepens its encounter with alterity. As we have seen, the established pattern of the story of interspecies miscegenation represents a male ape setting upon a female African.[41] In this passage, however, the female Yahoo, herself both human and animal, taking the place of the male ape, attacks the male Gulliver, a European human standing in for the female African. This intersection of alterities complicates and opens up the implications of the fable of the nonhuman being. Male and female sexual roles are reversed in Swift's version of the anecdote, and as a consequence African and European identities are su-

[40] Jonathan Swift, *Gulliver's Travels and Other Writings*, ed. Louis A. Landa (Boston: Houghton Mifflin, 1960), 215.

[41] Aside from this passage in *Gulliver's Travels*, there are no known counterexamples. Schiebinger asserts that "in these accounts it is invariably the male ape who forced himself on the human female. To my knowledge there was not one account in this period of a female ape taking a man or even of intercourse between a female ape and a male human" (95). See also Jordan, 238.

perimposed, so that Gulliver occupies the position of both male and female, African and European at once.

Such a confluence of affinities brings the movement of proximity to
bear upon the European reader himself in an assertion of identity that
prevents that racialist separation of the non-European from the European
that we have seen in Long's version of the story, as well as in the contemporary displays of non-Europeans alongside nonhuman new world curiosi-
ties. Neither Gulliver nor Swift's reader can stand clear of this story. It is
specifically structured to implicate its audience, in the same way that *Gulliver's Travels* as a whole, and Swift's satire in general, works to implicate its
reader, as the modern critical tradition of Swift has consistently con-
tended. But in this case we can see how Swift's distinctive and notorious
satiric form is structured by its particular manipulation of a well-developed
contemporary cultural fable. The intersections in this passage also suggest
an interdependency of affinities—male and female, African and European—such that the leap that produces a point of contact between the
poles of one pair of opposing positions corresponds precisely with the leap
that joins the other pair. In this sense, Swift's version of the miscegenation
story serves to extend the relevance of the fable of the nonhuman being,
linking its differences of species and culture with those of gender.[42]

In the next quarter of the century, in the course of his long pair of
chapters in *Of the Origin and Progress of Language* designed to prove
through the example of the orangutang that "language is natural to
man,"[43] Lord Monboddo reminds his reader variously and repeatedly of

---

[42] The influence of the fable of the nonhuman being is even evident in an anecdote in
Olaudah Equiano's *Narrative* (1789) describing Equiano's unexpected meeting with another "black boy" on the Isle of Wight. Here the distance is the effect of Equiano's partial de-
racination, which initially links him to the European side of the equation, but which is
quickly superceded by brotherhood:

> I was one day in a field belonging to a gentleman who had a black boy about my
> own size; this boy having observed me from his master's house, was transported at
> the sight of one of his own countrymen, and ran to meet me with the utmost haste.
> I not knowing what he was about, turned a little out of his way at first, but to no pur-
> pose; he soon came close to me, and caught hold of me in his arms as if I had been
> his brother, though we had never seen each other before.

The peaceful field, the physical distance, the "transport," "haste," and speed, the difference
as Equiano turns away, and the telltale embrace are all established aspects of our fable,
which is here recruited to the purpose of representing the complexity of African diasporic
identity. Olaudah Equiano, *The Interesting Narrative and Other Writings*, ed. Vincent Carretta
(New York: Penguin, 1995), 85.

[43] James Burnet, Lord Monboddo, *Of the Origin and Progress of Language*, 2d ed. (Edinburgh, 1774; reprint, New York: Garland, 1970), 1:360. Subsequent references are to this
edition; page numbers are given within the text.

the miscegenation story. Early in his discussion he recalls those claims "that [the orangutang] is very fond of women, whom they always attack when they meet with them in the woods" (274–275). He specifically quotes a well-known traveler, "Mr de la Brosse," who "made a voyage to Angola in 1738 . . . [and found] that these Orang Outangs, whom he calls by the name of *Quimpezes* . . . . carry away young negroe girls, and keep them for their pleasure: And, he says, he knew one negroe girl that had been with them three years" (277–278). He cites the miscegenation story as an indication of the orangutang's character: "they shew also counsel and design, by carrying off creatures of our species, for certain purposes, and keeping them for years together, without doing them any harm; which no brute creature was ever known to do" (289–290). And he recalls other "certain" evidence "that [the orangutang] copulates with our females, and [there is] the greatest reason to believe, that there is offspring of such copulation" (334), because "Keoping, the Swedish traveller . . . relates, that he himself saw the offspring of a woman by an Orang Outang, which having in it all the vigour of the wild race, immediately, when it was born, began to run about, and to climb upon every thing" (334n).

Indeed, Monboddo's description of the orangutang can be seen as a proliferative expansion of the anecdote of miscegenation, a repetition, in a series of episodes and assertions, of that distinctive dynamic of proximity. And for Monboddo, as for Swift, the human pole in that leap of affinity, though sometimes specified as non-European or "negroe," is clearly grouped with Europeans rather than separated from them: "our" species and "our" females constitute the link with the ape. Building on Rousseau's argument about language and the status of the ape in his *Second Discourse*,[44] as well as on Tyson's *Anatomy of a Pygmie*, Monboddo constructs an exhaustive and comprehensive encyclopedia of the affinity of the human and the nonhuman being, structured throughout in terms of the same trajectory of surprise and inevitability that marks the miscegenation story. In the long course of Monboddo's account, evidence for the connection between apes and humans is raised to an insistence on their identity. Monboddo notes for instance that Tyson's dissection demonstrated, surprisingly, a similarity between the "small" orangutang's body, tongue, viscera, and brain and that of man, and he concludes that "for any thing we know, the great Orang Outang may be still more like men such as we" (272). Like the contemporary London displays and shows, Monboddo is preoccupied with images of apes dressed in human clothes

[44] Lovejoy sees Rousseau's *Second Discourse* (1753), note j, as directly influential on Monboddo. See Lovejoy, *The Great Chain of Being*, 235; and "Monboddo and Rousseau," *Modern Philology* 30 (1933): 275–276.

and performing human actions. He cites numerous instances of apes walking erect, wearing clothing, "play[ing] very well upon the pipe, harp, and other instruments," "performing domestic offices," and learning "to sit at table; to eat of every thing; to make use of the spoon, knife, and fork; and drink wine and other liquors," "and, when they were looked at, . . . conceal[ing] with their hand, those parts, which modesty forbids to shew" (275–279).

But beyond these concrete displays of resemblance, Monboddo is especially concerned to project a shared sensibility that provides an affective identity between orangutangs and humans. Orangutangs, he contends, have been observed to weep and groan (274); they are "sensible of their captivity, and appear . . . melancholy" (279); they have a "sense of honour," and "if they are laughed at, they take it so much to heart, that they languish and die" (287). Indeed, possessed of "a mildness and a gentleness in [their] nature," they are

> capable of the greatest affection, not only to [their] brother Orang Outangs, but to such among us as use him kindly. And it is a fact, well attested to me by a gentleman who was an eye-witness of it, that an Orang Outang, which was on board his ship, conceived such an affection for the cook, that when, upon some occasion, he left the ship, to go ashore, the gentleman saw the Orang Outang shed tears in great abundance. (343–345)

This story condenses contemporary ideas about the orangutang's "humane" disposition (289). And as such it serves as a sequel and counterpoint to the miscegenation story, a testimony to a surprising but natural intimacy, based, in this passage, on the nonhuman being's expression of that very affective identity Monboddo takes to be constitutive of the human—a "great abundance" of tears. Affinity is balanced by distance even here, however, though the leap is a retrospective one: the affection of the ape and the cook is only evident upon their separation.

Monboddo takes note of the current debate about the biological classification of the orangutang in relation to the human—the hotly contested question of species—citing positions on both sides. That taxonomic question, however, is clearly subordinated to the concrete and visceral images and stories that enact the movement of proximity in Monboddo's text. Monboddo's essay, though it advances an abstract ontological point, adopts the vivid rhetoric and distinctive dynamic of the fable of the nonhuman being. And like other instances of this resonant fable, Monboddo's argument implicates the non-European human being in a direct analogy to the ape:

If . . . the Orang Outang be not a man, then those philosophers of
Europe, who, about the time of the discovery of America, maintained, that the inhabitants of that part of the world were not men,
reasoned well; for, certainly, the Americans had not then, nor have
they yet, learned all the arts of which their nature is capable. But I
think the Pope, by his bull, decided the controversy well, when he
gave it in favour of the humanity of the poor Americans: And for
the same reason, we ought to decide, that the Orang Outangs are
men. And, indeed, it appears to me, that they are not so much inferior to the Americans in civility and cultivation, as some nations of
America were to us, when we first discovered that country. (347–348)

Here, as in Long's conclusion to the miscegenation story, the identity of
the nonhuman being is inextricable from the contemporary encounter
with cultural difference. And for Monboddo the conviction of the affinity of apes and humans is a matter of human dignity: he argues emphatically that we do not "disgrace our nature, as we imagine, by admitting
the Orang Outang to a participation of it" (343). In fact, the denial of
this participation amounts to "a false pride, to think highly derogatory
from human nature, what the philosopher, on the contrary, will think
the greatest praise of man, that, from the savage state, in which the
Orang Outang lives, he should, by his own sagacity and industry, have arrived at the state in which we now see him" (360–361). This assertion
comes at a summary point in Monboddo's second chapter on the orangutang, and, like Gulliver's claim that he "was a real yahoo," it serves as a
statement of identification and identity. For Monboddo too, that leap of
affinity from the human to the orangutang entails the claim to a particular human identity. Though Monboddo and Swift make opposite assessments of the implications of this identity—from secular optimism to
Christian pessimism—both imagine human being by means of a difference from the non-European being, which they both construct in terms
of the nonhuman.

III

In describing the names of substances and their divisions into sorts or
species in the *Essay concerning Human Understanding*, Locke exemplifies
his claim "that *men* make sorts of things," not nature, with a very familiar
example:

Nature makes many *particular things*, . . . But it is not this real
essence that distinguishes them into species; it is men who . . .

range them into sorts . . . for the convenience of comprehensive
signs; under which individuals . . . come to be ranked . . . : this is a
man, that is a drill [baboon]: and in this, I think, consists the whole
business of genus and species. (bk. 3, chap. 6, §36)

Locke's image, unlike Monboddo's, assumes a separation between man
and ape, but a separation, like Pope's, that derives its meaning from its allusion to the contemporary movement of proximity between the human
and the nonhuman.

In the *Essay* that proximity is also developed in the representation of
another member of the nonhuman cohort of this fable, the parrot. The
parrot, as we have seen, is a major cultural locus of human attention and
expense in the eighteenth century; and this creature is also a favorite nonhuman exemplum in the philosophical discourse of the period.[45] Locke
uses the parrot to draw the distinction between "articulate sounds" and
language—"signs of internal conceptions": "for parrots, and several other
birds, will be taught to make articulate sounds distinct enough, which yet
by no means are capable of language" (bk. 3, chap. 1, §1). Locke's implication, that language is a means of defining man, sets the terms for the
complex debate on language which Monboddo later engages in his *Origin
and Progress of Language* and which becomes, as Monboddo develops it, a
debate about the status of the human. Monboddo's argument is that the
orangutang resembles man in every respect except speech, and hence
"that language is not natural to man" (358). But Locke's linking of language and man does not eliminate the possibility of a much nearer proximity between the animal and the human. In book 2 of the *Essay*, the nonhuman being appears as a "very intelligent rational parrot," and a means
to the definition of a "*Man*":

> the *Idea* in our Minds, of which the Sound *Man* in our Mouths is
> the Sign, is nothing else but of an Animal of such a certain Form:
> Since I think I may be confident, that whoever should see a Crea-
> ture of his own Shape and Make, though it had no more reason all
> its Life, than a *Cat* or a *Parrot*, would call him still a *Man*; or who-
> ever should hear a *Cat* or a *Parrot* discourse, reason, and philoso-
> phize, would call or think it nothing but a *Cat* or a *Parrot*; and say,

---

[45] On the parrot's various connections with the contemplation of difference, in the figure of the non-European "savage," the woman, or the "defective being," especially as defined
by the capacity for speech, see Felicity A. Nussbaum, "Speechless: Haywood's Deaf and
Dumb Projector," in *The Passionate Fictions of Eliza Haywood: Essays on Her Life and Work*, ed.
Kirsten T. Saxton and Rebecca P. Bocchicchio (Lexington: University of Kentucky Press,
2000), 194–216.

the one was a dull irrational *Man*, and the other a very intelligent rational *Parrot.* (bk. 2, chap. 27, §8)[46]

"*Man*" acquires his identity as an animal "of a certain Form" by means of his simultaneous separation from and identification with the rational parrot, whose possible proximity to man as an "intelligent rational" being makes him the test case for human identity.

This argument is succeeded by a long anecdote extracted from the *Memoirs* of Sir William Temple about a particular nonhuman "Talker" (bk. 2, chap. 27, §8). Locke quotes Temple's account of his attempt to verify the story of this parrot:

> I had a mind to know from *Prince Maurice*'s own Mouth, the account of a common, but much credited Story, that I had heard so often from many others, of an old *Parrot* he had in *Brasil*, during his Government there, that spoke, and asked, and answered common Questions like a reasonable Creature . . . I had heard many particulars of this Story, and assevered by People hard to be discredited, which made me ask *Prince Maurice* what there was of it.

And next, Locke quotes Temple's quotation of Prince Maurice's story:

> He . . . told me short and coldly, that he had heard of such an old *Parrot* when he came to *Brasil*, and though he believed nothing of it, and 'twas a good way off, yet he had so much Curiosity as to send

[46] Locke's pairing of the cat with the parrot suggests that the issue of speech, mechanical or not, was less significant than the general sense of the growing intimacy between man and animal. After our cohort of monkeys, parrots, and lap dogs, the cat, another animal newly embraced in this period as a household pet, was an additional locus for the encounter with alterity. The most famous pets in the literary canon of this period are cats: Samuel Johnson's Hodge and Christopher Smart's Jeoffrey. Cats figure prominently not only in Smart's *Jubilate Agno* (1763) but also in Thomas Gray's *Ode on the Death of a Favourite Cat* (1738) and Anna Seward's *An Old Cat's Dying Soliloquy* (1784). Margaret Doody has argued that an intimacy with animals—cats and other species—is especially common among eighteenth-century women poets; "Sensuousness in the Poetry of Eighteenth-Century Women Poets," in *Women's Poetry in the Enlightenment: The Making of a Canon, 1730–1820*, ed. Isobel Armstrong and Virginia Blain (New York: St. Martin's Press, 1999), 3–32. Johnson provides the non-European perspective on the imaginative status of the cat; describing the native Americans: "Johnson. 'Now what a wretch must he be, who is content with such conversation as can be had among savages! You may remember an officer at Fort Augustus, who had served in America, told us of a woman they were obliged to *bind*, in order to get her back from savage life.' Boswell. 'She must have been an animal, a beast.' Johnson. 'Sir, she was a speaking cat.' " James Boswell, *Life of Johnson*, ed. J. D. Fleeman, rev. ed. (Oxford: Oxford University Press, 1953), 912.

for it, that 'twas a very great and a very old one; and when it came
first into the Room where the Prince was, with a great many *Dutch-
men* about him, it said presently, *What a company of white Men are
here?* They asked it what he thought that Man was, pointing at the
Prince? It answered, *Some General or other;* when they brought it
close to him, he asked it, *D'ou venes vous?* it answered, *De Marinnan.*
The Prince, *A qui estes vous?* The Parrot. *A un Portugais.* Prince, *Que
fais tu la?* Parrot, *Je garde les poulles.* The Prince laughed and said,
Vous gardez les poulles? The Parrot answered, *Ouy, moy et je scay bien
faire;* and made the Chuck four or five times that People use to
make to Chickens when they call them. I set down the Words of
this worthy Dialogue in *French,* just as Prince *Maurice* said them to
me. I asked him in what Language the *Parrot* spoke, and he said, in
Brasilian; I asked whether he understood *Brasilian;* he said No, but
he had taken care to have two Interpreters by him, the one a *Dutchman,* that spoke *Brasilian,* and the other a *Brasilian,* that spoke
Dutch; that he asked them separately and privately, and both of
them agreed in telling him just the same thing that the *Parrot* said.

Temple's summary deliberately leaves unanswered the question of the
rational parrot:

I could not but tell this odd Story, because it is so much out of the
way, and from the first hand, and what may pass for a good one; for
I dare say this Prince, at least, believed himself in all he told me,
having ever passed for a very honest and pious Man; I leave it to
Naturalists to reason, and to other Men to believe as they please
upon it; however, it is not, perhaps, amiss to relieve or enliven a
busie Scene sometimes with such digressions, whether to the purpose or no. (bk. 2, chap. 27, §8)

Locke's story reproduces a formal dynamic typical of the fable of the
nonhuman being. This text places multiple impediments between the "rational parrot" and the incredulous contemporary human audience: both
geographical distance and layers of language and narration. The parrot is
"a good way off" from the Prince, to whom he must be transported, but
this new world story itself is another "good way off" from the metropolitan
locus of its telling. The Prince's account is twice retold by Temple and,
then, by Locke, and the parrot's own language is twice or thrice translated: from "Brasilian" into Dutch, from Dutch into French, and finally
from French into English, by Locke's English reader. But these impediments to the connection of parrot and human dissolve at the point of the

parrot's dialogue with the Prince, an event that produces that leap of affinity characteristic of this fable. Human and nonhuman suddenly make direct contact in this strange interspecies repartee, and even the Prince's own "short and cold" demeanor is through this contact transformed into a "laugh."

The nonhuman participant in this dynamic of proximity is linked to the non-European human in the same way that Monboddo's nonhuman reminds him of the "poor Americans." Here, the parrot's opening observation alludes to the cultural oppositions in his new world setting: "*What a company of white Men are here?*" In the Brasilian colonial state, the "white men"— French, Dutch, and Portuguese—are immediately singled out by the "rational" parrot, in contrast to a nonwhite group with which the parrot by this observation implicitly links himself. Although Locke's story is designed to demonstrate "the *Idea* of a *Man*" by separating the human from "an Animal of [a different] Form," namely the rational parrot, the dynamic of the story locates human identity through its proximity to that same animal—a nonhuman being whose status is shared by the non-European. Locke's use of Temple's anecdote demonstrates a conjunction of nonhuman and non-European that often accompanies the fable of the nonhuman being. And the anecdote demonstrates this conjunction at the same time as it shows our fable's deep implication in the constitution of a human identity. "Man" is conceived through the story of an animal that sees itself as a native.

The parrot makes other appearances in the philosophical discourse of the eighteenth century. Charles Bonnet in *The Contemplation of Nature* (1766) follows Locke's argument about the connection between language and man, but without entertaining the possibility raised in Locke's parrot story of a "very intelligent rational parrot." Bonnet argues that "to *speak*, is to connect our *ideas* with *arbitrary* signs that *represent* them. The phrases which the parrot repeats with so much exactness, do not prove that he has any ideas annexed to the words he pronounces: he could pronounce equally well the terms of the most abstracted sciences. Who does not see that this is an exercise purely automatical?"[47]

This heritage of the use of the parrot to define the problem of the human in British epistemological thought also accounts for David Hume's employment of the figure in his footnote to "Of National Characters" (1758) in the *Moral and Political Essays*, where the parrot is directly identified with the non-European in order to distinguish both from the European and the human:

47 Charles Bonnet, in *The Contemplation of Nature* (1766), 2:182. Cited in Markman Ellis, *The Politics of Sensibility: Race, Gender and Commerce in the Sentimental Novel* (Cambridge: Cambridge University Press, 1996), 75.

I am apt to suspect the negroes, and in general all other species of men (for there are four or five different kinds) to be naturally inferior to the whites. There never was a civiliz'd nation of any other complexion than white, nor even any individual eminent either in action or speculation. No ingenious manufactures amongst them, no arts, no sciences. On the other hand, the most rude and barbarous of the whites, such as the ancient *Germans*, the present *Tartars*, have still something eminent about them, in their valour, form of government, or some other particular. Such a uniform and constant difference could not happen, in so many countries and ages, if nature had not made an original distinction between these breeds of men. Not to mention our colonies, there are *Negroe* slaves dispersed all over *Europe*, of whom none ever discovered any symptoms of ingenuity; tho' low people, without education, will start up amongst us, and distinguish themselves in every profession. In *Jamaica*, indeed, they talk of one negro, as a man of parts and learning; but 'tis likely he is admir'd for slender accomplishments, like a parrot who speaks a few words plainly.[48]

Hume's example of Francis Williams, the Cambridge educated mathematician, places Williams, like Locke's parrot, at a geographical and narrative distance from the European and the human, or in Hume's case the white "species" of men. Here again in this brief evocation of our fable, the nonhuman being is the ultimate test case for human identity, while the movement of proximity is condensed into the image of the speaking parrot with its evocation of that sudden affinity of human and animal.

But the parrot, or his feathered prototype, appears elsewhere in the print culture of the eighteenth century, linked as in the philosophical discourse with the contemporary encounter with the non-European. In this era of pet-keeping, feathered beings are a common metaphor for new world peoples. Pope's *Windsor Forest*, for example, alludes in its triumphant encomium to the *pax britannica* to the "Feather'd People" who will flock to the shores of the Thames:

Then Ships of uncouth Form shall stem the Tyde,
And Feather'd People crowd my wealthy Side,
And naked Youths and painted Chiefs admire
Our Speech, our colour, and our strange Attire!

[48] David Hume, "Of National Characters," in *Essays: Moral, Political and Literary* (Oxford: Oxford University Press, 1963), 213 n. 1. The essay was originally published in 1742; this note was added in 1758 and slightly revised in 1777.

The feathers link the feathered dress, conventionally associated with native Americans, with the exotic birds themselves, fashionable imports from the new world, whose presence as a subtext is felt subtly in the image of nesting in "native Groves" in the lines that follow:

> Oh stretch thy Reign, fair *Peace!* From Shore to Shore,
> Till Conquest cease, and Slav'ry be no more:
> Till the freed *Indians* in their native Groves
> Reap their own Fruits, and woo their Sable Loves.[49]

The image of "wooing" in the "native Groves" of the new world is another constituent of the trope of feathered people, more clearly evident in the later opera *Love in Mexico* (1790), where the Indian maiden Isagli describes her lover Alkmonoak through this same figure: "I would deck our wigwam for my love's approach with all the variegated plumage of our luxuriant Indian groves. It shou'd be my ozier cage, and my love, my Alkmonoak, my sweet bird—he should be my bird of paradise and convert my hut into a Heaven."[50]

This image of feathered non-Europeans appears elsewhere in the poetic discourse of the eighteenth century: Thomas Gray's *Progress of Poesy* (1757) sees the same blending of human and nonhuman in the forests of the new world:

> And oft, beneath the odorous shade
> Of Chile's boundless forests laid,
> She deigns to hear the savage youth repeat
> In loose numbers wildly sweet
> Their feather-cinctur'd chiefs and dusky loves.[51]

Such passages, though they do not develop the fable of the nonhuman being in its full dynamic form, indicate a ready exchangeability in contemporary culture, by which a familiar companion animal and a non-European human could be seen through the same imaginative lens.

In this context, another famous cage bird from the canonical literary culture of the period provides a fully elaborated representation of the fable of the nonhuman being: the starling of Laurence Sterne's *Sentimen-*

---

[49] Alexander Pope, *Windsor Forest* in *Poems of Alexander Pope*, vol. 1, ed. E. Audra and Aubrey Williams (London: Methuen, 1961), lines 403–412.

[50] *New Spain; or, Love in Mexico* (1790), 2.3. Cited in Benjamin Bissell, *The American Indian in English Literature of the Eighteenth Century* (New Haven: Yale University Press, 1925), 140.

[51] Thomas Gray, "The Progress of Poetry," in *The Poems of Gray, Collins, and Goldsmith*, ed. Roger Lonsdale (New York: Longman, 1969), lines 58–62.

tal Journey (1768). Early in that novel, Yorick, fearful of the legal reper-
cussions of his traveling to France without a passport, pauses in the midst
of his own fantasy of imprisonment in the Bastille:

> I was interrupted in the hey-day of this soliloquy, with a voice which
> I took to be that of a child, which complained "it could not get
> out."—I looked up and down the passage [of the hotel], and see-
> ing neither man, woman, nor child, I went out without further
> attention.
>
> In my return back through the passage, I heard the same words
> repeated twice over; and looking up, I saw it was a starling hung in
> a little cage.—"I can't get out—I can't get out," said the starling.[52]

Yorick's story here emphasizes that characteristic transition from distance
to proximity that marks the fable of the nonhuman being. Yorick's musing state resembles Gulliver's soft descent to his bath in the stream; his
going out upon hearing the "voice" describes a physical remove like that
of the "rational parrot" from Prince Maurice; and this distance is answered by a surprising encounter with a speaker who is "neither man,
woman, nor child," but who engages Yorick in a dialogue like that between Prince Maurice and the parrot:

> I stood looking at the bird: and to every person who came through
> the passage it ran fluttering to the side towards which they
> approached it, with the same lamentation of its captivity.—"I can't
> get out," said the starling——God help thee! said I, but I'll get thee
> out, cost what it will. (96)

It is at this point that Yorick makes the leap of affinity, internalizing the
starling's experience and acting on his understanding of the starling's
words with a sudden energy and force: "I turned about the cage to get to
the door; it was twisted and double twisted so fast with wire, there was no
getting it open without pulling the cage to pieces—I took both hands to
it" (96).

Yorick's dialogue with the starling ends with his failure to liberate the
bird: "I fear, poor creature! said I, I cannot set thee at liberty—No,' said
the starling—'I can't get out—I can't get out,' said the starling." Their exchange transcends identification and serves, for the human participant,
as a test case for an assertion of identity:

[52] Laurence Sterne, *A Sentimental Journey Through France and Italy*, ed. Graham Petrie
(London: Penguin, 1967), 96. Subsequent references are to this edition; page numbers are
given within the text.

I vow, I never had my affections more tenderly awakened; or do I remember an incident in my life, where the dissipated spirits, to which my reason had been a bubble, were so suddenly called home. Mechanical as the notes were, yet so true in tune to nature were they chanted, that in one moment they overthrew all my systematic reasonings upon the Bastile; and I heavily walked upstairs, unsaying every word I had said in going down them.

Disguise thyself as thou wilt, still slavery! said I—still thou art a bitter draught. (96)[53]

Yorick's own prospective imprisonment in the Bastille has prepared him for the analogy with the caged starling, but his intensely experienced contact with the bird far exceeds such an identification—so far that he even repudiates his previous concern with his own fate to privilege the starling's plight. So powerful is the movement of proximity in Yorick's contact with the bird that Sterne can deliberately raise and directly supercede the debate over animal language that provides the contemporary context for the nonhuman "Talker" in its other redactions. This passage, in its evocation of the "mechanical" notes of the starling, echoes Bonnet's assertion of the "purely automatical" speech of the parrot. But that allusion is broached only to be set aside: "yet" and "in one moment" all that matters is that overwhelming proximity, which propels its audience into a direct and unquestioned relationship with alterity. That leap of affinity with the nonhuman expresses Yorick's consciousness of the "soul" within himself (137), those "affections" and "undescribable emotions" (137–138) that make him a man of feeling. And significantly, the nonhuman agent that generates Yorick's sentimental identity in this passage is ultimately figured as non-European. The imprisonment of the starling is a "disguise" for the institution of slavery, and the bird itself, in this last phase of the fable's dynamic unfolding, is an African slave in the new world. Both the turn to the constitution of identity and the implication of the non-European characterize the structure of the fable of the nonhuman being, as it projects the encounter with the nonhuman being upon the contempo-

---

[53] Many critics have taken up Sterne's image of the starling. Wilbur L. Cross described it as an observation upon slavery; see *The Life and Times of Laurence Sterne*, 3d ed. (New Haven: Yale University Press, 1929), 3. Jonathan Lamb sees the figure as symptomatic of the sentimental conjuncture of pleasure and pain; see "Language and Hartleian Associationism in *A Sentimental Journey*," *Eighteenth-Century Studies* 13 (1980): 285–312. In his edition of the *Sentimental Journey*, Gardner Stout calls attention in his annotation to this passage to the allusion of the starling to Sterne's family name; see 197 n. 66. And Michael Seidel sees it as an allusion to Crusoe's parrot; see *Exile and the Narrative Imagination* (New Haven: Yale University Press, 1986), 115. Ellis takes up a theme similar to my own; he sees Sterne's starling as an allusion to Hume's parrot (74).

rary problem of cultural difference with all of its implication in power and exploitation.

IV

When the fable of the nonhuman being is centered upon the life and fate of the lap dog, the non-European figure that we have seen variously shadowed in this imaginative venture of affinity consistently takes the shape of the African slave. An early emblematic passage in Sarah Scott's sentimental novel, *The History of Sir George Ellison* (1766), makes this connection of nonhuman and non-European explicit. In the opening pages of the novel, Sir George makes his fortune in trade in Jamaica and marries a widow who brings him "a considerable plantation, cultivated by a numerous race of slaves."[54] Opposed to the institution of slavery, but "sensible he could not abolish [it], even on his own estate" (10), Ellison, like Savillon in Mackenzie's *Julia de Roubigné*, undertakes to reform the treatment of his own slaves, much against his wife's wishes and sentiments. Mrs. Ellison "was above those soft timorous whims which so much affected him; . . . and never flinched at any punishment her steward thought proper to inflict" (12).

This discussion between Ellison and his wife, conducted in the abstract mode typical of this didactic narrative, is suddenly interrupted by the anomalous appearance of Mrs. Ellison's lap dog, which evokes an effusion of that very sentiment its owner has pointedly denied to her slaves:

> She was turning the conversation to another subject, when a
> favourite lap-dog, seeing her approach the house, in its eagerness
> to meet her jumped out of the window where it was standing; the
> height was too great to permit the poor cur to give this mark of
> affection with impunity; they soon perceived that it had broken its
> leg, and was in a good deal of pain; this drew a shower of tears from
> Mrs. Ellison's eyes, who, turning to her husband, said, "You will
> laugh at me for my weakness; but I cannot help it." (13)

The distance, the surprise, the sudden "eagerness," the tears, and the "natural" or inevitable nature of Mrs. Ellison's connection with the dog, all follow the formal structure of the fable of the nonhuman being. Here Mrs. Ellison

---

[54] Sarah Scott, *The History of Sir George Ellison*, ed. Betty Rizzo (Lexington: University Press of Kentucky, 1996), 10. Subsequent references are to this edition; page numbers are given within the text.

occupies the place of Yorick, the man of feeling, whose very nature is constituted by his leap of affinity with the nonhuman, or of Gulliver, who acknowledges, when the female Yahoo leaps from the bank into his embrace "that I was a real yahoo in every limb and feature." This emblematic scene both thematizes that movement that joins human to nonhuman—as the nonhuman leaps into the human embrace—and also directly implicates the link to the non-European that we have seen to be a persistent dimension of the imaginative experience of alterity. Ellison's response to his wife reflects on the relation between the African slave and the nonhuman being:

> "My dear," replied Mr. Ellison, "you will one day know me better than to think I can laugh at any one for a token of sensibility; to see any creature suffer is an affecting sight; and it gives me pleasure to observe you can feel for the poor little animal, whose love for you occasioned his accident; but I confess I am surprised, though agreeably, to see such marks of sensibility in a heart I feared was hardened against the sufferings even of her fellow creatures." (13)[55]

In this passage, the lap dog's leap into affinity generates the same debate about species as the miscegenation story, and the same constitution of identity. Long finds that apes and Africans are "nearly allied"; Gulliver cannot deny that he is of the same species as the Yahoo; and Mrs. Ellison's proximity to the lap dog indicates, in the context of this redaction of the fable of the nonhuman being, an equivalent proximity to the Africans who are her slaves—a proximity that she must be at pains, ineffectually, to deny: "Sure, Mr. Ellison, you do not call negroes my fellow creatures?" Ellison's response provides a definition of the human and an assertion of identity that serves as the climax of this anecdote, a climax characteristic of the fable of the nonhuman being: "Indeed, my dear, . . . I must call them so, till you can prove to me, that the distinguishing marks of humanity lie in the complexion or turn of features. When you and I are laid in the grave, our lowest black slave will be as great as we are; in the next world perhaps much greater" (13).[56]

Mrs. Ellison's affection for her lap dog refers to a satiric theme of misogynist writing in the eighteenth century—that of the intimacy of the lap dog and the woman of fashion. Pope's "Men, Monkies, Lap-Dogs, Parrots, perish all" evokes this theme in its suggestion that the perverse values

[55] Ellis, in a close reading of this passage, argues that "the reader is invited to read the lap-dog as a metaphor for the slaves" (98), and, relatedly, that Scott's lap-dog "has a structural affinity with the . . . starling in Sterne's *A Sentimental Journey*" (96).

[56] Wheeler cites this line as a key indication that even as late as 1766 skin color was not necessarily held to determine human value (146).

of the social world of Pope's poem are aligned to a specifically female sensibility for which, as for Mrs. Ellison, lap dogs have a privileged place. Indeed, these particular canine nonhumans were represented as participating in the private lives of their mistresses with an intimacy that was clearly sexual, as when Belinda's lap dog "wakes his Mistress with his Tongue" (1.116). Jonas Hanway, in his "Remarks on Lap-dogs" (1756), specifically links women with the problematic of human proximity with the nonhuman:

> I think a woman of sense may entertain a certain DEGREE of affection for a BRUTE; I do not mean a HUMAN brute, but a DOG, for instance, which is a faithful animal, and preferable to a monkey, because a dog has no vile resemblance to the human species, as monkeys have. Most dogs are SYCOPHANTS, but they are FAITHFUL, which is more than can be said for the generality of parasites of our species. . . .
>
> But alas! the BEST things may be abused, all the kind intentions of providence perverted! Thus we may sometimes see a fine lady, act as if she thought the DOG, which happens to be under her proper care, is incomparably of more value, in her eyes, than a HUMAN creature, which is under the care of any other person, or peradventure, under no care at all. From hence we may conclude, that an immoderate love of a brute animal, tho' it may not destroy a charitable disposition, yet it often weakens the force of it.[57]

In fact, in suggesting alternative affinities for the "fine lady"—either monkey or lap dog—Hanway's comments illustrate the imaginative connections among the nonhuman cohort that shapes this contemporary negotiation with difference, a negotiation that also readily leaps beyond the bounds of species to embrace differences of culture and of gender.

The lap dog, with his peculiar connection to the woman of quality, is the protagonist of Francis Coventry's popular midcentury satiric novel *Pompey the Little* (1751). This picaresque circulation novel[58] uses the ca-

---

[57] Jonas Hanway, *A Journal of Eight Days Journey*, containing "Remarks on Lap-dogs," (London, 1756), 69–70. Cited in Ellis, 97.

[58] Such works, like John Phillips's poem *The Splendid Shilling* (1705), Joseph Addison's autobiography of a shilling in *Tatler*, no. 249 (11 November 1710), or Charles Johnstone's *Chrysal; or the Adventures of a Guinea* (1760–1765) represent the movement of an object or, in Pompey's case, an objectified being through an economic circuit or change of hands. See Christopher Flint, "Speaking Objects: The Circulation of Stories in Eighteenth-Century Prose Fiction," *PMLA* 113 (1998): 212–226.

nine pet, "little *Pompey*,"[59] as a means of moving from one social site to another, and thereby generating a series of set satiric scenes. Pompey, born into the home of a "celebrated Courtesan" of Bologna (7), is taken to England by a fashionable gentleman on his return from the grand tour, and thence passes through the houses of the vain Lady Tempest, a social-climbing City family, an "ancient Virgin" (50), a Captain of the guards, an enthusiastic female Methodist, an inn keeper, a blind beggar, a pair of polite and good natured sisters, a prosperous widow milliner, a great Lord, a penniless poet, the vaporous Mrs. Qualmsick, a Cambridge scholar, yet another fashionable Lady, and finally back—in a framing move that emphasizes the connection to the female figure—into the hands of Lady Tempest. As the protagonist of a full-length novel, taking the place of the human hero, the pet Pompey condenses the contemporary interest in the status of the nonhuman. And in the course of his adventures, the lap dog provides various perspectives on the fable of the nonhuman being; in fact, the novel could be seen as an encyclopedia of the redactions of the themes of this cultural fable.

The novel displays at length the intimacy between this particular nonhuman being and the woman of fashion, first through the summary account of Pompey's life with Lady Tempest:

> Lady *Tempest* . . . soon ushered him into all the Joys of the Town. He quickly became a great Admirer of Mr. *Garrick*'s acting at the Playhouse, grew extremely fond of Masquerades, passed his Judgment on Operas, and was allowed to have a very nice and distinguishing Ear for *Italian* Music. . . . he attended his Mistress to all Routs, Drums, Hurricanes, Hurly-burlys and Earthquakes, . . . and was extremely proud to shew *his collar at Court*. (30)

This theme is engaged again, with more explicit sexual innuendo, in the account of Pompey's intimacy with another mistress, the fashionable Aurora, with whom

> he was a great favourite. . . . *Aurora* . . . caressed him with the fondest tenderness, and permitted him to sleep every night in a chair by her bed-side. When she awoke in a morning, she would embrace him with an ardour, which the happiest lover might have envied. (132)

---

[59] Francis Coventry, *The History of Pompey the Little or the Life and Adventures of a Lap-Dog* (1751), ed. Robert Adams Day (London: Oxford University Press, 1974), 10. Subsequent references are to this edition; page numbers are given within the text.

Coventry also uses his nonhuman "Hero" (17) as a means of reflecting on contemporary assumptions about "learned" animals. Pompey demonstrates a "Sagacity" that ascends to ridiculous heights of proximity. In the opening "Panegyric upon Dogs" of the first chapter, the author informs us of "the Capacity they have often discovered, for playing at Cards, Fiddling, Dancing, and other polite Accomplishments" (2). And Pompey masters these accomplishments early in his career, when Lady Tempest cultivates the lap dog's talents as a partner at cards:

> As to his own Part, his Lady was at the Expence of a Master, per-
> haps the great Mr. *H——le*, to teach him to play at Cards; and so
> forward was his Genius, that in less than three Months he was able
> to sit down with her Ladyship to Piquet, whenever Sickness or the
> Vapours confined her to her Chamber. (31)

Even the question of language, usually evoked in the appearance of the talking bird, is suggested in the claim the narrator makes, in the course of this same opening "Panegyric," that he has "heard of a Dog's making a Syllogism; which cannot fail to endear him to our two famous Universities, where his Brother-Logicians are so honoured and distinguished for their Skill at that *useful* Science" (2). Local satire, like this against the university, is the main effect of *Pompey the Little*, where, as in contemporary satiric verse, the dog is used simply to demonstrate the deficiency of the human target. Pope's well known epigram, "Engraved on the collar of a Dog which I gave to his Royal Highness," illustrates this specifically satiric use of the canine species:

> I AM his Highness Dog at Kew;
> Pray tell me Sir, whose Dog are you?[60]

But the lap dog's presence in this text has a larger purchase on the imagination than those local satiric effects would suggest. Pompey calls up the various dimensions of the experience of alterity figured through the nonhuman cohort of our fable, and projects that experience directly into the realm of the non-European. For instance, in the course of Pompey's peregrinations, Coventry provides a sample disquisition on the debate about species. In his attendance upon Lady Tempest, Pompey witnesses a "curious Dispute on the Immortality of the Soul"

[60] Alexander Pope, [Epigram], in *Eighteenth-Century English Literature*, ed. Geoffrey Tillotson, Paul Fussell Jr., and Marshall Waingrow (New York: Harcourt, Brace and World, 1969), 681.

between Lady *Sophister* and two physicians. Their argument specifically addresses the relation of men to animals, and ultimately focuses on the lap dog himself, whom Lady Sophister points out as an apt and immediate example of her claim for the proximity of the human and the nonhuman:

> "the *Indians* you know believe their dogs will bear them company to heaven. . . . For instance now, there's lady *Tempest*'s little lap-dog"—
> —"My dear little creature," said lady *Tempest*, catching him up in her arms, "will you go to heaven along with me? I shall be vastly glad of your company, *Pompey*, if you will." (39)

Here Lady Tempest's embrace signifies that intimacy between the woman of quality and the lap dog that shapes the plot as well as many of the specific satiric effects of this novel. But that connection is also an emblem of the larger problematic of difference in which the species debate and the fable of the nonhuman being participate.

The same topic, the relation of men to animals, is taken up at the end of this text, in the debate in the Monday night authors club held in "a little dirty dog-hole of a tavern in *Shire-lane*" (169). There Pompey and his current master, the poet Mr. *Rhymer*, meet "a free-thinking writer of moral essays, a *Scotch* translator of *Greek* and *Latin* authors, a *Grub-street* bookseller, and a *Fleet* parson" (169). The human discussion that follows has a nonhuman analogue, represented in the participants' canine pets:

> By odd luck, every one of these great advancers of modern literature, happened to have a dog attending him; and as the gentlemen drew round the fire after supper in a ring, the dogs likewise made an interior semi-circle, sitting between the legs of their respective masters. (169)

This human/nonhuman colloquium, drawn in a manner to exaggerate its polarities, takes a very familiar tack:

> "Why this is my paradox, sir," replied the free-thinker; "I undertake to prove that brutes think and have intellectual faculties. That perhaps you'll say is no novelty, because many others have asserted the same thing before me; but I go farther sir, and maintain that they are reasonable creatures, and moral agents."
> "And I will maintain that they are mere machines," cries the par-

son. . . . "Sir, you may be ashamed to prostitute the noble faculty of reason to the beasts of the field."

. . .

[the free thinker says] "but I will maintain that brutes are capable of reason, and they have given manifest proofs of it. Did you never hear of Mr. *Locke*'s parrot, sir, that held a very rational conversation with prince *Maurice* for half an hour together? what say you to that, sir?" (171)

The circled dogs serve as either a mockery or a mimicry of the claim to nonhuman rationality. On one hand, as satire, this passage seems to expose the excesses of the position of affinity; the dogs depicted in the absurd role of rational disputants make such a claim to a human-like faculty ridiculous. But, on the other hand, this scene, like the novel as a whole, testifies to and participates in the attraction of the dynamic of affinity, with its allusion to the authority of "Mr. *Locke*" and the "intelligent rational parrot," and with its vivid image of the conferring dogs, whose critique of proximity entails a performance of it. Even as a satiric indication of the human disputants' failure of rationality, the dogs still sit in a human place.

This complex play with the contemporary figure of the nonhuman is matched in *Pompey the Little* by an insistent, pervasive, and wholly implicit analogy between the lap dog and the African slave. The dog's name comes from contemporary slave-naming convention, where Pompey, Caesar, and other imperial names were an ironic commonplace. In the first pages of the novel, we learn that "Master *Pompey*" is presented "with a Collar studded with Diamonds" (9), a material link between slavery and dog fancy. In the eighteenth century, such elaborate collars were made interchangeably for Africans and for dogs, and sold in the same shops. F. O. Shyllon supplies a vivid context:

That a collar was considered as essential for a black slave as for a dog is clear from *The London Advertiser* for 1756, in which Matthew Dyer, working goldsmith, at the Crown in Duck Lane, Orchard Street, Westminster, intimates to the public that he makes "silver padlocks for Blacks or Dogs; collars, &c". In *The London Gazette* of March 1685 a reward was advertised for bringing back John White, a black boy of about fifteen years of age, who had run away from Colonel Kirke's. He had a silver collar about his neck, upon which were the Colonel's coat-of-arms and cipher. And in *The Daily Journal* of 28 September 1728 is an advertisement for a runaway black boy, who had the legend, "My Lady

Bromfield's black, in Lincoln's Inn Fields", engraved on a collar round his neck.[61]

We can trace the connection between slaves and pets still further in this text. When Lady Tempest loses Pompey in St. James's Park, she places an advertisement for his return in the London papers. This appeal runs for a month:

> *Lost in the* Mall *in* St. James's Park, *between the Hours of Two and Three* in the Morning, *a beautiful* Bologna *Lap-dog, with black and white Spots, a mottled Breast, and several Moles upon his Nose, and answers to the Name of* Pomp, *or* Pompey. *Whoever will bring the same to Mrs.* La Place*'s, in* Duke-street, Westminster, *or Mrs.* Hussy*'s, Mantua-maker in the* Strand, *or to* St. James*'s Coffee-house, shall receive two Guineas Reward.* (43)

Lady Tempest's advertisement is directly modeled upon the increasingly frequent notices for the return of runaway slaves, in which the physical description, including color, the naming of distinctive features, and the specification of a monetary reward—often of "Two Guineas"—were standard components:

> RUN AWAY, From Captain STUBBS. A Yellowish Negro Man, about Five Feet Seven Inches, very flat Nose, and a Scar across his Forehead, he had when he run away, a white Pea-Jacket, a Pair of black Worsted Breeches and Stockings, and a black Wig. Whoever will bring the said Negro Man to his abovementioned Master, Capt. STUBBS, in Prince's Square, Ratcliff Highway, shall receive Two Guineas Reward.[62]

In the first half of the novel, Pompey is passed from one aristocratic household to another in the same way that young Africans were often exchanged. Shyllon describes this situation, as well:

> That having small black boys was popular among Duchesses and Countesses of the period can be seen from a letter which the

---

[61] F. O. Shyllon, *Black Slaves in Britain* (London: Oxford University Press, 1974), 9. Aravamudan also describes the contemporary pet/slave analogy (33–49). And David Dabydeen documents the frequent parallels represented between Africans and canine pets in the visual art of the period. See *Hogarth's Blacks: Images of Blacks in Eighteenth Century British Art* (Surrey: Dangaroo Press, 1985), 26–30.

[62] From a plate taken from a page from the *Public Advertiser* (British Museum); cited in Shyllon, facing 116.

Duchess of Devonshire wrote to her mother towards the end of the
eighteenth century:

    Dear Mama, George Hanger has sent me a Black boy, eleven
years old and honest, but the Duke don't like me having a black . . .
if you liked him instead of Michel I will send him, he will be a
cheap servant and you will make a Christian of him and a good boy;
if you don't like him they say Lady Rockingham wants one." (12)

In *Pompey the Little* the canine pet is the unacknowledged counterpart
of the African slave. The imaginative status of both pet and African is
thrown into relief by this analogy. The cultural currency of pethood—its
import and efficacy in contemporary experience—is evidenced in this
conjunction of the idea of the pet with the historical events that accompany European global expansion—the exploitation of cultural difference
through the institutionalization of new world slavery. And the African in
turn is strangely reconstituted through the European intimacy with the
nonhuman. Figured as nonhuman beings within the dynamic of proximity that structures this cultural fable, non-Europeans are both radically
alien and also intimately connected with the European human beings
who find their own identity through this paradoxical movement.

V

Animals helped Europeans imagine Africans, Native Americans, and
themselves. The many figurative lines of connection between our cohort
of nonhuman beings and the non-European human beings who had become vividly present to European experience in the eighteenth century
suggest that the fable of the nonhuman being served as a powerful and
common resource for structuring the encounter with cultural difference.
This fable repeatedly raises questions about the nature of the human, just
as it also repeatedly implicates itself with the unprecedented forms of
"ruthless exploitation" that mark modern Europe's engagement with the
peoples of the globe. In the imaginative world of our fable, each of these
themes constitutes the other. To ask, "What have we here, a man or a
fish?" is to confront the subjugation of one human being by another, and
to recognize the historical forces that accompany that subjugation. To assert that "I could no longer deny that I was a real Yahoo" is to lay claim to
an identity defined in terms of the exploitation central to those modern
forces. The fable of the nonhuman being gives the problem of the human
a specific historical location and significance—in the eighteenth century
and in the imaginative encounter with the expansive promises and the
unprecedented exploitations of modernity.

Very often, in these several redactions of our fable, that problem is re-solved in favor of a narrowing, a containing, an exclusion, or a prescrip-tion, as in Long's racialist distinction between "black men" and Euro-peans, Hume's claim that "negroes" are "naturally inferior," or Coventry's and Scott's satires on the fashionable woman's affection for her pets. In-deed, like our fable, other modern attempts at an engagement with the nonhuman find their way back to an ideological project consolidating a particular sort of human identity, and thus provide a foregone conclusion to their story of the encounter with alterity.[63]

Donna Haraway's reading of the history of primatology largely sup-ports this structure of appropriation and retrenchment. Haraway sees twentieth-century primatology as "simian orientalism":

> western primatology has been about the construction of the self
> from the raw material of the other, the appropriation of nature in
> the production of culture, the ripening of the human from the soil
> of the animal, the clarity of white from the obscurity of color, the
> issue of man from the body of woman, the elaboration of gender
> from the resource of sex, the emergence of mind by the activation
> of body. To effect these transformative operations, simian "oriental-
> ist" discourse must first construct the terms: animal, nature, body,
> primitive, female. Traditionally associated with lewd meanings,
> sexual lust, and the unrestrained body, monkeys and apes mirror
> humans in a complex play of distortions over centuries of western
> commentary on these troubling doubles.[64]

Perhaps the clearest—certainly the most straightforward—conclusion we can draw from our reading of the fable of the nonhuman being is about our own need to see ourselves in the beings around us, to use those beings to our ends. But Haraway's position itself seems to license some-thing else. She writes about primates, she claims, because "all members of the Primate Order—monkeys, apes, and people—are threatened" (3). Her motive mirrors Pope's joining of the human and nonhuman in his image of the encounter with an ultimate, leveling dissolution: "Men, Monkies, Lap-dogs, Parrots, perish all." In this context Haraway self-consciously represents her role as that of a collaborator with the nonhu-

---

[63] Recent discussions of anthropomorphism, in various fields, exemplify such conclu-sions. See John S. Kennedy, *The New Anthropomorphism* (Cambridge: Cambridge University Press, 1992); or Mary Midgley, *Beast and Man: The Roots of Human Nature*, 1978; rev. ed. (London: Routledge, 1995).

[64] Donna Haraway, *Primate Visions: Gender, Race, and Nature in the World of Modern Science* (New York: Routledge, 1989), 11.

man, because "primates . . . are wonderful subjects with whom to explore the permeability of walls, the reconstitution of boundaries, the distaste for endlessly socially enforced dualisms" (3).

But Haraway's exploration leaves the main question open. One image, for instance, central to Haraway's account of "Rehabilitants and Surrogates: Modeling Social Problems after World War II," echoes one of the central tropes of our eighteenth-century fable, the interspecies embrace. Haraway describes how the intimacy of humans and apes in the rehabilitation projects of the mid twentieth century, "where white women teach captive apes to 'return' to the 'wild'" (2), exceeds the numerous accommodations of "gender, decolonization, class, race, and other large historical constructions" that inevitably circumscribe such projects:

> the emotional complexity of the relationships among women and chimpanzees in these stories of exile and rehabilitation is stunning. The forms of love and knowledge in these narratives are rich, often wrenchingly painful, and far from innocent extensions of the possibilities of animal-human contact imagined and enacted within western culture in the Third World. The narratives tell of profound loss and also of major achievements—by people and by animals. The people and the animals in these stories are *actors* enmeshed in history, not simply objects of knowledge, observers, or victims. The 1986 photograph of Janis Carter in an embrace with Lucy, then an adult rehabilitant in The Gambia after nine years, captures part of the tone of these narratives of relationship. (129–130)

This powerful image of contact, which Haraway reproduces on a full page, shows a chimpanzee and a woman in an intimate embrace. Seated partly facing one another in the underbrush, with a leafy jungle in the background, their arms are wound around each another; the animal's hand is visible at the human's waist as it circles behind her back, as is the woman's as it appears from behind the animal's shoulder; the human's cheek rests on the back of the animal's head, and the animal's face fits against the human's neck.[65] Is this simian orientalism, or something else, for which Haraway has no name?

Our fable, too, often leaves its central question—the limits of the human—unanswered. The bathing scene of *Gulliver's Travels* throws into mutual suspension the status of human, animal, man, and woman alike. Monboddo's approach to the question, "*What is man?*" (313) through an

---

[65] Figure 6.1. "Janis Carter and Lucy embrace on Baboon Island in the River Gambia in 1986, a year before Lucy's death."

extended gesture of affinity with the orangutang denies the conventional boundaries of the human. And the vividly realized encounter of human and nonhuman elaborated in the story of Prince Maurice's parrot far exceeds the requirements of Locke's argument that the idea "*Man*" is "nothing else but of an Animal of such a certain Form": the parrot's conversation with Prince Maurice defies the primary distinction between human and animal, that of reason.

In his account of "The Family Pet," Marc Shell describes what it might mean to deny these boundaries, defy these dualisms, and to leave open the question of the human:

> The tendency to erase—and, if you want, also to rise above—the ordinary distinction between human and animal beings suggests the first potentially disturbing question raised not only by the ordinary definition of *pet* but also by the institution of pethood itself. Another way to put the same question is, "what is a human being?"
>
> . . . .
>
> Family pets are generally mythological beings on the line between human kind and animal kind, or beings thought of as being on the line between. Yet sometimes we *really* cannot tell whether a being is essentially human or animal—say when we were children, or when we shall become extraterrestrial explorers. Sometimes we really cannot tell whether a being is our kind or not our kind, our kin or not our kin; we cannot tell what we are and to whom. If there were no such beings as pets, we would breed them, for ourselves, in the imagination.[66]

We did breed them, in the eighteenth century. And the cultural fable they generate enables us to imagine an open possibility: if we *really* cannot tell "whether a being is our kind, or not our kind," then we might refuse the "ordinary" exercise of distinction, we might see something else in alterity, and we might understand "what we are and to whom" in a new way. This surprising leap is the positive promise of modernity, a promise tied as closely to its "ruthless exploitation" as the Negro woman to the orangutang, the parrot to the colonial aristocrat, or the lap dog to the frivolous lady of fashion..

[66] Marc Shell, "The Family Pet," *Representations* 15 (1986); 121–153; these quotes, 123, 142.

Index